50% NAMASTE, 50% FUCK YOU

50% NAMASTE, 50% FUCK YOU

A Sensitive Soul's Guide to Finding Happiness in the Chaos of Life

By JR Hutchinson

ISBN: 979-8-9887381-0-7

Contents

Introduction

The human world we live in is a crazy place. Always has been and likely always will be. But it's a beautiful place when you learn to see beyond the chaos and tragedy that plague it. I didn't always believe that though. I wanted to, but…I didn't know how to see beyond the shit of a life I had lived. I was miserable, to be honest. *Fuck my life* wasn't just a funny phrase to me. It was my reality. I had spent so much of my life being unhappy that I was incapable of knowing that I was unhappy. The crap life I had experienced was just normal to me. As a matter of fact, I didn't even know what happiness really was. I thought I did…but I really didn't. All I knew was the frigid and empty tundra of my life.

On top of living this unhappy life, I was a very sensitive soul who felt everything in ways that most people couldn't remotely understand. I was different, to say the least. Large groups of people were nearly intolerable for me to be among. Light, noises, smells, and feelings were amplified a hundredfold in this human body of mine. I'd often have an awareness of things I couldn't explain. I could look at someone and feel the trauma they had experienced in their life without them saying a word. All I had to do was be near them for a moment or even just look at a person in a picture, and I could feel all the chaos and/or beauty that existed within them. And this doesn't even scratch the surface of how sensitive I truly was. I lived a cold and unhappy life, feeling every ounce of everything and nothing, all at the same time.

Imagine being born alone in a dark and frozen forest with no access to direct sunlight or fire. All you know is the cold and the darkness. Your senses are amplified so you can survive this extreme environment. You can see light above the treetops, but it's high above you. You've never touched it, so you don't know what it is other than a light off in the distance. The sunlight is no different to you than the light of a full moon. Until one day several large trees divinely fall, and the sunrays come beaming through to the ground and touch your skin for the very first time. Once you feel that warmth, you don't want to stay in that cold and dark forest anymore. You want to go where you can feel the warmth of the sun until it thaws your frozen soul.

Now that you've seen and felt the warmth and light of the sun, you want to leave that forest and live among the sun-drenched lands you can only imagine exist beyond it. But you've never been beyond that forest and have no idea how far away this theoretical land is, or if it even really exists. You feel it though…deep in your defrosting soul. You feel that there's a place the warm sun shines and that there may be even other people there who are just like you.

So you leave all you know behind and embark on a journey to find this place you can only feel and imagine exists. The forest is like a maze, though, and it takes you years and countless circles and dead ends before you finally find the path out. Along the way you come across evidence that there are others wandering that forest just like you. Turns out you weren't alone after all; the others were just too far off in the distance to be seen. But you've now found the path out and finally can say without doubt that the sun-drenched land you felt in your soul existed–actually does exist. Before you permanently leave that cold and dark forest, you decide to go back and leave path markers for the other wandering souls to find so they can make their way to the warmth of the land beyond, just as you have.

The cold and dark forest is clearly a metaphor for human life as we know it. And the sun is the happiness we all long to feel while we live in it. I'm sure many people can relate to that, especially the countless sensitive souls who live among this world. Sensitive souls who aren't always seen or heard but are here and are the guardians, guides, and teachers of this beautiful and sun-drenched existence.

This book was written as a guide to those gentle yet powerful souls who are more sensitive than most people. To those who don't fit in, feel weird, and may struggle being in crowds. To the givers who get the shit kicked out of them by the takers. To the artists, romantics, tree huggers, and social justice fighters. To the healers, clairvoyants, intuitives, and seers. To the witches and wizards very few even know exist. To the souls who feel alone in a world full of people, the ones who walk between the worlds everyone else creates. To those who typically refer to themselves as spiritual but not religious. To the progressives who truly believe everyone and everything are equal. Call them old souls, empaths, introverts, introverted extroverts, highly sensitive people (HSPs), star seeds, light workers, indigo children, hippies, or whatever. There's really no one universal term to define them. But they are the future of this world, and this book was written with them in mind. It was written by one of them.

50% Namaste, 50% Fuck You consists of ten down-to-earth, heartfelt, and brutally honest life lessons, all of which are infused with a wickedly sarcastic and humorous undertone...wrapped in a cozy blanket of love, kindness, and wisdom.

Throughout the book I will guide you through this series of fundamental life lessons, utilizing examples from popular movies, television shows, and music. I use these types of examples to highlight how the universe speaks to us through creativity, painting a picture that allows you to find love and guidance all around you when you open your awareness to that divine voice.

I also present examples and stories from my own life to bring the authenticity, perspective, and practicality of these lessons into clear view. You get an unfiltered view of how I was beaten down by the lessons I faced until the day I hit rock bottom, experienced a divine intervention, and finally learned to manifest something I had never experienced before—happiness...true happiness. Through darkness I found light, and I found it in what most would perceive as one of the darkest moments of my life.

Join me on this thought-provoking and emotional journey of enlightenment that will make you laugh, cry, and most importantly, think about life from a different perspective. A journey that is designed to light a pathway in that dark forest for other sensitive souls to follow and find their own true happiness, no matter what challenges they face along the way.

These ten lessons aren't steps though...they're a philosophy. A philosophy that will guide you to a place of peace, harmony, and love within yourself that will stretch as far as your eyes can see, your mind can imagine, and your heart can feel. In the end you will come out a little bit wiser and loaded with an arsenal of tips that will help you better navigate and experience this grand lesson we call life.

LESSON 1:

Actions and Vibes Speak Louder Than Words

Wordplay

Words, words, words...oh how beautiful and powerful they can be, yet also so confusing—and even dangerous. Potent little fuckers, to say the least. In the most basic terms, words are simply a method to communicate a message to someone else, a message that should be straightforward and factual. However, there's so much interpretation required to decipher a person's words. They often have multiple meanings and can vary from one culture to the next. There are so many rules around usage, whether they be formal rules that are generally static or informal rules that change regularly, that understanding someone by words alone can be a daunting and sometimes impossible task. Add to that the idea that a person's words may or may not be completely truthful...well, it gets downright frightening to navigate.

In order to get the full picture of what someone is actually saying, one must learn to understand the energy being emitted regardless of the words being used. You must listen for the echoes of truth that are impossible to hide.

As I write this, I'm listening to a song called "Beautiful,"[1] written and performed by Carly Rae Jepsen and Justin Bieber. One of the lyrics from that song goes: "It's how you take my breath away, feel the words that I don't say, I wish somehow I could say them now."[1] The part about feeling the words that aren't said is a key aspect of understanding the truth of what someone says, regardless of what they say with their words. For the true meaning of any word, phrase, or paragraph, whether it be written or spoken, can be found in its shadow. It's found in the energy that permeates everything.

To find and understand that true meaning, you must open yourself–your mind, body, spirit, and your energy field–to access a place that unequivocal truth exists. And yes, such a place does actually exist. There you will find the meaning behind any word ever written or spoken. You can also find the meaning behind a look someone gives you, even from an animal or an insect. In this place you can even find the emotions someone is feeling whether they physically express them or not. Access to this place is something we all are born with, and everyone uses it every single day, even though they likely don't realize it. It's really just a matter of learning to recognize it, trust it, and strengthen your ability to understand it in a more logically defined and physical manner. Before I get further into this, let's start with the basics of communication.

Words are tools used to communicate in this physical world we all live in, and as with any other tool, how that tool is used can vary dramatically depending on who is wielding it and for what purpose. For example, a hammer can be used to pound a nail into a wall to hang a picture. That same hammer can also be used to pound a rock to break it into pieces. Same hammer–two results. That hammer can even be combined with another tool to achieve something it can't perform on its own. A chisel, for example, to etch a design into stone.

The reality is, that hammer can be used to achieve many different things, even things it isn't traditionally intended to be used for. In the end, what that hammer does depends completely on the intentions of the person using it. Words are the same way. One word can have many meanings depending on how it's used, what other words it's combined with, and ultimately, the intentions of the person using it.

Take, for example, the word *bullshit*. It could be used to crudely identify a bull's fecal excrement, or it could be used to crudely imply that someone or something lacks truth or accuracy. Add in an undertone or two with the word, and it can morph into any number of meanings. For example, if you and I were having a conversation right now, and you told me I was going to win the lottery tonight, and I replied, *Bullshit*, what am I really saying? That there's bull excrement nearby? No, of course not. That's pretty obvious. What am I saying then? I obviously am disagreeing with you but in what way? Am I angry? Am I being sarcastic? Maybe I'm being sarcastic in a lighthearted and humorous way or maybe in an angry way? That word can be used with any one of those undertones. So which is it? There are many answers but only one truth, and the true answer depends exclusively on my intentions.

Unfortunately, seeing someone's intentions isn't quite as easy as seeing or hearing their words. This is why people often prefer in-person or verbal conversations. Seeing and/or hearing a person's physical and vocal expressions while they talk helps you decipher their intentions. You can infer much of their intentions by looking at their demeanor while they speak. However, a person can sell dishonest words with dishonest expressions. That's how actors work, right? They say words that, in reality, are not true to them and sell you on the deception using their expressions.

No wonder the world is the way it is. It can be so confusing to know the truth of any given situation. The world is a mixed batter of misunderstandings, lies, and truth. Add in a dash of emotions, a dollop of toxic masculinity, and a generous pour of selfishness and *voilà*–you've got the human world as we know it. A fucked-up mess. Depressing huh? Well, it's not that bad actually. It is if you look at the world from this narrow perspective...but where it all leads to is a beautiful thing. After all, you inevitably drop more than a few balls while learning how to juggle.

Some might say you should take a person's words at face value and leave it at that. However, as great as it would be, that simply isn't realistic. Why? Simply put...people lie. That may sound cynical, but it's absolutely true. People lie all the time, and it may be more widespread than you're consciously aware of.

When you think of a lie, what comes to mind? You probably think of someone intentionally lying, for example, to cover up a mistake or to manipulate a situation to their favor. The reality is, though, that most lying is done unintentionally. When people lie unintentionally, it can be because they were told a lie and are unknowingly spreading it. Or they may be lying to themselves and are incapable of accepting the truth they have buried away somewhere in their conscious or subconscious mind. Worse yet, they may be doing a combination of both. Unintentional lies can be the most difficult to see through. People lie all the time, and words are their tools to pull the wool over your eyes, whether they mean to or not.

In order to see the truth behind someone's words, there are two facets one must learn and master before they can accurately and consistently weed out the lies in any given situation. Those two facets are the following: (1) observing a person's actions, and (2) analyzing the energy that's being emitted, otherwise known as getting a vibe.

Using either one of these alone is quite powerful, but the combination will give you an almost superhuman ability to see straight through even the densest pile of bullshit. Observing a person's actions is, at least partially, something everyone already does, whether they realize it or not. So I will start with it and dig into the energy aspect a little bit later in this lesson.

Show Me the Money

Simply observing a person's body language, emotional expressions, and verbal queues is something we all learn to do from an early age. For example, is the person yelling the words with an angry facial expression or giggling with a sheepish grin? Do they have their arms crossed, are they pacing back and forth, or is their face turning red? Those are immediate observations that can be made and interpreted. However, you can take it a step further. This is where the title of this lesson comes into play. Actions and vibes speak louder than words.

Imagine for a moment that someone told you they were going to give you a million dollars. Your immediate reaction is going to be disbelief, right? Why? Because people generally don't give away a million dollars–duh! After all, a million dollars is nearly impossible to come by for 99 percent of the population. So most people can't even hand it out at all, let alone hand it out willy-nilly. Now imagine if someone told you they were going to give you one dollar. You're much more likely to believe that simply because one dollar isn't an overly large amount of money that's unbelievable to imagine someone giving away. On the contrary, it's a relatively small amount of money, and people give away dollars on a regular basis.

I give these as examples because one is so unbelievable, and the other is very believable. The truth of the matter is that both scenarios are equally believable or unbelievable. Both are simply statements that someone will do something, and either one could be a lie or the truth. The tried-and-true way to know if the words are the truth or a lie is to observe the actions of the person saying them. If they give you the million dollars, then they were speaking truthfully. If they don't, then they weren't. The same goes for the one dollar. Two dramatically different offers provide the same path to identifying the truth.

People can say many things, whether they be small or grandiose, but their actions ultimately define whether they're true or not. It's literally impossible for someone to lie with their actions. Someone could lie when they tell you they are going to give you a million dollars, but if they actually give it to you, then it becomes truth. Vice versa: A person could be completely honest when saying they'll give you even just one dollar. But if they don't do it, then it becomes a lie, even if it's an unintentional one.

Actions define truth in the vast majority of circumstances. There are no ifs, ands, or buts about it. As a matter of fact, you can theoretically understand the truth of a situation by completely ignoring words and only considering the actions. I love actions! They are so defined, solid, and undeniable. Words can be beautiful, but they are mushy, moldable, and oftentimes meaningless. Actions are truth, and if you focus on them, they can enlighten you, regardless of what words are being said, why they're being said, how beautiful or ugly they appear, and if the person saying them is aware of the truth or not.

Die Hard Fucker!

Looking for a person's actions isn't always an in-your-face kind of thing. Sometimes you have to be patient and wait for the truth to reveal itself over time. You also need to look in the shadows to find the truth. When I say "the shadows," I'm referring to more subtle actions or lack of actions where they should exist. Looking at the lack of actions is one of the most useful resources in my action-observing arsenal.

A great example of observing subtle actions comes from the movie *Live Free or Die Hard*,[2] the fifth installment in the series of *Die Hard* movies starring Bruce Willis. In one scene John McClane, a New York City cop, and Matthew Farrell, a small-time computer hacker, are being escorted by federal agents to the Department of Homeland Security (DHS) in Washington, DC, where Farrell is to be interviewed. Farrell has unknowingly written an algorithm for the bad guys of the movie that, you later find out, will allow them to hack into a top-secret government facility. DHS agents are desperate to get information on these bad guys, so they need Farrell in DC as quickly as possible.

The streets are heavily congested en route to DHS, so the federal agent driving radios into the DC Metro Police Dispatch to request they clear a route for them. When the police dispatch operator comes on, Farrell quickly recognizes the voice as one of the bad guys, inferring that the bad guys have somehow hacked the police dispatch line.

Farrell has already lied to McClane previously but swears to him he is positive the voice on the other end of the radio is one of the bad guys. McClane clearly has a hunch Farrell is being honest and that the operator is potentially a villain. In an effort to weed out the truth, he picks up the radio to make what appears to be small talk with the operator. He says, "How's your day going over there? It's gotta be pretty crazy over there with all those 587s, huh?"[2] The operator replies, "Yes sir, we've had to dispatch all units."[2] McClane then replies with his typical sarcastic tone, "You had to dispatch all units for all the naked people walking around?"[2] McClane has caught the operator red-handed in a lie by baiting her with false information that would have been obvious to a real police dispatch operator. By doing this, he is able to validate what Farrell has said as the truth and avoid the trap the bad guy operator intends to lead them down.

What McClane is looking at when he baits the operator is not only what she says but also what she doesn't say. He is looking for her to question him on the validity of his comment. She doesn't though; she simply goes along with it, unknowingly revealing she has no idea what a 587 is. This tells him she isn't a real police dispatch operator. What she doesn't do plays at least an equal, if not more important, role in revealing the truth to McClane. This is a brilliant display of looking at the actions and lack thereof to shed light on the truth.

The Bullshit Bell

Another aspect of the aforementioned scene from *Live Free or Die Hard* [2] is McClane's hunch that Farrell is being honest and that there is something off about the dispatch operator. This is where the energy aspect comes in. Throughout all of the *Die Hard* movies, you become clear that McClane has great instincts for weeding out bullshit just like the fake dispatch operator is shoveling. The reality is, what the character is actually good at is picking up a vibe or energy that something is off. He then follows it to figure out exactly what is off about it by observing the actions of those who are ringing his bullshit bell.

In other words, he's picking up on the energetic vibration that is emitted when something is not matching the truth. Keep in mind that truth has an energetic vibration, so do lies. So when the vibe that McClane is picking up on isn't matching with the truth, he immediately starts getting the feeling that something is off. The great instincts he has aren't so much generic hunches, as is often assumed when someone has great instincts, but are actually his abilities to sense and recognize inconsistent energetic vibration and then react by implementing tools to reveal the truth. The tools are various methodologies of observing actions. Once the truth is revealed, then the energetic vibration changes and becomes consistent with the truth, which McClane keenly can sense as it changes.

Science has many tools and methodologies to measure different types of energy. Unfortunately science does not have tools to measure the type of energetic vibration I'm discussing here. Actually science doesn't really recognize this type of energy at all, simply because it doesn't have a way to identify, isolate, quantify, and replicate it. This is understandable but annoying nonetheless to those sensitive souls who know it as well as a best friend. Since this energetic vibration is overall undefined and unrecognized by science, it's commonly discarded as nonsense or pseudoscience. This is very unfortunate but doesn't change the reality that it does indeed exist or that it always has and always will.

Throughout my life I've spent countless hours contemplating this vibrational energy, all in an effort to better understand it and to refine my ability to accurately sense it. I'm not a scientist and have no interest in being one so will never be able to document my findings at that level. What I can do, though, is discuss it in the best way I know how, even at the risk of encountering criticism or of sounding nonsensical. What I know firsthand as someone who, like the character John McClane, is especially attuned to feeling the energetic vibrations that truth very consistently emits, is that it without a doubt exists.

Not only does truth emit an energetic signature, but everything on this planet also emits an energetic vibration of some kind. Different emotions emit unique vibes. Different thoughts do as well. The earth itself emits energetic vibrations–so, of course, do rocks, water, and air. The funny and complex thing about all of this is that numerous energetic vibrations can all exist in one place at one time. The earth, for example, emits all kinds of energetic vibrations. People and animals do too. In my opinion, humans have the most complex and erratic vibes simply because they have such a broad range of emotions, thoughts, and feelings all going on at one time. Plus they emit the same energetic vibrations that typically appear in all living creatures. So humans are simply loaded with different vibes, especially with bullshit vibes, which can make them downright unbearable to be around at times. This is especially true for those of us who see it so clearly.

Vibeology

I will give some tips and advice on how you can pick up on the vibe of truth, but before I do, I will say this: it takes time and patience to learn how to logically observe, differentiate, and process all of these energetic vibrations as a whole. But I can assure you that you and everyone else have the ability to do it. After all, humans are energy itself just taking the form of matter. Our spirits, which are who we really are, are energy as well. We are beings of energy inhabiting physical bodies made of a solid form of energy, otherwise known as matter. So we have the innate ability to sense all kinds of different energetic vibrations. It's literally who we are! Our physical brains just need to learn, or evolve, to understand and process those vibrations within the confines of their physical structure and capabilities. That is what takes time. Despite that time requirement, you can start feeling those vibes and implementing your awareness of them right away, regardless of how far you've already developed that ability.

Describing how to feel those vibes isn't a straightforward thing to do. Imagine if someone were to ask you how you move a finger, a toe, or an arm. Think about that for a moment. How would you describe how to move your finger? It's a hard thing to describe when you stop and analyze it. You just think about moving your finger, and voilà, it moves. Actually, you don't even really think of moving your finger. You more have an intention of moving it, and then it moves. It's not like you tell your brain, "Move left index finger up one centimeter, extend 80 percent, and point five degrees to the left." It's not a specific and detailed logical thought from you to your brain. It's just an intention from the spiritual you, and then your brain kicks in to decipher and define the technical action required to fulfill it. All in a ridiculously fast and almost instantaneous fashion. It's amazing shit when you really think about it–the most advanced piece of technology imaginable, in my opinion.

Feeling a vibe and distinguishing it specifically from any other vibe is kind of similar to the whole moving-your-fingers concept. There isn't a specific and detailed logical thought that will come into your brain telling you that you're picking up a certain vibe. It's more like the intention of moving-your-finger type of thing, where it's a bit vague. From there your brain needs to kick in and recognize it at the more logical and detailed level. It needs to learn that, though, just like it had to learn how to move your finger way back when you were a wee baby.

Yes, you read that correctly: your brain had to learn how to move your finger back when you were a baby. It makes sense, I know, but we forget about that stuff. Back when you were still in the womb, your brain had to learn how to control your body and connect the movements to the intention that your spirit set. It carried on with the process after you were born until it became proficient with all the coordination and technicalities involved in receiving an intention from your spirit and converting it into a technical function within your body. Now that you're much older, it's all second nature.

When it comes to vibes, your brain will go through the same process. It will be slow and clunky at first, just like a baby learning to control its movements, but with practice, it will get it down and become more and more proficient at it. And just like an athlete who trains their brain and body to become stronger and more efficient at whatever movements they need to perform their sport, the more you train at feeling and understanding those vibes, the stronger and more efficient you will become at it.

I guarantee that you are already picking up on vibes and have been doing so your entire life. Your brain just may not know exactly how to process the data into a clear logical thought. Depending on how you've developed your ability thus far, you may be quite good at it already. Or you may need quite a bit of work. Either way, what I'm about to describe will hopefully help you in your journey to become an advanced vibeologist.

Who Dat?

One of the most important aspects of evolving your vibrational perception is to contemplate it. Think about times where you've gotten a gut feeling about something. What were you feeling, and what stood out about it? If you've had it happen multiple times, then compare the feelings and try to identify similarities. Think back to a time when you walked into a room and noticed someone. What did you notice about them? Did you feel a sense of happiness? Were you creeped out? Did you feel sadness? It's easy to dismiss those feelings as random or meaningless, but they all mean something. Acknowledging these feelings, digging into them, and trying to understand why you're feeling them is exactly what is needed to grow your ability to connect to them and understand them at a logical level. The very act of doing so will trigger your growth.

In this process, you must be aware of and separate out any feelings that are resulting from something going on in your own life and try to narrow them down to feelings that are outside you. For example, if you pick up on sadness from someone, look back at yourself and analyze whether you were sad before you came into proximity of this person. If the answer is yes, then the feeling may be leaching over from your own life. If not, then you are clearly picking it up from an outside source.

When you perform this analysis, keep in mind that the feelings are not a mental thing at their core. They are simply feelings, just like the intention to move your fingers. It's vague until your brain kicks in and starts trying to process them on a logical level, which will happen automatically. Your part is to start the process of feeling it and have a desire to break it down and understand it. Set your intention to feel it and understand it. Set your intention at the core of who you are and let it flow from there. It's like pouring water down a hill. Once you pour the water, gravity kicks in. Similarly, once you set your intention, your brain will naturally kick in and try to understand it. It's really that simple.

Just like the baby learning to master control of their fingers, growing your abilities as a vibeologist will take time. Step by step, day by day, year by year, you will get stronger and better at it. Feel it, feel it, feel it. When you do feel something, then acknowledge it, accept it, and analyze it. It's easy to not pay attention to it or to blow it off, but you must open yourself to it. Opening yourself to it is the start of the process of understanding it.

Zen as Fuck

One of the best practices I've learned to help me pick up on, differentiate, and understand vibes is to meditate. I'm not sure of your experience with meditation, but I can tell you mine, and hopefully it will help you on your path. Please keep in mind, though, that I'm not a meditation expert by any means, nor am I claiming to be. I'm just a schmuck who has become very skilled at it over the years and approaches it with a unique perspective that may prove beneficial to you.

I was in my midtwenties when I first became interested in meditating, but I was very quickly turned off. Everything I read or was told was all about quieting the mind, which I struggled with. I have a very active mind–I might argue an overactive mind–and trying to quiet it was literally impossible for me. I'm a quiet-on-the-outside and noisy-as-fuck-on-the-inside kind of person, if you know what I mean! Needless to say, I got frustrated and repeatedly gave up on every attempt. Until one day after several years of trying, lightning stuck and divine inspiration hit me. I decided that those saying to quiet the mind are full of shit. I came to the awareness that what if I didn't try to quiet my mind at all, but instead left my thoughts there and just separated my spiritual self from them? Like what if I treated my thoughts like clouds in the sky? Let them float up there while I'm down on the ground relaxing in the soft sand of a fantasized Bora Bora beach? If a thought pops into my mind, I can put it up in the sky with the rest of my thoughts/clouds. Those thoughts can stay there until I'm done meditating, or they can float away if they're not that important.

That idea proved to be a pivotal moment for me. From that moment forward, I started successfully meditating. I quickly progressed to the level of being able to get into very deep states of meditation where information would flow to me in an almost psychic way. But here's the greatest thing I realized through my process of learning meditation: you can utilize meditation to get into a conscious state of deep awareness without having to take a deep dive as you do with traditional meditation. What I mean by that is you don't necessarily have to sit down, cross your legs, and close your eyes for a specific amount of time to get into a receptive state. Don't get me wrong; sitting down and doing traditional meditation is definitely great and serves a very valid purpose. But you can get into a deep state of awareness without hiding off in a quiet space for ten, twenty, or thirty minutes or whatever your practice is. You can get there whenever you need to while maintaining your normal fully conscious and aware state.

Getting into a conscious state of deep awareness is so helpful in picking up vibes. For me, it's simply about separating your spiritual self from your physical self while meandering through life as usual. As you get into this state, you enhance your vibe awareness and then allow your brain to start digesting all of it while you physically go about your normal activities. That might sound overly simplified, but I promise you it actually comes very naturally and is very easy. It just takes some practice and learning to become aware of it.

A simple way I get into a conscious state of deep awareness is to put my physical body in a safe situation where I can let it go on autopilot and not have to think or be aware of what's physically around me at every moment. There are no decisions to be made and no triggers for curiosity or fear. For example, I can hop on a treadmill set to a constant speed with nothing overly stimulating to look at, such as a video screen, hot chicks or dudes with their asses bouncing in front of you, or people coming and going triggering your nosy mind. When you get going on the treadmill, your brain becomes preoccupied with coordinating the technicalities on keeping your body moving. This acts as a distraction for your brain. And with nothing stimulating to look at, you–the spiritual you–can turn your attention inward and focus on whatever you choose.

This act of keeping your body moving and focused on that movement allows you the opportunity to separate your physical consciousness from your spiritual consciousness. As you bring your spiritual awareness to something and begin feeling it, your brain will naturally kick in and start to analyze and digest it on a logical level. That's good...don't fight it. Allow that to happen while you continue feeling it. Now guess what? You are officially in a conscious state of deep awareness. Seems easy huh? Trust me–it really is.

Now you may be asking yourself how your physical brain processes what you spiritually are feeling when you've purposely separated from it. Very good question! Yes, you are separating your spiritual self from your physical self but only to a very small degree. Enough to open the door and allow information and vibes in, but you're certainly not separating from your body by any means. So as you receive information or vibes, your brain will naturally have access and kick in to understand and process them. And no worries–you cannot accidently separate from your body and get lost or anything. It doesn't work like that.

This same process can be used while walking into the office after parking your car, sitting in a doctor's office waiting room, riding the subway home after work, etcetera. Start with something that really distracts your physical body, like using the treadmill or even walking up and down a set of stairs repeatedly, then work your way up to waiting rooms and subway rides that have less physical monotony to distract your body with. As you grow this ability, your brain will learn not bug you so much during this state, and you'll eventually be able to do it on a whim. When you achieve it, then it really helps you pick up on vibes, quickly identify your own feelings and vibes from those of an external source, and understand what they are and where they're coming from.

If you find it challenging not to get caught up in things going on around you while you try to access this conscious state of deep awareness, then I suggest trying noise-canceling headphones, earbuds, or regular headphones/earbuds with music that is engaging but not charged with a lot of intense emotions or energy that will distract you spiritually. I personally love music by *Enigma* to achieve this, like "Back to the Rivers of Belief"[3] or "Return to Innocence."[4] If I need to take a bit of a deeper dive, then I'll go with ocean sounds since the noise level is relatively consistent and dreadfully boring. It's perfect for tuning myself to energetic vibrations.

Honestly, though, the music that works for one person may not work for someone else. The music that will trigger this for you is very much dependent on your connection to and perception of the song. For example, sometimes Enigma's music does it for me. Other times "Sailing,"[5] by Christopher Cross, will do it. The *NSYNC version of "Sailing"[6] can do it for me as well. Or I especially love "Go West,"[7] by the Pet Shop Boys. My own vibe can very much alter which song does it for me, so I simply go with whichever feels right.

An exception to my rule on choosing music that isn't charged with a lot of intense emotions or energy is foreign-language music. Sadly, I only speak English, but I love listening to music in other languages that I literally do not understand a word of. I have an entire playlist of Latin music that's sung completely in Spanish. I find it to be a great training tool in understanding what's being said behind people's words. If you can't understand their words, then you have no choice but to feel those vibes. For this reason, the intense emotions and energy is actually beneficial rather than a potential spiritual distraction. Any of Karol G's songs are my go-tos, especially "Tusa."[8] I could look up the translation of that song, but I really don't need to. I can feel exactly what she's saying without understanding her physical-world words. Knowing the words could actually ruin it for me as they may oppose what I pick up on. As I've said, people lie unintentionally. Singers and songwriters are certainly not excluded.

Sometimes the best method for getting into a conscious state of deep awareness is simply quietness, which is where the noise-canceling headphones/earbuds come in. I've tried every brand out there and give my top billing to Sony without doubt. (And, no, they are not paying me for that shout-out, but I am willing to whore myself for them, if they're willing…hint, hint, Sony marketing executives.) Not only do their headphones/earbuds kick serious ass with music sound quality, but their noise canceling is superior as well. I'm definitely an earbud guy and especially love their WF-1000XM4s. Some days I wear them eight hours solid to block out the bullshit coming out of people so I can focus on the truth their emitting…well, that and not going fucking insane listening to their verbal diarrhea!

One final and simple way to practice getting into a conscious state of deep awareness is to quietly observe people from a distance. For example, try going to a busy public place, maybe a mall or a park, and sit off by yourself where you can see the other people that are there, but you don't have to interact with them. Pop those noise-canceling earbuds in and just observe the people. This is basically practice. You don't need to meditate while doing this. You don't have to put any pressure on yourself to do anything other than be nosy. Look at the people, but don't focus on what they're saying. You don't know these people, and you likely will have no idea what they're talking about or doing. This is the point. Their words are meaningless in this situation, so just observe them. Feel for their vibes. Try to understand these people without knowing what they're talking about. Observe their actions, how they hold themselves, and what their emotional expressions are. This doesn't take long at all. Grab yourself a cup of coffee or tea and sharpen your vibrational awareness. Before you know it, you will unknowingly be in a conscious state of deep awareness. The more you do this, the better you will get. And the better you get, the easier it will be to turn it on whenever you choose.

Are We There Yet?

I touched on patience a couple times earlier in this lesson, but it's time to dig into it a bit deeper. After all, patience is a key element of finding truth when it's hidden. The deeper it's hidden, the longer it can take to find it. Sometimes it can take days, weeks, months, and even years to find the truth. Think of yourself as an investigative reporter who has gone deep undercover to bust some crooked and powerful politician. Gathering the evidence to bust them isn't going to come quickly. But with time and patience, you'll gain all the intel you need to not only bust them but also publish that Pulitzer Prize-winning article you've always dreamed of.

As humans in this modern world, we're subliminally mind fucked to want instant gratification. Words provide that without a doubt—words like *yes* and *no*. Do you love me? Yes. Are you lying? No. Did you have a great time? Yes. Do I look fat in this outfit? No. You see… instant gratification. However, are those words true? You won't get instant gratification when you ask that question. It may take a little or a lot of time to reveal the truth, but if you grant yourself the time to discover it, then you'll inevitably find yourself swimming in a sea of truth.

Take, for example, two people who have been in a long-term relationship. Maybe they're even married. But one of the people frequently questions if the other loves them. That person's partner says they love them, but for some reason, they keep asking themselves if it's true or not. This person is perplexed over these feelings and can't shake this need for validation of that love. And they typically feel like it's all in their head or their own insecurity that's at the root of it. But is that really the situation, or do we have a case of emotional manipulation and gaslighting?

The truth of whether this person's partner loves them is right there in plain sight but can't always be seen in a particular moment or answered with a question. No, this person will need to observe actions, or lack thereof, over the course of time to get to the undoubtable truth.

The first step is to trust and accept the vibes they are getting. Like the vibe that makes them doubt their partner's love in the first place. Instead of them attempting to dismiss those feelings as nonsense or being manipulated into dismissing them, they should try doing something different that nobody can manipulate away from them. Try accepting their feelings as information. Information that is begging for their attention. They don't have to accept the feelings as the absolute truth in that moment. No, just accept and acknowledge it as information. Maybe it's information that's warning them that their partner doesn't love them or is a manipulative fucker. Maybe it's information that they have deep-seated insecurities that need to be addressed before it damages their relationship. Or maybe it's information that something else is happening that they haven't grasped yet. Whatever it is, it without a doubt is information. Accept that, and let's look at actions to validate what exactly those feelings/ information may indicate.

When observing actions in this case, the first thing we can look at is the very fact that this person is questioning their partner's love for them. It's a huge fucking clue! And it's one that typically shows up after having unintentionally missed or ignored much more subtle clues over a longer course of time. If someone loves you, then they will do things that show it. There is never a case where someone won't show you they love you, if they truly love you. Fuck their words! Look at their actions to know if they truly love you.

For example, when you're sick, do they stick around to take care of you? And are they happy doing it? Do they go to the store to buy you tissues and various remedies? Do they do the chores around the house while you're sick, or does everything go to shit unless you take care of it? Do they make you soup and pick up your snot rags off the floor because you were too sick to put them in the trash yourself? Or do they leave you at home while they go out with their friends and have a great day? Or maybe they stick around but piss and moan about what they're missing or about having to take care of so much while you're sick. These are all actions that speak to the truth. Actions that you may not be able to see in an instant. They are actions that take place over time.

Let's look at a few more examples. You have hobbies and things you enjoy, right? Does your partner engage with you in these hobbies regularly? Maybe you like playing *Pokémon Go* in your downtime. Does your partner play it with you and listen to you when you tell them about it? Even if they aren't the biggest *PoGo* fans, do they at least have an account and join in sometimes? And do they appear to enjoy it? If they absolutely hate playing *Pokémon Go* yet you love it, does that mean they don't love you? No. But if they never engage with you over it in any way, then that is certainly an important clue. Even if they hate it, their love for you will override that feeling, and they will want to support you in some way. They may not want to play it, but maybe they buy you an event ticket or even just an Adventure Box because they heard you when you told them that the event was coming up or that your supplies were running low. Or maybe you plan to attend Go Fest in person, and they help you plan that trip, regardless of whether they go with you on the trip or not. These are all actions that show you they love you. And they are actions that are revealed over time.

Here's another one. Maybe you love going to local art exhibits. Does your partner go with you to these exhibits? If so, how often? Do you have to drag them along, or do they genuinely seem to engage in it with you? If they do join you, are they on their phone all the time or make you feel like they don't want to be there in some other way? Maybe they're not a huge art fan like you, but they go occasionally to support you and genuinely try their best to engage. Maybe they're major introverts and dread being around all the people, so instead they drive you to the events and pick you up afterward so you can enjoy yourself and have as many drinks as you feel like? Or maybe they don't join in at all, and you have to ask them for a ride so you can enjoy the wine? But you don't get to enjoy the wine because they are too busy whining about how they're going to miss hanging out with their friends that they see every fucking weekend? Again all of this says so much. They don't have to love everything you love, but if they do love you, their actions will reflect their love for you in one way or another. People can hide the truth for a short time. But not forever...especially in relationships.

Let me put one more example out there for consideration. Affection, kissing, and sex. Does your partner hold your hand, rub your shoulders, or massage your scalp? When you're sleeping, do they snuggle with you? How do you feel when your partner kisses you? Do they summon you to kiss them, or does their love and passion for you draw you in? Do they know how you liked to be kissed, and do they act on that? Or is it all about them and they take what they want when they want it? Do you have sex regularly? Do you want to have sex with them regularly? Do you feel like they want to have sex with you regularly? When you do have sex, do you and they enjoy it? Do they act like it's the most disgusting or most amazing thing in the world? How do you feel after sex–like your world was just rocked or like you want to crawl under a rock?

All of these actions and feelings/vibrations say so much my friend. And the truth behind them can't be seen in an instant. Patience is needed to observe them over time and in accumulation. Nobody is perfect, and no relationship is perfect. Even the best people and relationships can't be amazing all the time. But when you take the time to observe and reflect, you can start to see patterns emerge that speak to a truth that is buried deep beneath the surface. A truth that will be revealed no matter if someone wants it hidden or not. Actions and vibes over time can reveal even the deepest and darkest truths. It's inevitable. Even the ones that you yourself may not want to expose.

Keepin' It Real

In order to be an all-powerful truth seer, there is a very important task you must commit to every day from here on out. That task is to simply be honest with yourself, no matter how difficult the subject matter may be. If you can't look at the truth within yourself, then how could you ever see the truth in someone else? Not so easily, that's for sure. Granted, there is a spectrum to being honest with yourself, but you at least have to be somewhere on that spectrum in order to uncover truth in the lie-filled world we live in. It takes truth to see truth. The more honest you are with yourself, the brighter the truth will shine for you to see.

Being honest with yourself is a complex subject that can't be fully discussed in the context of just this one lesson. As a matter of fact, learning to see the truth within yourself will be covered throughout this book in various and sometimes subtle ways. By the end of the book, you will be much better equipped to take a truly deep dive into the depths of who you are and what you may be hiding from yourself. However, in this moment let's stick to simply committing to being open and honest with yourself. Just having that desire and commitment is the very first step on the long journey of self-discovery and enhancing your superpower of truth vision.

Bullshitometer

I hope the words I've written in this lesson and, more importantly, the intention I have behind them, are helpful to you in achieving that superpower of seeing straight through the bullshit that plagues this world. Before this lesson concludes, though, I want to leave you with a story based on a real-world situation from my life, a situation where I picked up on the vibe of a lie and patiently hunted down the truth using my arsenal of action-observing tools.

This story comes from a situation I once experienced while working for a large corporation. I had worked at this company for about ten years at the time, and a new management team had come in after a consistent lack of growth. It first started with a new chief executive officer, then a new chief operations officer, then new directors, and so on. It all took a little time for these newbies to be hired on and start getting involved at a level that directly affected me. I was the equivalent of an operations supervisor at the company's headquarters in San Diego, California. About two years after the CEO came on board, a new director of operations was brought on to oversee the area of the company I worked in and would be someone I would directly interact with regularly.

After a few months on the job, this new director told everyone in the department that he would be scheduling one-on-one meetings as a way to get to know us on a personal level. Sounds lovely, right? When he made this announcement, though, something triggered me. My bullshitometer started going apeshit! Something was off, and it was clear to me he wasn't being completely open and honest about his intentions for the one-on-one meetings. I wasn't sure exactly what, but I was for sure picking up on something. I could just feel it in my bones. I just didn't have any physical world proof of it…yet.

A week or so later, the new director of operations met with me and proceeded to talk about what my future goals were and offered advice on how to advance should I want that. He talked quite a bit about his career and kept everything very lighthearted. He even mentioned being part of a grunge band in the 1990s and loving to make music–so much so that he built a recording studio in his house. Somewhere in the middle of all this casual conversation, he slipped in a question that caught my attention. He asked if I had any interest in relocating to Dallas, Texas, where the company housed its main distribution center.

By this point I had worked with this guy for a few months, and we had built the type of relationship where I felt comfortable to be blunt and honest. The truth was that I really wasn't particularly interested in moving to Dallas, but I didn't want to fully shut him down since I could feel something was going on. So I simply said, "Money talks." I explained that my son was in a school he loved and thrived at, plus I was comfortable in San Diego and was born and raised in California, so moving just wasn't something I had in mind at the moment. But, I emphasized, if he needed me to move, and there was a financial incentive, then I'd certainly consider it. He accepted that and moved on to other lighthearted topics before wrapping up the meeting.

After the meeting, I was even more convinced of the dishonesty of the situation. When he asked about moving to Dallas, I could feel that vibe so strong that this being a get-to-know-you session was load of bullshit. A load of bullshit wrapped around a whole lot of lighthearted and honest banter in an attempt to cover up the foul stench of his lie. That feeling spoke so loudly to me that I knew something big was going on.

In the days following the conversation, I heard from other employees in the department that they had all been asked the same question about their interest in moving to Dallas. That raised some more red flags for me and was now a series of actions to start backing up the vibes I had felt. Logically I started questioning why he was asking this. The distribution center was just that and nothing more.

Was there a plan to expand the operation in Dallas to include office workers? Was there a chance my department would be moved to Dallas? He certainly wasn't coming right out and saying what the plan was. This lack of transparency was another clue to the truth and was equally based not just on what was being said, but also on what wasn't being said. I kept this all in the back of my mind, and I began watching diligently for any more actions to indicate what might be in the works.

A few months later, a new manager in my department was hired after the former manager was fired for harassing employees and generally making a mess of things to boot. There was nothing unexpected about this new manager being hired, but I did find it interesting that the position was never officially posted on the company's career page or any other public job site. The new manager was hired outside the traditional process of posting the position publicly, which was another action, or lack thereof, to be considered. Why would they do that? What purpose could it have served? Why would they scout someone without going through the traditional channels and publicly listing the job responsibilities? All very good questions and all speaking to the truth that was sitting right there in front of me yet couldn't directly be seen.

After hearing of the new manager's name, I did a little digging in an effort to understand who they were and their backstory. This new manager had lived in San Diego for many years, working for a competitor down the road, but had originally hailed from Texas. When she joined the company, it was announced that her position would now also oversee some parts of operations at the distribution center in Dallas. Big shocker...not! With all that said, it came as no surprise when it was announced that the new manager would also be based out of Dallas and travel back and forth from there to

San Diego on a regular basis. Of course this raised my alert level even more as these were actions that were backing up the idea that something was going on that they weren't being honest about. It was obvious that at least some part of my theory was coming to fruition.

On the very first day of this new manager's official start date, I had the opportunity to sit down with her for a couple of hours to help her get acquainted with the various aspects of the department that I supervised. It was also a get-to-know-you session. She seemed very nice, and we immediately got along quite well. So I decided to deploy some tactics that would help me uncover what the future plans were, if any, and determine how they could potentially affect me down the line. After all, this person was hired outside the standard process, so she likely would have at least some awareness to changes since she appeared to be part of them.

We had built a nice rapport by the end of the conversation, so I decided to come right out and casually ask her if there were plans to move some of the department to Dallas. I had already mentioned that I was a very straightforward person and preferred to cut to the chase. She learned that quickly with this bold question. Now keep in mind that I'm no fool and very much realized the likelihood that she would tell me anything was slim to none, assuming there was anything to tell in the first place, of course. But I wasn't asking this question expecting a straight answer. I rarely come across someone who loves the truth as much as I do. Especially to a point where they'll just come right out and say it. I've always found that a person who is being dishonest will avoid the truth like the plague. One of the best ways to get the truth from someone who is being dishonest is to watch for signs they're running from it. This was my goal for the question, to observe her reaction and evaluate what it could reveal to me about the truth of what was going on.

Immediately after I asked this question, she very quickly, and with a clear panicked vibe, answered with an absolute no and assured me that there was nothing to be concerned about and that nobody would be losing their jobs. In that moment, I knew she was lying. First, I could feel it. The vibe was so clear. Second, she panicked. I could tell that by how quickly she replied and the demeanor of her straightening her back and her eyes widening. Third, her reply was not only quick but also spot-on to an obviously scripted answer. I could determine it was scripted because this was her first day on the job, and she immediately jumped to an absolute no and said nobody was losing their jobs. That told me the subject had been discussed with her prior to this conversation. She was prepared for it, though obviously not expecting it so soon.

The response I would have expected if the subject had never been covered with her prior to our meeting would have been slower; she would have needed a moment, even a brief one, to quantify what I was asking and what the proper response should be. And she certainly wouldn't have jumped right to the subject of people losing their jobs. She might have realized that as a potential concern after a moment or two but not instantaneously. I hadn't said anything about anyone losing jobs, and my approach wasn't accusatory or anything of that nature; it was very casual and slipped in on a "Hey, so what's the plan?" kind of gig. Not an "OMG, are we being laid off?" kind of thing.

Had the manager never discussed the subject prior to this moment, then her reply would have been something like a pause and "No, not that I've heard." There would have been a vibe of confusion. She might have even paused and clarified the question with me. But no, she jumped right away to a firm no, saying that nobody was losing their jobs. That spoke volumes to me. I knew she was lying.

I knew there had been discussions with her about the subject and what the answer should be, and I knew it likely involved people losing their jobs. I learned all this by watching the subtle actions and lack thereof. But I still didn't have the full truth. I didn't know for sure what the future plans were. That would come in time with a little more patience.

After this conversation I was quite confident in what I had discovered. So I decided to pass my findings onto three coworkers I was friends with and informed them that there might be a layoff coming down the line. Yes I know. This was probably a little inappropriate, but I like to cut the bullshit and get right to the point. I'm not one to hide such important information from people I'm friends with. In this conversation I told them my guesstimate was that it would be in one to two years based on the timeline of the company's busy season and the logistics involved with moving the department to another state. Two of the people believed what I said and accepted my assessment. One thought I was being paranoid and blew the whole thing off as me being negative. I explained to him that I wasn't being negative; I was simply stating what I had witnessed and observed firsthand. I told him that he was obviously free to believe what he chose, but I challenged him that if he saw what I observed as negative, then it was his own negative perception, not mine. It was a little tense there for a minute, but we were all friends and quickly agreed to disagree.

After this conversation with my three friends, one of them pulled me aside and asked me if I thought we'd all be laid off. I told him no. I said I thought he would be spared but the rest of us would be let go. This friend was obviously somewhat relieved to hear me say this but asked me why I thought he would be spared. I said it was for a few reasons. First, he was the lowest paid out of our group. Second, the company likely wouldn't want to risk tribal knowledge loss by eliminating everyone so would likely keep a skeleton crew on site and reevaluate once the supposed transition settled in. Third, his teenage daughter was fighting cancer, and the management team weren't the type of folks to layoff someone with a sick child unless there was a big cost savings, enough of a cost savings to quell the guilt of laying off someone with a deathly ill child, which wouldn't be the case since he was the lowest paid in the group. I told him that all of those things combined would likely result in him staying on longer than anyone else.

Subsequently, and much to my dismay, word of what I had told my three friends started to make the rounds. Before I knew it, everyone was wondering if the department would be moved. In one of the regular department meetings with the new manager, someone decided to do what I had done and come right out and ask. This time the manager was better prepared and didn't panic. This time she replied very calmly and confidently, telling everyone that the department absolutely was not moving, and added that nobody needed to be worried about their jobs. She even went so far as to guarantee that there was nothing to be concerned about. Despite that more confident answer, the vibe came through to me loud and clear that she was once again lying. Of course my logical mind wondered if she could be telling the truth since she was much more convincing this go-around, but I couldn't ignore the vibe.

After that meeting, the three coworker friends I had originally told my theory to came to me and questioned if I was right or not. Of course the one who didn't believe me was now convinced even more that I was just being negative. The other two were now questioning it all as well. I reiterated my belief and findings, but they were no longer convinced. They weren't mad at me or anything, but I could feel that they no longer believed what I said. I was ok with that though. I didn't tell them in the first place just to convince them. I told them what I knew in the hopes of helping them navigate the future. They were my friends, and I didn't want them to be caught off guard when the truth came out. Ultimately it was their choice whether they believed and accepted it or not.

Unfortunately for me, the vibe around the entire department took the same path as it did for my friends. Nobody truly believed in what I had said, and I was seen as somewhat paranoid. At that point I regretted telling anyone anything about what I observed and decided to limit any further discussions. I never stopped believing in what I knew though. I had absolutely no doubts.

About six months later, I was in Dallas on one of my now monthly trips there when I received a text from the manager saying she was at headquarters in San Diego. The message asked me to step outside the building so we could speak privately. I immediately could sense what was happening. As I dialed the number from my cell phone, I feared she would answer with someone from human resources on the line as well, indicating layoffs were in play...and much sooner than I had suspected. Sure enough, after she picked up, she informed me that an HR rep was in the room with her, and I was on speaker.

What proceeded to be explained to me was that half of my department was moving to Dallas but that it wasn't the half that I worked in, and they wanted to assure me that nothing was happening to my job or anyone else's on my team. I asked what was happening to the folks on the other side of the department. The manager said they were all being laid off with exception of one who would be kept on to help train the new Dallas crew and preserve tribal knowledge. I so badly wanted to throw her words back in her face and remind her how she had promised everyone six months earlier that nobody would lose their jobs, yet here we were with half the department being laid off. But I didn't. I kept my mouth shut since I felt it wouldn't serve any purpose other than to point out that she was a liar, which would fall on deaf ears and not achieve anything.

As the manager wrapped up the conversation, she asked if I had any questions for her or the HR rep. I asked if they could confirm I had heard correctly that my job as well as my team's jobs were not affected. They both confidently confirmed that. I also asked if there were any plans to move my team's positions to Dallas at any point in the future. This question was one they had not spelled out specifically, which is exactly why I asked it. Remember what I said about dishonest people avoiding the truth? Well, they both got awkward, stumbled over their words, and couldn't put together a firm answer. Then all of a sudden, the call went absolutely silent as they had clearly placed me on mute so they could discuss an answer. That was all they needed to say or not say. I already knew the truth that they clearly were attempting to hide. My team was next, and it would play out for my colleagues exactly as I had called it six months earlier. After a moment they came off mute and proceeded to assure me that there were no plans to move my or my team's roles to Dallas and that there was nothing to be concerned about. I thought to myself, What fucking liars! What I replied was much different of course. I simply said, "Great," and we ended the call.

With this major revelation now revealed, I decided that once I got back to the office in San Diego, I would go to my three friends to discuss the events that had transpired and tell them what had occurred on my call with our manager and the HR rep. All three of them had already been made aware of the news and were now singing a new tune; they were starting to accept that they had been lied to. At one point in the conversation, their minds naturally started questioning everything. And they wondered if maybe this time the manager was being honest, and their jobs wouldn't be eliminated. I told them, "Come on, guys–the truth is right in front of you. You just need to push aside your fear of the truth." They just needed to push aside the lie-filled words and only look at the actions, which were screaming the truth to them. They just needed to not be afraid of what that truth was. We all were in the same mindset that we didn't want to be laid off, but it was obvious that would be the case.

One year later, my side of the department was laid off with exception of the one person with the daughter who had cancer and who is, thankfully, in remission.

Now you might be asking yourself what the benefit was of digging out the truth in this case. It feels like there was a lot of anguish in knowing what was coming. True–there was anguish, but all of us were able to prepare for what was coming. I decided to take the layoff, whenever it came, as an opportunity to break away from the corporate bullshit that I had spent too many years dealing with and use the time to heal the many wounds I had incurred. One of the others had been actively interviewing and quickly found a new job after the layoff because of that knowledge and effort. The last one decided to retire if he got laid off. So we all had the time to plan and adjust rather than be smacked upside the head out of the blue.

And That's a Wrap, Folks...

The moral of this story I shared and of this lesson is to listen to your vibes and don't dismiss them. Pay attention to actions and allow them to reveal the truth to you. Vibes and actions don't lie, so use them as tools to look beyond words and see the truth. Accept the fact that people are fucking liars, even the best of them. They may be lying intentionally or unintentionally. They may be aware of the lie or may not. They may have been lied to and are unknowingly spreading it. They may be manipulating you or just trying to manipulate themselves. Regardless, lies are everywhere, and the only way to see through them is to feel the vibrations of the energy being emitted and patiently observe the actions that show the truth for what it is. Be aware and accept that actions and vibes speak louder than words.

LESSON 2:

You Are Not Your Thoughts

The Beast Within

For anyone who's introspective, the question of who you are will eventually come to mind. After all, self-awareness is a defining element of advanced intelligence under traditional human scientific constructs anyway. So it's understandable that we would contemplate this question at some point in our lives, if not for our entire lives. I certainly have pondered it myself throughout my life and eventually settled in on the basics of an answer. I say basics because it's such a deep question that I'm not sure anyone has truly reached a level of physical evolution where they could completely understand and have the ability to physically communicate who they really are. However, I do believe we are capable of coming to an understanding that will allow us to define it from a very basic perspective. The answer I defined for myself came to me not through thinking alone though. It came through feeling for the answer, and then letting my brain digest the information I received until I came to a construct that made some sense in the world as I physically knew it.

The knowledge I've gained throughout my life became very handy one evening when my then thirteen-year-old son came to me for help in falling asleep. This was common for him to do at the time as he has a very active mind just as I do, yet he hadn't quite gotten to the point where he could limit the influence of his thoughts on his overall level of inner peace.

Every evening he went through a process of getting ready for bed that, in part, helped him unwind before hitting the sack. He cut off any use of electronics several hours before bed, he showered to wash away as much of the day's influence as possible, and he gave himself plenty of time to do all the necessary tasks. This allowed him to crawl into bed in the most relaxed state possible. He did this because, even though he's so young, it all helped him relax his mind and body to a point where he could quickly and more consistently drift off to sleep.

My son had never had an issue staying asleep; it's just the falling asleep part that got him. I had taught him many techniques to help him in his journey, and he'd made great progress over his limited years. Overall, I'd say he actually fell asleep quite quickly on most nights.

When he did struggle, then he'd simply come downstairs, where I was usually sitting in the dark with my earbuds in watching a TV show or movie on my computer, and asked me to come upstairs with him to retuck him in. I rarely watched anything on a traditional TV at that time in our lives for a variety of reasons, but the main one was that on my computer, I could easily and more comfortably watch without creating any potential disturbance for my son while he was trying to fall asleep. Turning all the lights in the house out when he went to bed and not having TV noise proved very beneficial for him. I also made sure the temperature in his room was no more than seventy-two degrees Fahrenheit, and if it's not too cold, I'd turn a small fan on low to create some background noise and a subtle, yet comforting, circulation of air. Anything I could do to help him was certainly worthwhile to me.

It was about 9:30 p.m. on this particular night when I felt a tap on my shoulder. I watched TV with my back to the stairs, so with the lights all off and my earbuds in, I rarely could see or hear him come down before the shoulder tap occurred. His preferred bedtime was 9:00 p.m., so it had been thirty minutes since he had gone to bed that evening. This was typically the time he'd come down when he was having a hard time drifting off. So I immediately knew what the situation was. As usual I took out my earbuds and asked him how he was doing. He replied with his typical answer and said he was having a hard time sleeping. He then asked me to come upstairs with him, also as usual.

We walked up the stairs in the dark since he hadn't turned on his bedroom light before coming down. Both of us had great night vision so rarely felt it necessary to turn a light on before we headed upstairs. Once we got to his room, I flipped the switch on a small nightstand lamp so he wouldn't have to feel his way into bed and risk stubbing a toe. His nightstand lamp was American Craftsman style, to go along with the Disney Grand Californian Hotel® theme of his room, and it had a sixty-watt equivalent LED soft-white light bulb in it. The lampshade was amber in color and had dark-brown horse shapes embedded into it that added an extrathick layer of shade in those spots, dimming the light more than a traditional lampshade. I turned that light on rather than the much brighter ceiling light to keep the mood more relaxed and conducive to getting into a sleepy state.

After he crawled back into bed, I pulled his covers up to just below his chin, covering his arms and shoulders in the process. At this point, one of two scenarios typically occurred. If he was feeling relaxed enough, then we'd just chat about a lighthearted subject, get in a good hug, and then we say all the I love yous and good nights before I turned the light off and departed. Or if his thoughts were more of an issue, then he'd bring them up so we could talk about them.

When the latter occurred, I'd kneel next to his bed so we could have a more in-depth chat. In this scenario he'd bring up what was bothering him, and we'd discuss it for a few minutes to settle whatever the concern may have been. Most often the chat only went on for a few minutes and ranged from something more minor, like discussing his homework load and any concerns about getting it all done on time, to psychologically deeper subjects, like him worrying about something going on in the world that was triggering for him.

On this evening the scenario was on the heavy side, very heavy from his perspective actually, and turned into a rather in-depth and lengthy discussion. One that I feel that, in the big picture, was actually good that he experienced, even though it was tough and emotionally charged for him to handle in the short term.

What he brought up to me this particular evening was that he was bothered by some repetitive *bad* thoughts that had been coming up a lot recently. He told me that these thoughts were getting worse and worse, and he was afraid of them. I could see tears welling up in his eyes as he finished telling me this. At this point I started to feel the weight of his feelings and wanted to help him set his mind at ease as quickly as possible. I then asked him to share the bad thoughts with me. He replied, with noticeable hesitation, saying that the thoughts were so bad that he didn't want to even say them out loud. With him being so noticeably upset, I didn't want to push him too hard on it and risk upsetting him even more than he already was. However, I wouldn't be able to help him if I didn't know what the thoughts were. I also knew he was aware of that so wouldn't have brought the subject up if he wasn't willing, at least on some level, to tell me.

I proceeded to gently encourage him to say what these thoughts were. It took a few repetitions and reassurances that it was ok to say it, and I wouldn't judge him in any way. He then told me that the thoughts were horrible and evil. He was borderline shaking when he added to it that they were such bad thoughts that he was afraid he was evil. This comment raised my level of concern. Fear started to fill my own mind in that moment. What if he was really having some seriously bad thoughts? What if he was thinking about murder or something? I had to quickly snap myself out of that thought process, as I recognized instantly that I was letting my own brain-based thoughts and fears get the best of me. After all, I knew my son very well and I had no hesitation in saying he was literally the gentlest person I knew. Seriously he wouldn't even step on a bug, let alone think about murdering a person.

I of course reassured myself that that the thoughts he was hesitating to share were likely just exaggerated in his mind. I needed to be open-minded, though, and prepared for anything. So I carefully pressed on and once again comforted and reassured him that it was ok to say out loud. The tears were now starting to pour down his face. I reached over, wrapped my arms around him, and whispered that it was ok. My heart broke to see him in such anguish. The pain he was feeling was quite literally pouring out of him, but he held strong and started to tell me what the bad thoughts were. With embarrassment palatable, he hesitantly said, "666" and then whispered, "The devil."

Now that he finally was able to tell me what the bad thoughts were, I was instantly drawn into a state of understanding and relief. Knowing my son as I did and how similarly our brain's functioned, I could already sense what it was about these thoughts that were so disturbing to him. And how it was elevated to the point of tears and having a fear that he was somehow evil.

To confirm what I suspected, I proceeded to ask him what it was about those thoughts that were bothering him. He explained that the number 666 and the word *devil* kept popping into his mind repeatedly, and he couldn't make them go away. He continued by telling me that those were words that represented evil, and the fact that they kept popping into his mind made him fear that he was having evil thoughts and maybe was evil himself. I of course quickly assured him he was not evil and that these were simply thoughts that had nothing to do with who he was. I knew that confirmation from me would immediately give him some relief, which is why I started my reply off with it. But I also knew he would need more than that in order to come to terms with these thoughts.

I went on to explain that we are not our thoughts. We are spiritual beings experiencing life in physical bodies, which was something we'd talked about a number of times before, so it was a familiar concept to him. He was getting older, though, and capable of understanding this from a broader perspective, so I felt it was an appropriate time to expand upon it. I went on to explain to him that our bodies are basically organic machines, and that our brains are the central processing units for those machines. I explained that our brains do many, many things to keep our body running and that it never fully rests. Even during sleep our brain keeps running, although in a different state than when we're awake. Our brains are designed to constantly run and process information. Part of that information processing is for it to try to understand words, images, sounds, ideas, concepts, and so many other things. I emphasized to him that what he was experiencing was simply his brain analyzing information and that information can sometimes get stuck in a loop, especially if it's something we're sensitive to for any reason.

I went on to give him an example to help him grasp this concept. I told him to think of a piece of food he was trying to eat that was large or tough. He would have to chew it over and over again until it was small enough to swallow. I then told him that information in his brain was similar. His brain sometimes needed to chew on it awhile before it could swallow it. I followed that up by assuring him that the bad thoughts were just that. Thoughts from his brain and not from him. I could sense more relief falling upon him, but I needed to dig even deeper to truly seal the deal.

I asked him why he felt the number 666 was bad or evil. He basically said that it was because it represented the devil, and the devil is evil. I challenged him on that notion by asking how he knew that. He replied that his mother (my ex-wife) had told him so and that he had seen stuff on the internet about it. I asked him if that made it true. I think he picked up that I was challenging him on this idea as I could sense that he was starting to feel doubtful and confused on how to answer. I stopped him from thinking any further about his reply and explained to him that the world often can instill information upon us and that it can be easy to simply accept that as truth, especially when it comes from someone who is loved and trusted. However, I told him that he should always validate information he receives blindly until he himself knows it as the truth. Otherwise he could end up unintentionally believing in lies.

I wanted to give him an example to solidify this in his mind, so I googled the origin of the number 666 on my phone and explained to him what I was looking up. I had previously seen a TV show where the backstory of the number 666 had been discussed at some length. It had stuck with me because up to that point, I had also believed or maybe feared that it indeed represented evil. After watching that show, I had done some research on my own to validate if what was presented was accurate or not, since it drastically changed my outlook on the subject. Everything checked out in my research, so I had decided on my own to rewrite my view on the number. I now wanted to present the same information to my son in hopes it would help him as well. I quickly found one of the web pages that I had used in my previous research, which summarized the many the different origins of 666. I then began reading through it out loud for him.

Before I proceed I definitely recommend to my readers to do your own search on this subject, evaluate it on your own, and come to your own conclusion. I'm certainly not trying to push any particular view. I'm simply expressing my and my son's point of view as it relates to this story.

After reading through the backstory of the number 666, I asked him if with this new knowledge he still felt that 666 represented the devil, or the beast as he now understood as the more formal terminology. He had already interjected some questions throughout my reading of the backstory, and it took a bit of time to go through it, even though I was skimming to a certain degree, so he was able to come to a quick answer. "No," he replied. I asked him why. His reply, in summary, was basically that it appeared like it stemmed from a coded term referring to the Roman leader Nero Caesar, who was a brutal tyrant. Nero was a bad person to say the least, and it's fairly easy to see, once you understand the backstory, how the number 666 mutated over time into the current generalized concept of referencing the devil or evil. We went on to discuss and concluded that the number 666, as it pertains to evil, was simply a false belief. Or my preferred term…a lie.

With his new point of view on the number 666, he was now starting to feel less fearful of it. He was realizing that the fear that had built up in him was a construct of his mind, all based on false information. With his fear of 666 now breaking apart and fading into nonexistence, I decided to tackle the concept of the devil and prove the same point. This time I didn't need to pull up a web page on the backstory of the devil. I already had a summary reasonably organized in my noggin, which was surprising actually because I generally have a shitty ability to regurgitate information on the fly.

I proceeded to explain to him the convoluted backstory of Satan, or the devil as he was referring to it, and how much of the concept was created slowly over time, with layer after layer of different ideas being placed on top of each other and mutating into what we currently see as this horrible overlord of hell and evil, an opposite of God per se. I explained that once you understand the backstory and how it all came to be, you start to realize that it's just another lie that was created over time and passed down, generation after generation. As expected he now put the concept of the devil in the same category as the number 666.

With the truth of 666 and the devil/Satan illuminated in his mind, I dove back into how our minds process information. I reiterated that what our brain is thinking isn't the same as what we, as spirits, are thinking. And it certainly doesn't define who we are. I went on to explain that, over my own life, I've struggled with repetitive thoughts myself and how they were oftentimes things I perceived as bad. I told him that I use to stress and fear so much that I thought maybe I was going nuts. I explained how it took me years, literally a good portion of my life, to break it all down and understand what was really going on. Our physical brains and our spiritual selves are different and separate from each other. And if you focus on it, you can learn to decipher which is which, so you don't drive yourself batshit crazy over it.

I explained to my son how I now know that when something is stuck in my head, or I'm hung up on some worry, it's just my brain chewing and trying to swallow something that's a little too big for just a few chews. I shared that I've learned to cut myself some slack and understand it's not me. It's just my brain cranking away as it's designed to do. I show myself compassion and reiterate to myself that it's ok–it's really ok.

I also reiterated and elaborated that our bodies are essentially machines with Central Processing Units (CPUs…i.e., brains) designed to run all the time. Our brain needs to run so just give it the room and compassion to do what it needs to do. We can help it along by trying to understand what it's getting hung up on. Give it information and time to contemplate so it can break something down quicker and easier. We need to show our brain some love and kindness and trust it to do its job. We need to trust ourselves as well–our true selves, the spiritual us–that energy that is who we are behind our brains.

Before I wrapped up this conversation with my son, I wanted to give him one more tip to help him when brain-based thoughts get overwhelming or feel like they're out of control. I shared with him that something I learned to do was to say a positive mantra. Not only say it but repeat it over and over in my physical mind. I explained to him that more often than not, things that get stuck in my head have a negative connotation, at least to me anyway. I found that a great way to combat that is to have a positive and comforting mantra that I can put into my brain and run it on repeat. What I've found is that my brain can't think multiple things at the exact same time. It can bounce from one thought to another, and it can do it so quickly that it may feel like multiple thoughts at the same time, but it can't actually think multiple thoughts on top of each other. With that being the case, I can take a mantra and force-feed it to my brain and have it run on repeat over and over so that there's no room for another thought to exist.

I continued by explaining that if you–your spirit/true self–feed some other data into your physical brain, then it will have no choice but to take it. You may have to be diligent and intentional about it, since it can very quickly and easily flip from one subject to the next, but it is possible to override what it thinks about. I told him that it's like chewing food and not getting it down, so you remove the food from its mouth. Once it's had a little break, then it will either not need to chew that thought anymore, or the break will have given it much-needed energy to now chew it up properly.

I explained that he could make up any mantra he wanted. Anything that was easy to repeat over and over again and was charged with positive energy. I gave him mine as an example, which is this...all is good, all is great, all is wonderful, all is amazing. And then I told him I repeat it over and over again. I told him that I think it rhythmically so my brain can take it and run it on auto play. Before I know it, whatever thoughts that were hung up are either gone or diminished to a point they don't bother me. And if they start to come back, which is common, then I simply run it again until I'm at peace.

The nice thing about a positive mantra is that not only do the thoughts of these words replace other thoughts, but also, because they're positively charged, they overpower and eliminate negatively charged thoughts as well. So it's a double whammy! I told him I use my mantra all the time, even at times when I'm just in a crappy mood or if I see or hear something that triggers me. The positive energy that my spirit, the true me, gives to my physical brain and body through this mantra are powerful. It's like turning on a light in the dark. Just a little bit of light illuminates the darkest of rooms. I explained that the light of a positive mantra is an invaluable tool to overcome the darkness that can exist in our physical minds.

In the end, this conversation helped my son in ways that will last a lifetime. It woke him up to the reality that our brains are amazing and powerful pieces of technology, but they are not who we are. Our brains are not us. The thoughts in our brain are not us. Thoughts from our brain are simply part of the functionality necessary to grow in and navigate this physical world. He woke up to the reality that lies are all around us, and we need to question everything until we personally know it as the truth. How lies can wreak havoc on our minds and affect us in deep and profound ways. How we need to be compassionate and loving with ourselves and treat our brain and body with care and understanding, so it can learn, grow, and evolve as we need it to. My son woke up to the reality that we are our spirits and that our bodies are simply the vessels in which we travel this physical world. By the end of this conversation, my son was able to finally get that rest he so desperately desired. And he went to sleep a little wiser than when he had awoken.

You Be Trippin', Bro

I once had an interesting experience that highlighted to me how exactly my brain works as well as everyone else's, I'm sure. It was a challenging experience indeed but one I don't regret one bit. Through it I got an inside look at my brain's processing of information, which has proven to be an invaluable piece of knowledge I can now share with others. Put on your seat belts, kids, as I take you on a wild, wild trip…

One evening some time ago, I decided to give marijuana a try. I had never tried it before but had been curious for a number of years. I also was searching for something to replace beer in a special weekly ritual I enjoyed, as I had sadly discovered that I was allergic to alcohol. Yes, you read that correctly...I'm allergic to alcohol. It's fucking depressing to think about, to be honest. Do you know how devastating it was to find out I could no longer drink beer? *Oh... my...God...*devastating! The reason for this devastation might come as a surprise though.

I was never much of a fan of alcohol until I was in my late thirties when I found a beneficial use for it. Now, now, I know what you're probably thinking. Found a beneficial use? Seriously? Duh, the buzz is beneficial all on its own dipshit! Yeah, yeah, I know that, but I honestly never liked alcohol or the buzz that came along with it. Alcohol always made me feel...well, yucky. It gave me the worst headaches, no matter how much I drank, and the buzz just wasn't worth it. Little did I know that the yucky feeling was a direct result of the allergy. The one and only type of alcohol I would drink, and on rare occasion, was beer...Guinness, to be specific. I don't know what it was about Guinness, but it simply didn't make me feel as bad as other beers or alcohols. And I enjoyed the taste. That could be because of my Irish roots. Guinness probably ran through my ancestors' blood like water does in a river. Or maybe it has less of whatever I'm allergic to in it. Regardless, it was the only alcoholic drink I would even consider taking down.

One day when I was in my late thirties, I had read a story about how some Buddhist monks would use alcohol as a tool in their meditation practices. What the story went on to say, basically, was that the monks would drink to a point where they'd loosen up but not lose control. Once the alcohol took full effect, they'd get into a deeper state of meditation. I found the concept fascinating and wanted to try it. So I bought myself a pack of Guinness and went for it. I didn't achieve the full result I was looking for right away, but I did find it beneficial. From that point forward, I began using Guinness in a once-weekly meditation ritual. Before I knew it, I started experiencing some amazing shit. It sounds crazy, I know, but I'm absolutely serious. Once I got the hang of it, I could get into a meditative state where knowledge would flow to me with less interference than without the alcohol.

Now before you go getting any crazy ideas, this type of meditative state certainly has its uses but absolutely is not something you can do daily. Alcohol, no matter what anyone says, is toxic to our human bodies. You can have some, and your body will process and eliminate it without too much issue. Too much, though, and you will simply be poisoning it. So don't go getting any dumb ideas that you'll get buzzed every day under the guise of meditation. It simply doesn't work like that. However, within reason and with some practice, it is a useful meditative tool.

For me I found that three 14.9-ounce cans drunk in quick succession over about thirty to forty-five minutes did the trick. Early evening worked best for me, and I preferred it served in an ice-cold glass usually between 6:00 p.m. and 7:00 p.m. And very importantly, I needed to go into it with a positive vibe and relaxed mind. Quite often I would watch a movie that I felt energetically drawn to as long as it was all positive vibes. And yes, I can meditate while watching a movie. Call me crazy if you will, but I swear I can. It's kind of like the conscious state of deep awareness I noted in lesson 1—just more intense and you're not nearly as with it. Think of it as an alternate form of meditation.

My favorite movies to perform this ritual with are the Disney® masterpieces *Moana*® and *Coco*. There's just something about those movies that crack me right open during this ritual. Once I enter this meditative state, I literally feel my body loosen its grip on my spirit. Now keep in mind that your body and spirit are separate entities, but they are connected to each other. Breaking the connection presumably only happens when the body dies. I don't know that for sure, but it makes sense. When I'm in this meditative state, the alcohol seems to loosen that connection a tad bit. Just enough to allow information to come through that normally is blocked either by the brain or by the tight connection the two inherently have. This loosening grip doesn't last long. Like maybe thirty minutes to an hour, I'd estimate. During that time I can simply connect to information and/or knowledge that I already have access to, but it just flows with less interference. This ritual was something I very much enjoyed on a weekly basis. Any more than that and my body would become too resilient to the alcohol, and the grip wouldn't loosen as much.

With this ritual being so beneficial to me, having to eliminate it because of an allergy to alcohol was the shits. But I respect and love my body, so I do what I must. Letting go of this ritual is what led to my endeavor with marijuana. I was curious if I could achieve something similar with it. It was a long shot but worth trying. I absolutely despise smoke, though, so puffing the magic dragon wasn't an option for me. So I did a bunch of research on edibles and the various strains available. Once I narrowed down what seemed like the best option for me—a citrus-flavored gummy in case you're curious—I went ahead and ordered them online and picked them up in person the same day.

Later that night I decided to give the edibles a go. I followed my typical ritual of getting in the right frame of mind and tuning my vibe to right channel. Then I popped one just as was recommended, since it was my first time. About thirty minutes later, I could start to feel it kicking in. Fifteen minutes after that, I started to feel it peak and then start dwindling away. At this point I wasn't particularly impressed. I don't know how to describe the feeling it gave me, but it certainly wasn't the loosening effect I was used to. It really wasn't much of anything actually. My feet got a little warm, and I was a bit tired. Other than that, it was just meh.

After about an hour, I felt like the high had completely worn off. I started to wonder if I should have another. The recommendations I had been given were to wait two hours before taking another though. By that point if you aren't feeling much, then it would be safe to take just one more. So once the two-hour mark came up, I went ahead and took one more. About thirty minutes later, I started to feel a much stronger effect, though still not what I was looking for. After another thirty minutes, I was getting supertired and decided the whole thing was a bust. I figured I'd just call it a night and go to sleep. There was a problem though. I was supertired, yet I couldn't sleep; I was almost wired like on an intense caffeine high or something.

What proceeded to occur was what I now would refer to as a bad trip. Though I felt nearly nothing from the first gummy, the second appeared to have amplified its effects tenfold. What I started to feel was not the loosening effect I was looking for but instead was a tightening effect. My thoughts seemed like they started racing faster than I had ever experienced before. I was so tired and just wanted to sleep, but the thoughts in my mind were just going apeshit. The feeling of being so tired you could just crash in place yet so wired was becoming excessively disturbing. I started to feel a sensation I had not experienced in many years. An old enemy that would rear its ugly head at the worst of times...panic. I was starting to freak out.

I had long ago conquered my panic attacks, but here that feeling was roaring back with a fierce intensity. I knew I needed to do something, but what? All I could think of doing was to lean on all the techniques I had learned on my journey of defeating fear and panic, to pull on the spiritual knowledge I had gained over those years.

The first thing I did was make sure I was breathing properly. Slowly in and out. Deep breath in, hold it...deep breath out. Again, deep breath in, hold it...and deep breath out. I continued with this while I sat upright on my sofa with my legs crossed in a mediation-type pose. I then began rubbing my belly in a circular pattern. I always had found that to be very grounding for me in my states of panic, and it was working this time as well.

Despite these efforts, I could feel my brain freaking out still. I wasn't spiritually freaking out, but my brain was. This was a very interesting thing. I was clearly aware of the thoughts from my brain–separate from me–my spirit, the real me. There was a very clear separation without any doubts. I spiritually was able to think separately from my brain. It really didn't feel like thinking though. It was an awareness rather than thinking. Imagine an old-fashioned hard disk drive in a computer versus a new solid-state drive. The hard disk drive (i.e., my brain), was cranking away at full rpm scouring through information. The solid-state drive, on the other hand (i.e., my spirit), already had the information, and there was no spinning. No thinking or searching. I was just there, along with all my knowledge. I was separate from my brain and my body, yet it wasn't a relaxed connection like I would feel with alcohol. I was gripping onto my body and brain as tightly as I could, trying to regain some level of control.

As I became aware of the separateness of me from my brain/body, I started to become aware that I was struggling for control of it. Imagine playing a video game, and the controller is tripping out, so your avatar in the game is doing all kinds of crazy shit. You keep wiggling the joystick and pressing the buttons, but the avatar isn't reacting as it should. You gently move the joystick to the right to move what you think should be one step, but your avatar goes twenty steps to the right, twenty steps to the left, and then jumps. You're like, What the fuck! That's how I was feeling. Like I was desperately trying to control my avatar with a malfunctioning controller.

Once I realized this, it actually made it a bit easier to deal with. I didn't have full control, but at least I understood it was malfunctioning, and I just needed to proceed cautiously. So I kept breathing and rubbing my belly. As I did this, I could see my brain thinking, cranking away like a madman. The thoughts were wild–not in the sense of what the thoughts were about, but uncontrollable like a wild animal. I didn't know what to expect, and I was at their mercy.

All of a sudden, a fearful thought came into my brain, and I felt my body start to panic. The thought was about being out of control. I realized my brain had taken the awareness of my spirit and run those twenty unexpected steps further than would normally occur. Spiritually I was calm, but physically my brain and body were panicking. I realized I needed to be more careful with what I was thinking spiritually, as my brain would pick up on that and run with it. In an effort to stop my brain from running amok with a fearful thought, I decided to repeat my positive mantra over and over again. This helped. My brain became preoccupied with the functionality behind repeating the mantra, and that, combined with the positive vibes, gave me the ability to calm it down.

By this point, I was sitting cross-legged on my sofa, stoned out of my mind, carefully breathing in and out, rubbing my belly, and forcing my brain to repeat a mantra over and over again. I was in bad shape, but I had stabilized the situation. My brain was still full-on tripping, but my spirit was ok.

I didn't know how long this trip was going to last. After all, this was my first time, so I had no reference point for when my brain and body would come down. I just sat there repeating what I noted previously, over and over again. At this point I had no reference to time either. I couldn't have told you if I had been in this state for ten minutes or ten hours. Looking at a clock was low on the priority list, not that my brain could have really comprehended it anyway. I was still in deep. I had to keep a tight focus on the breathing, belly rubbing, and mantra-repeating; otherwise, my brain would have slipped and started panicking again.

At times the thoughts would creep back in, and I'd have to put the mantra back in play to block them. It was an exhausting battle. My body was so tired; spiritually I was exhausted, but I couldn't stop with the routine. I tried lying down to go to sleep, but the moment my body started to drift off, the thoughts would come racing in with a powerful intensity. I couldn't control it in that state, so I sat back up and kept up with the routine. I couldn't keep going like this all night though. I needed to do something different. So I decided to start walking around the house. I lived in an open-concept condo at that point in time, so it was easy to walk from one room to the next. I just got up, kept breathing carefully, rubbing my belly, and walked aimlessly from the front room through the dining room to the kitchen and then back around. I was in auto mode in a sense.

Walking around the house actually helped, as it was another controlled distraction for my brain, and I was able to chill a little bit on the mantra. Thoughts started to pop up in between the mantra, and it seemed ok for the most part, depending on the thought of course. If a fear-based thought came to mind, then the panic would start, and I'd have to push it out with the mantra. As the non-fear-based thoughts came in, I let them be, mainly because I was exhausted and needed a break from the death grip I had on my physical consciousness.

An interesting thing happened while I was walking aimlessly through the house. I started to observe the thoughts of my brain in a way I had never experienced before. Not only was I hyperaware of the separation between my mind/body and me—my spirit—but I was also experiencing the thoughts of my brain with clearly defined separation from each other. Each thought was like a movie playing within a small movie theater, which was housed within a megaplex of countless other thoughts/theaters. Each theater had a single door that could be seen and accessed from a central corridor, which seemed to extend on forever. I spiritually would open an illuminated door and step into a thought/theater. In it was one thought playing on the screen, and there were thousands of subthoughts that made up all the scenes in the movie. For example, if a thought as a whole was about needing to go to the bathroom, then the subthoughts were the nuances of executing such an action.

From the center hallway of my megaplex mind, I could see the infinite number of darkened doorways to each thought/theater. And I could see which thought was in focus by noticing the lights on in that theater. As I stepped into a lit up thought/theater, I could see what it was playing on screen. The subthoughts/scenes were scattered among the theater, and my brain was trying to organize them to create a coherent story to show on screen. Just as it was all coming together and beginning to make some sense, my brain changed focus and moved to a different thought/theater. The thought I had been in was still there, but the lights were out, and the movie wasn't playing any longer. I then moved to the theater that was now lit up and playing a different thought/movie. Once again, it was a mess, and my brain was trying to put the scenes together. Before I knew it, regardless of whether the scenes were organized or not, off the lights went, and my brain was off to a different thought.

I followed each thought and observed my brain as it bounced back and forth between thoughts. Some thoughts it left behind would become a focus again, and the movie would pick up where it had left off. It was organized chaos, but it was enlightening to observe. I was seeing how my brain was processing information from the inside. Chaotic but beautiful. It was like looking at the inside of a functioning machine.

This carried on for I don't know how long until I eventually started slowly regaining control of my brain and body. The fear-based thoughts couldn't get in as easily, and the separation between me and my brain/body was becoming less observable. I eventually stopped walking and went back to the sofa, where I got into the seated position and continued carefully breathing, rubbing my belly, and repeating the mantra as needed. My guess is that it had been a few hours at this point, but I'll never know for sure. It was clear to me, though, that I was finally coming down.

Considering my progress, I was willing to try lying down again to see if I could sleep. It honestly scared me, because I didn't want those fear-based thoughts to come roaring back in, triggering a panic attack. I thought maybe I should stay up a little longer just to be on the safe side. So I pushed on. Before long I was starting to drift off while in the seated position. As I drifted off, I seemed to be ok, so I eventually laid down and allowed my brain and body to sleep.

Honestly, that experience was kind of fucked up, and I didn't like it at all. It wasn't the worst thing I had ever experienced, but I definitely wouldn't voluntarily do it again. And without a doubt, marijuana was not going to be a possible substitute for alcohol in my weekly meditation ritual. Something wonderful came out of the experience though. So wonderful I wouldn't undo the experience if I could.

Observing the clear separation of my mind and body from me, my spirit was enlightening and awakening. I had already understood and fully believed in the concept of all this, but the experience gave me an enhanced awareness to it that has carried on ever since. And observing the thoughts as I did…boom! Mind blown! Wow, this was seriously enlightening. It was like taking a tour of my brain and learning how thoughts work inside it. This knowledge has given me a deep awareness and perspective that allows me to understand everyday situations so much differently. Anytime I feel fear, I can much more quickly and easily recognize if it's a fear from my brain or an energy I'm picking up on spiritually. The same even goes for things I'm attracted to. I can quickly recognize if it's my brain that likes it or if it's an energy I'm connecting to. All I can say is, the experience was profound. Scary as shit in the moment but life-changing. I am so much more aware of what is me and what are thoughts from my brain.

What About Bob?

The human brain is a powerful tool. The analysis it's capable of running (i.e., thoughts), along with the simulations, memory storage, sensory processing, and countless other quantitative and functional tasks, is immeasurably profound. Especially considering the speed at which it performs all of these functions often simultaneously and without our conscious awareness. As spirits navigating this existence in these human bodies, our human brains are some of our greatest allies and friends. When we don't understand it, though, or if we lose control of its power, it malfunctions, or we simply misuse it, then it can turn into a major pain in the ass. Understanding it and how it functions is key to preventing that from occurring. Having compassion for what it's doing, what it's trying to achieve, and its limitations are key elements of that understanding.

A great example of how the brain can turn into the aforementioned pain in the ass comes to us from the 1991 movie titled *What About Bob*,[9] starring the hilariously funny and divinely wise Bill Murray. In the movie, Murray plays the character Bob Wiley who, according to his new psychiatrist, Dr. Leo Marvin, played by Richard Dreyfuss, is an almost paralyzed multiphobic personality who is in a constant state of panic.

The movie begins with Bob making his way to Dr. Marvin's office to begin treatment. En route you see Bob struggle with hypersensitivity as well as fears of germs and enclosed spaces. As he leaves his building, he has to use tissues to open doors. As he walks through New York City, he has to use a mantra to manage the chaos around him. And once he gets to Dr. Marvin's building, he opts to take the stairs up to the forty-fourth floor, rather than taking the claustrophobic elevator. It's clear that this poor guy is struggling in his life, despite the classically lighthearted and funny delivery by Murray.

Bob was referred to Dr. Marvin by his former psychiatrist, Dr. Fensterwald, who was closing down his practice in a clear effort to get away from Bob and his eccentricities. Dr. Marvin, who you learn is a self-centered and egotistical dickhead, agrees to interview Bob after Dr. Fensterwald butters up his massive ego by telling him that Bob needs someone brilliant like him. Dr. Marvin of course takes the bait and unknowingly sets Dr. Fensterwald free from all that is uniquely Bob and transfers it directly to himself.

After this call between Dr. Marvin and Dr. Fensterwald, Marvin informs his secretary that a Bob Wiley may call, and she should schedule a short interview with him after he returns from his vacation. His secretary responds to him by saying that Bob has already called twice and is his next appointment. Shortly thereafter Bob stumbles out of breath into Dr. Marvin's office after having climbed the forty-four flights of stairs.

What awkwardly proceeds in Dr. Marvin's interview with Bob is an abbreviated but relatively traditional psycho analysis. Bob describes his long list of symptoms while Dr. Marvin listens and attempts to get to the core issues. At one point Bob mentions he had been married previously but had left his wife because she liked Neil Diamond and he didn't. Dr. Marvin challenges Bob on this notion by clarifying with him that, despite Bob being an almost paralyzed multiphobic personality who is in a constant state of panic, his wife didn't leave him, but rather he left her because she liked Neil Diamond?

Bob, who appears a bit startled by this clarification, then asks Dr. Marvin if he is implying that maybe he didn't leave her because she liked Neil Diamond, but that maybe she left him? Dr. Marvin bluntly tells him, yes. Bob then begins repeatedly saying, "Ow, ow, ow, ow," grabbing his stomach and flailing about. After a moment he settles down and takes a deep breath. He then looks at Dr. Marvin with a wide-eyed and almost relieved look on his face and says, "Dr. Marvin…you can help me. For the first time in my life, I feel like there is hope. I feel like I can be somebody."[9]

Dr. Marvin admits to Bob that yes, he can help him. He begins by giving Bob a copy of his newly released book titled *Baby Steps* and explains that the book is about setting small and reasonable goals for yourself, one day and one tiny step at a time. Dr. Marvin gives him some examples, like don't think about what you must do to get out of the building; instead think about what you have to do to get out of the room. Then deal with the hall as another step and so on and so forth. Bob enthusiastically takes to this idea and bravely starts making his way around Dr. Marvin's office, literally taking tiny steps as he maneuvers. Bob is certainly excited to use this new technique.

Dr. Marvin then opens his office door and tells Bob, "This should give you a lot to digest while I'm on vacation."[9] Bob begins to panic. Dr. Marvin explains to him that he will be on vacation with his family for one month beginning that afternoon but that they can schedule a session for after Labor Day when he returns. Still panicking, Bob asks him what he can do if he needs to talk during that time. Dr. Marvin tells him he will have an associate that will be glad to talk if needed. And of course he'll be back, so they'll get to talk…after Labor Day.

As Bob baby-steps his way out of the office, Dr. Marvin assigns him the task of reading *Baby Steps* during this downtime. Bob then repeats the words "baby steps"[9] over and over again as he makes his way out the main door, through the hall, and to the elevator. Once to the elevator, he repeats his new mantra onto the crowded lift. As the doors close, a huge smile beams across Bob's face, excited that he is conquering his fear with Dr. Marvin's technique. The next thing you hear is Bob screaming as the elevator descends to the first floor.

What occurs in the coming scenes is Bob struggling to deal with the fact that he can't speak to Dr. Marvin while he's on vacation. He attempts to call Dr. Marvin's phone service to see if they'll give him his number, but they refuse. It's becoming clear why Dr. Fensterwald wanted to get away from him. He has clearly relied on his psychiatrist to make it through his day. Eventually Bob resorts to lying in an attempt to get Dr. Marvin's contact information. He fails initially and in various ways, but eventually he gets a post office box by charismatically pretending to be a police officer supposedly investigating Bob Wiley's suicide. Of course he doesn't really commit suicide, but the answering service doesn't realize this and gives him the doctor's mailing address in an effort to support the investigation of his supposed death.

With the mailing address in hand, Bob decided to use his new baby steps technique to board a bus to Lake Winnipesaukee, New Hampshire, where Dr. Marvin is vacationing. He doesn't have the doctor's home address there, but it's enough to get him close. Once he arrives in this small town, he begins randomly screaming Dr. Marvin's name until he eventually finds him exiting the local grocery store with his family.

I don't want to spoil the rest of the movie in case you haven't seen it, so I will keep the rest of what I say of it narrowly limited to the point of why I'm sharing it in the first place. What proceeds is Bob clinging to Dr. Marvin like a scared puppy, desperately trying to get him to talk with him in an effort to ease his psychological pain. Dr. Marvin refuses to speak with him, gets seriously annoyed, and tries to get rid of him at every turn. In this process, though, Dr. Marvin's family gets to know Bob and really likes him. Bob likes them as well as they fill a void missing in his life. He fills a void for them as well, a void created by Dr. Marvin's massive ego.

As the movie continues, Bob's challenges begin to fade away. It becomes clear that he's not the psychopathic stalker that Dr. Marvin now thinks he is. He's actually a very kind, fun, generous, and sensitive guy who just needs love and support from genuinely kind people to overcome a large number of varying psychological symptoms caused by what I personally define as a very powerful and hyperactive brain.

You see, at the heart of Bob's issues are his excessive brain-based thoughts. You learn throughout the movie that he's exceptionally intelligent and thinking of everything all the time. And that constant bombardment of unmanaged and uncontrolled thoughts have spiraled into a perpetual state of psychological chaos. Unlike what people who didn't know Bob thought of him and even those that did know him–like his current and former psychiatrist–Bob is just a normal person deep down. A normal person who has struggled to manage his excessive thoughts. They weigh him down like a wet blanket, and he doesn't have the know-how to understand what they are and how to manage them. He just thinks he is nuts.

At one point in the movie, Dr. Marvin selfishly concocts an idea he hopes will rid him of Bob for the remainder of his vacation. He writes Bob a prescription not for pills but for him to take a vacation himself, a vacation from his problems. Now this may have been a selfish maneuver by Dr. Marvin, one that he naively thinks will take place back in New York City, but it ultimately is exactly what Bob needs. It is a mind-blowing moment for Bob and creates an opportunity for him to finally show himself some much-needed compassion. Compassion to take a break from those excessive thoughts that have been plaguing him for so long. As he does this, Bob reveals to Dr. Marvin's family just who he really is. This wonderfully caring and fun guy who just wants to be loved and enjoy his life. As he begins to do that, he ends up positively impacting the lives of those around him. Except for Dr. Marvin, sadly, whose ego-based psychological issues trigger his own chaos.

In the end, Bob's life is changed for the better. Bob learns to show his brain compassion and how to separate his true self from his powerful yet excessive brain-based thoughts. Now those thoughts likely never stop for him. He just learns how to separate from them and find a happy place where he can let them be what they are without them controlling him. And it's this very notion that is the basis of this lesson. You are not your thoughts. Your thoughts are simply a function of your brain. They are a form of analysis that is necessary for you to live and function in this world. Each brain is a little different, though, so how one person's brain functions isn't exactly how someone else's functions. Each person has to learn how to maneuver that joystick, so their avatar doesn't go too many steps further than they intend.

Please note that my comments about the fictional character of Bob Wiley are simply my observations based on my own experience of dealing with such things, as well as my intentions behind this book. I'm not a psychiatrist or medical doctor and am not making any kind of medical diagnosis for this fictional character, or for anyone, fictional or real, for that matter. I'm simply highlighting the reality that we all have a little bit of Bob Wiley in us and how the thoughts we all have can easily spiral out of control, leading to a form of psychological chaos not that much different than what Bob Wiley experienced in various forms. We're all just scared puppies looking for someone to help us through our psychological pain. We all desperately need and yearn for unconditional love and support, especially from ourselves.

Girl, You So Crazy

As this lesson concludes, I would like to leave you with this gentle reminder. Your brain is an organic computer, and it can run some amazing analysis and simulations. It's easy to get lost in that, though, and lose track of what's real versus what's a creation of your physical mind.

I've been very fortunate to experience some crazy shit in my life—crazy shit that triggered me to learn how to separate myself from my brain and understand how my thoughts are a product of my brain's functions. For me what triggered the enhanced awareness was a variety of life challenges. They were the pathway to school per se. But it wasn't the life challenges that taught me the awareness. It was the school itself that did the teaching. Access to this school starts with your interest in enrolling. Once you choose to enroll, the lessons will start to come on their own. So if you desire an enhanced awareness to you versus your brain/thoughts, then just be interested in it. Open your mind, your energy, and your intentions to it. It will naturally come once you do.

Finally...here's a brief reminder to always be kind to your body and brain. And be kind to you as well. You and your avatar are amazing and doing the best job possible in a really tough situation. Your brain can be a little fucking crazy at times, and that's ok. You can be a little fucking crazy at times too, and that's ok as well. This experience we call life is fucking crazy, and you got it–that's ok. Nobody ever said it wouldn't be crazy. Once you understand what life is really about and why we're experiencing it, you'll understand why the craziness was necessary and what an amazing job you did navigating it. You'll compassionately understand, without any doubts, that you are not your thoughts.

LESSON 3:

Flow with Life like a Leaf in the Wind

Wax On, Wax Off

What do you think of when you hear the word *flow*? I think of effortless movement, like waves flowing effortlessly onto the beach, water flowing harmoniously down a river, or a leaf flowing gently in the wind. A wave doesn't dictate what beach it'll land on; it simply does its thing, and the moon pulls it to its destination. Water in the river doesn't say, "I want to roll in the rapids or meander through the shallows"; it just goes where it's drawn. The same goes for the leaf in the wind. The leaf simply goes wherever the wind blows. It doesn't matter if it lands on the ground, on a bush, or on a pile of shit. It just goes where it goes and accepts its destination with grace and ease. It's all effortless and just happens.

Being human obviously isn't the same as being a wave in the ocean, water in a river, or a leaf in the wind. However, there is a flow to our lives, just like there is for anything else in nature. Unlike the wave, water, and leaf, though, we do have an influence on where we flow. With influence comes a challenge to learn how to consciously choose to flow with the energy of life—energy being the wind and us being the leaf. Before we can do that, we must learn about control. For if we don't find the balance in control, we can end up wasting our time trying to consciously control something we can only control through our spirits and through the universe itself. We must learn to find balance in the control we have physically versus spiritually and leverage that against what we don't have direct control of.

Throughout my younger life I had been confronted repeatedly with lessons involving control. It was rarely obvious to me in the moment though. It wasn't until I looked back that I could see the pattern emerge. As time went on and the lessons involving control piled up, I started to become aware that control was a big and complicated lesson for me to learn and fully understand.

Early on I was confused over why there was such an emphasis placed on control. After all, I wasn't a controlling person, so why were so many of life's lessons about it? Eventually I came to learn that this confusion stemmed from an overly simplified view of what control is. I was thinking too one-dimensionally. I honestly was not a controlling person in the sense of everybody needing to do what I said or me always needing to be the leader. On the contrary, I was always open-minded and receptive to people's input, and I was more than happy to let someone else take the wheel.

Professionally I frequently found myself in leadership roles, simply because I was a jack-of-all-trades, very knowledgeable, personable, and an outside-of-the-box kind of thinker. I couldn't stand micromanagers so was always conscientious not to be like that. I genuinely was pretty mellow yet influential. I could be stubborn at times but definitely not controlling. Managing people was a gift, and I definitely knew how to influence without pushing.

On the personal side, my now ex-wife was supercontrolling, and there was absolutely no room for me to be as such. I certainly took control over anything I was so graciously granted authority over, home repairs, yard work, or taking out the trash. But I definitely wasn't controlling in the relationship itself. If anything, I was too much of a pushover. Wait, no—I was definitely too much of a pushover. Yet here were these lessons about control hitting me over, and over, and over again. In time they forced me to reevaluate my understanding of what control is.

As life lessons came and went, I began to understand what my issue was with control. It took me a really long time to truly understand and master it. I started with gaining an awareness of it by looking beyond that one-dimensional perspective I mentioned. I eventually learned that my issue wasn't that I was trying to control anyone or that I was a micromanager. My issue was that deep down my life felt out of control, and it wasn't flowing with the energy of life. My life was chaotic as I resisted that flow. I was tumbling through life rather than flowing with it.

Most of my professional life, I had worked in a corporate environment, where I desperately grasped onto any element of my job that gave me even the slightest bit of creative freedom. If it hadn't been for those elements, I'd just be a lifeless robot doing a meaningless job. Day after day being told what to do, what the priority was, and how I should think. I was forced to drink the corporate Kool-Aid® and pretend to love it as it choked me on the way down.

On the personal side, I was married to a very selfish, egotistical, controlling, and manipulative asshole, whose only interest in me was the money I made from my meaningless job and what I could provide her. That relationship manifested from a childhood growing up with a very selfish, egotistical, controlling, and manipulative asshole of a father along with a mother who, like me, had fallen into a bad relationship from her own bad childhood and didn't know how to teach me anything otherwise.

After a lifetime of feeling out of control, it was progressively getting worse. An unpleasant situation indeed. Other than my son, nothing in my life was enjoyable or inspiring. It was out of balance. Being out of balance for so long created a desperation for change. That desperation resulted in me trying to force change anywhere I thought I could...and I emphasize *thought*. So yeah, it turned out that I did have control issues after all. It wasn't a result of me being an overall controlling person though. It was a result of my life being out of control and spiraling into a minefield of counterproductive actions in an attempt to gain the control I so desperately needed.

Am I Being Punk'd?

Forcing change gradually became a big issue for me as I became consciously aware of my misery. For example, at one point in my life, I had sought a different job that paid more and elevated my position on the corporate ladder. It was 2012 and I had already ended the relationship with my now ex-wife. We were still legally married and living under the same roof since our son had some medical issues that required one parent to stay home with him full time. I couldn't afford to support two households, so moving out simply wasn't an option. Well, it could have been if I was a selfish dick, but that's genuinely not who I am.

Even though I was sticking around for the benefit of my son, that didn't tip the scales enough to create the balance I so desperately needed. So I had a nifty idea that if I were to find a different job that paid more, then–bada bing, bada boom–problem solved. I could then afford two households. As lovely as that sounded, I wasn't listening to my intuition so was headed into one of those minefields I mentioned previously. And I was destined to trip over one.

After this decision to look for a higher paying job, I found a job posting online at a company in the same industry I had worked in for many years. It was a start-up, though, and the position required specific experience, which I definitely had. I thought I fit the bill so went ahead and applied. Sure enough, a couple of weeks later, I got a call and discussed the position with the head of the company. As soon as I started speaking with this guy, warning signs started going off that this wasn't the right path. My desperation blocked me from recognizing those signs, though, so I kept on with the interviews and negotiations.

The process ended up taking several months and even resulted in me being invited to have drinks with this guy and his team at a trade show in Orlando, Florida. Looking back I remember so clearly how awkward it was having drinks with them. I was so uncomfortable being around them. I mean, they were friendly and all; I just didn't feel like we jived, you know? My anxiety was through the roof, and conversations felt forced at best. I felt like I needed to act like someone different in order to convince them I was the right person for the job. Turns out I was pretty good at that, too, because I finally was offered the job as director of operations.

As soon as I got the job offer, I could feel it was the wrong move. Something inside me was screaming not to do it; I blew it off as nerves though. I had read so many times that if you want change, then you need to accept discomfort to make it happen. If you aren't comfortable with a promotion, then take it anyway and fake it until you make it. With that in mind, I took the job.

Once I had accepted the new position, I informed my then current employer of my resignation. My boss at the time really liked me, and

I figured she would try to make me a relatively small counteroffer. However, she actually didn't offer me a pay increase at all. Instead, she offered me a bonus to stick around–$25,000 to be precise. She didn't offer me a pay raise because the powers that be had frozen increases as a result of financial challenges the company had been facing. The only thing she could do for me was the bonus, which was a loophole in the freeze, and it certainly was a nice chunk of change.

I was a little shocked with the bonus offer to be honest. My gut told me to take the deal and stay there. My brain told me to take the other job because it had better long-term opportunities. I knew I couldn't go anywhere at my current employer. I had been in the same position for several years, and there was no room for growth. I was making $75,000 a year, plus now I was being offered this one-time bonus. Here was this other company, though, that I would be getting in at the ground level, making $90,000 plus bonuses. This company was owned by a billionaire tycoon, so it was well financed and seemed to have minimal risk. It was a no-brainer. Yet here I was with this feeling telling me to stay with my then current employer and take the bonus, feeling that I wasn't fitting in with this new company, and having anxiety through the roof when I thought of taking that offer. I didn't listen to it though. My logical brain told me to go with the logical choice. So I did.

Once I started with this new company, I immediately began having issues. The nice guys who invited me for drinks turned out to not be so nice. Toxic masculinity, big egos, and fake-it-until-they-make-it kind of guys. I tried to continue fitting in with this crowd, but it wasn't going to be easy. I am not a macho guy by any means, and fitting into that is far outside my comfort zone. I did all I could to pretend, but things went downhill fast...very fast.

It was just two weeks after I started with the company that the top dog asked me to lunch to talk business with him and the head of finance. I didn't think much of it until we arrived at the restaurant and sat down. The look on his face turned sour as we began to talk. He proceeded to degrade and berate me for not achieving more in my first two weeks. I just about fell out of my seat when he came at me with this. His face was red, and he was making a scene. He was going off about how we had discussed in the interviews that he would like to see a portion of the distribution that was currently being outsourced be brought in-house. He had indeed asked during the interviews if I could facilitate that, and my answer had been an absolute yes. However, I had told him at the time that, based on volume, it would be best to wait until we reached a specific amount of sales before doing it; otherwise, it would be too cost-prohibitive. He agreed at the time and said it was something for down the line. That was the last I had heard of it until this very moment. Now, all of a sudden, he was saying it should have already been done. I was at an absolute loss trying to understand how this was happening.

Needless to say, the meeting was going terribly at this point, and I was completely caught off guard by all that was being said. As shocked as I was, what he said to me next was literally unbelievable to me, even to this day.

The top dog proceeded to tell me that I had until the next day to bring that portion of the operation in-house. I was sitting there thinking, This has got to be a joke. Is he serious? This is something we discussed at a very high level in an interview a month prior. Once I started with the company, he hadn't even brought it up, let alone defined a timeline. Was I being punk'd or something? No, I wasn't, and yeah, he was very serious.

I very calmly and politely told him it was impossible to bring this portion of the operation in-house in just one day. I explained this was a huge undertaking and would require building out a department, making custom equipment purchases that had multi-month-long lead times, hiring, training, and negotiating out of the contract with the existing vendor–a contract that was signed by him long before I started with the company. I told him it was a six-month project at a minimum, and we still didn't have the sales to make it cost-effective. I had hoped he would come to his senses with this information, but no, it just pissed him off even more. He quickly stood up, stormed out of the restaurant, and drove off in a huff like a temperamental two-year-old.

Once the top guy left, I looked over at the finance guy and asked him what happened. He simply shook his head and told me that reaction was very typical of the boss. Oh my...what had I gotten myself into?

Once the finance guy and I got back to the office, the top guy didn't speak or even look at me for the rest of the day. Of course I did everything I could to come up with an alternative to present him the next day, but I didn't make it that far.

I was scheduled to visit a vendor the next morning before coming into the office. When I arrived at their facility at 7:00 a.m., I found the head of finance sitting in his car in the parking lot. After I parked he got out of his car and walked toward me. I could feel the weight of what was about to take place. In the short conversation that proceeded, he told me that the top guy was so angry with me that he couldn't even speak with me face to face and, on his behalf, asked that I resign. I of course refused. He then fired me on the spot and handed me my final paycheck.

Yep, you heard it correctly. I was fired after two weeks, and I was devastated. But I was also relieved. I had accepted that job as a way of escaping the misery I had been in, but I ended up walking into an even more miserable situation instead. So yeah, it sucked, but there was definitely a sense of relief to be done with it.

As I was driving home from this horrendous experience that fateful morning, my cell phone rang. I looked down at my phone and recognized the number; it was my former employer's main line. Normally I wouldn't have picked up the call while driving, but something told me to do it. In this moment I stopped resisting and picked up. In the brief time it took for me to recognize the number and pick up, I pondered who could be calling. All I could come up with was, maybe it was a former coworker friend checking in on how things were going. I had no idea what I would say if that were the case. I would be so embarrassed to admit to the shit show that had played out. Much to my surprise, though, the person on the line was my former boss.

After a brief greeting, she asked how things were going with my new job. I was hesitant to give the whole story, so I downplayed it for the moment and only told her that it wasn't going very well. She paused for a moment and then proceeded to tell me that she was relieved to hear that, the reason being that things were getting rough on her side as well, and she was hoping I'd consider coming back. A rush of relief came over me as I started to respond. I of course proceeded to accept the offer, minus the $25,000 bonus sadly. But I was relieved to not be unemployed, as the devastation of that had already turned my stomach before she called.

After this unexpected experience, and accepting my old job back, I became consciously aware of the universe setting me back on course. All the pressure came off as I started to flow with the energy instead of resisting it. I didn't necessarily like where I appeared to be going in the moment, but it was better than where I had just been, and I was certainly appreciative of that.

In that moment I started to become aware of the energy of life and how I needed to flow with it, appreciate it, and not judge it or try to dictate where it flowed. In that moment I started to understand and appreciate that the big picture is difficult to see when you're zoomed in so closely in the moment. I needed to pay attention to that flow and trust where it was taking me.

As time went by, I learned why it was taking me where it was taking me, and it all eventually made total sense. So I no longer judge it in the moment…I simply trust it. I flow wherever it goes and know it's where I need to be in that moment.

The moral of this story is that I knew right off the bat that accepting this other job was wrong. I felt it in my bones. But I was blinded by desperation. I came up with a logical reason to discard what my intuition and the universe were telling me. The signs were all there the entire time; I just didn't open myself to them. I was resisting the flow of energy and trying to force what I thought rather than accept what I felt.

The energy was flowing in the direction of me keeping my existing job. When I was offered the bonus to stay, it was the universe flowing even stronger in that direction. I didn't flow with it though. I decided to resist, and the pressure immediately began to build up. It only took two weeks before the pressure became too much, and the energy found a way to get me back where I needed to be.

I might say the whole experience was a failure, but I won't. Why? Because I learned from it. This experience was a highlight for me that, in part, brought my attention to how I ignored the flow of energy.

So even though the experience was an utter failure, it was also an astonishing success.

Oh, Korra

After that experience, and after many others, I began to feel the energy flowing. I began to hear it whisper to me the direction I should go. I definitely made some mistakes along the way, but that was ok; it was simply part of the learning process. Over time every single lesson I faced taught me something invaluable. Piece by piece I was being taught what being controlled was, what being out of control was, what forcing things does, what balance is, and ultimately how to enjoy life and live in harmony. I was learning how to flow with life like a leaf in the wind, which is why the title of this lesson is this phrase. The phrase itself, though, wasn't inspired by a direct experience I encountered. It was actually inspired by an episode of a TV show I once watched with my son, which highlighted to me the concept of flowing rather than forcing.

It's very typical for me to be inspired by movies, books, TV, music, etcetera. I find creativity to be a very subtle way in which the universe speaks to me—and most likely all of us. The particular TV show episode that inspired the title of this lesson spoke to me so clearly and stuck with me so deeply that I carried it with me until this moment so I can share it with you now.

One December day, I sat down in my front room where my son was watching an animated TV show that I had neither seen nor recognized. I didn't always watch the animated shows he watched, but this one caught my attention. I was immediately drawn to it in a special kind of way that I had spent my entire life learning to consciously recognize and understand. It was calling to me. The universe was speaking to me in its natural language and bringing my attention to this show. The name of the show was *Avatar: The Last Airbender®*.[10]

In case you've never heard of this show, it's kind of a cult classic, circa 2005, and is about a world that is divided into four nations: the Water Tribe, the Air Nomads, the Earth Kingdom, and the Fire Nation. Some of the people who are native to each of these nations have the ability to manipulate the element that is the symbol of their nation. So, for example, some people of the Water Tribe can manipulate water, those of the Air Nomads can manipulate air, and so on. The manipulation of these elements is something they call *bending*. There is one person in this world who can manipulate, or bend, all four elements though. This person is given the title of *avatar*.

There is only one avatar at a given time, and when that avatar dies, their spirit will reincarnate in a newborn child. Each time an avatar reincarnates, their physical body will be born into a different tribe, rotating in succession. The avatar is responsible for keeping balance among all the nations, which is partially why they're born to a different nation upon each rebirth.

This particular show is about twelve-year-old Aang, who is the eighty-second avatar and is born to the Air Nomads. Aang is the last airbender because of a failed attempt by the ruthless leader of the Fire Nation, the Fire Lord, to kill off the avatar as a child before he could master all four elements and become too powerful to defeat. With the passing of Avatar Roku, the eighty-first avatar, everyone knew the eighty-second avatar would be of the Air Nomads since Roku was of the Fire Nation. But who the avatar actually is isn't clear until the Avatar child is older. Because the Fire Lord didn't know who the new avatar was, he simply ordered that all airbenders be killed.

Avatar: The Last Airbender®[10] aired for three seasons, and each season is named after a book, with each episode titled as a chapter in each book. The premise of the show is that Avatar Aang must learn to master all four elements to defeat the Fire Lord and restore balance and peace to the world. In each episode Aang learns an important lesson that eventually leads to him mastering all four elements. To gain the mastery of each element, he must find another bender of that element to mentor him. Mastery of each element isn't necessarily easy and challenges him each step of the way.

As the seasons/books progress, one key element that Aang must learn is balance. He can't force the elements to bend. He has to flow with them and allow them to bend through him. Anytime he tries to force the energy to go where he wants, he ends up metaphorically, and sometimes literally, falling on his face. Flowing with the energy is key. Eventually he masters all of the elements and ends up encountering the Fire Lord in an epic battle.

I won't give any more details about what happens in the series in case you decide to check it out yourself, which I highly recommend you do, no matter your age. You might think it's just an animated TV series, but it's far more than that. There are many great lessons it teaches if you can open yourself to it. For me and my son, it was a great bonding experience that spurred many conversations about life–all in a lighthearted setting that made it easy to discuss and connect to. We both loved the series so much that we were anxious to watch the spinoff series about the eighty-third avatar, which contained the episode that inspired the title of this lesson.

In this spinoff series titled *The Legend of Korra®*,[11] you learn how Korra is the eighty-third avatar and is born to the Water Tribe. She very quickly masters three of the four elements, with the remaining element being air, the most challenging for her to learn.

In book one, chapter two, titled: *A Leaf in the Wind* [12], Korra begins her air-bending training with her mentor Tenzin, the late Avatar

Aang's son. Tenzin walks Korra through what appears to be a simple task. There are a series of gates–which looked more like doors to me–in a formation and are held upright on a centered pin. The gates are lined up in a woven pattern to form a gauntlet-type device. Tenzin tells Korra she must make it through this gauntlet without touching the gates. She immediately smirks, thinking it'll be easy. You, as the viewer, can't help but think the same thing because, though the gates are all close together, there's plenty of room to walk between them without touching them. However, she and the viewers quickly come to realize that it's not going to be that simple.

With Korra's confidence at a high, Tenzin then activates the device by using his own air bending abilities. Each of the gates in this gauntlet starts rapidly spinning, and you can now see that the gates will be very difficult to pass since they're no longer in their fixed positions, and the pathways between them aren't nearly as defined. As each gate spins, you question if there's even room to pass as one edge of a gate comes into close proximity of another. The speed at which the gates are spinning is such that you can't even see when the edges get close together, let alone see how to navigate between them. They're literally like propellers on a plane or helicopter, spinning so fast you can't see the actual propellers, or individual gates. You just see a blur. In addition the spinning creates a vortex of wind that would affect one's ability to control their body as they move through the gauntlet. Getting through it now looks nearly impossible.

With the gauntlet at full speed, Tenzin pulls out a leaf, holds it up in front of the gauntlet, and releases it. As the leaf is sucked in and begins passing effortlessly through it, Tenzin tells Korra, "The key is to be like the leaf...flow with the movement of the gates."[12] Tenzin then asks his young airbender daughter, Jinora, to demonstrate. As Jinora enters the gauntlet, you get to observe this young child flowing through it with smooth, gentle, and effortless movements. While Jinora is passing through the gates, Tenzin tells Korra, "Air bending is all about spiral movements. When you meet resistance, you must be able to switch directions at a moment's notice."[12]

This scene caught my attention. I was fascinated to watch this leaf move through the gauntlet so effortlessly. And then to watch Jinora do the same thing…wow! So impressive! All of it made sense of course, but I was just fascinated with how much of a metaphor this is for life.

Korra, with her typical fearless bravery, ends up giving the gauntlet a try, and as you can imagine, she smacks into the first gate. Her problem is that she is trying to force her way through it. She quickly becomes frustrated and gave up for the day. Over time and through various life challenges, she learns to not force her way. She learns to flow with the energy, which is physically represented by the wind, as it moves around each gate. The energy knows the path and inherently makes its way through. After learning to flow with that energy, Korra successfully gets by each gate and through the gauntlet.

In time learning to flow with the energy rather than forcing it not only gets Korra safely through the gauntlet but also gives her the ability to air bend and move the air as she desires. What I've learned is that life is just like the gauntlet and air bending. Once you learn to flow with life like the leaf on the wind, then things get much, much easier.

The Only Way around It Is through It

Learning to flow with the energy of life isn't easy by any means, though it does get easier the more time you spend being aware of and observing it. It's something that challenges even the most attuned and awake people. Recognizing the flow of this very subtle energy, which you can't physically see, is like watching the wind. You can't see the wind itself, but you can feel it blow against you. You can see the effects of the wind, but you can't actually see the energy that is driving it. Flowing with the energy of life is similar in the sense that you can't directly see it. You can feel it though. You can feel how it affects your physical energy; you can feel it in your gut, per se. You can see how it affects things around you.

When you see a leaf floating in the air, you know it's the wind that is moving it. When you get laid off from your job, meet a new friend, lose someone you care about, get pregnant, have a girl or a boy, get stuck in traffic, arrive at Starbucks and find no line, etcetera–you can see the effects of the flowing energy of life. That flowing energy is moving your life in different directions, no matter how significant or insignificant those effects may appear to you.

You can resist the flow of energy if you'd like, but doing so will only make the energy flow more turbulent. The energy will go where it needs to go, and you can't consciously control it, just like the leaf can't control where the wind blows. You can control your awareness to this energy, though, and you can control your choice to resist it or not. You can also control whether you trust and respect it as well. Just keep in mind that this energy is part of you, it's part of the collective energy of the earth and the universe, and it's how your higher self and your spirit guides move you through life. This energy is you and deserves your trust and respect.

A great example of flowing with life is me writing these words right now. As I sit here, I have no fucking idea what I'm going to write. I'm flowing with the energy that has brought me to this point though; I'm flowing with the energy and where it's taking me. Yes, I have made a conscious choice to write. But that conscious choice came in the form of me accepting the path that the energy is taking. I'm not judging it or arguing with it. I'm not resisting it. Logically speaking my brain is like, *What the fuck dude? You're nuts to be writing this, and it's a waste of your time. People are going to think this is all hippie bullshit.* That's in my brain though; it's not the energy. I am neither my brain nor the thoughts of my brain. They are merely tools for me to use to help navigate this physical world.

Sometimes what my brain thinks is spot on. Like, *Don't touch that hot pan.* Sometimes it's wrong, like, *Don't write those words… nobody is interested in what you have to say.* I understand that both are simply fear. Fear is a natural function of the brain and is designed to warn you when there is something to be fearful of. It's my spiritual responsibility to listen to what it has to say and then decide if it's a valid fear or not.

For my brain, the fear of someone not liking what I'm writing is no different than the fear of touching a hot pan. Both are negative situations, and my brain is simply providing me the data to evaluate. I decide what data to listen to and what can be disregarded. I feel for the energy all around and within me and then decide if the thought flows with it. If yes, then the thought is valid. If no, then it's not valid. My brain fearing rejection is absolutely a legitimate fear. It doesn't match the energy I feel, though, so I choose to disregard it as an invalid fear. That decision is mine and mine alone. It's me choosing to flow with the energy of life.

If I were to choose to listen to those fears of rejection and not to write what I'm writing, then I would be resisting the flow of energy. I can do that if I choose; nothing is stopping me from it. But I would then be resisting the flow of energy, and that would come with a side effect, just like there's a side effect of disregarding the fear of a hot pan. In that case I would get burned.

Resisting the flow of energy is like trying to stop the flow of water in a river with your hand. You can do it temporarily, but the water will crash against you and build up pressure as it does. The longer you resist it, the more tired you become of the water constantly pushing against you.

Resistance takes effort, and any kind of effort requires use of your own internal energy. Imagine holding a glass of water in your hand for one minute. No big deal, right? Now imagine holding the glass of water for ten minutes. Getting annoyed but still ok. Now imagine holding it for an hour. You're getting seriously tired and have long since started to cramp up. Now imagine holding it for an entire day or even holding it forever. Eventually you either drop the glass of water, or you stand there uncomfortably getting depleted of energy until you do.

Some people resist so much that they end up miserable. I'm choosing not to resist, not to drain my internal energy. I understand the difference between my thoughts and me, I recognize and feel the energy of life. So I sit here now, and I write, disregarding the legitimate fear of rejection and accepting the other thought in my brain that sees the possibility that someone will read what I'm writing and like it. My words, or the intentions behind them, might be helpful to someone out there. That thought matches the energy I feel. So I go with it...I flow with it. I flow with the energy around me, with the energy that's in me, with the energy that's inspiring me, and with the energy of life.

Listening to this energy isn't always straightforward. We all can feel it, but it takes willingness to grow and understand it. This energy is part of you, your true self. Remember, you are energy. So you have an inherent ability to sense it. The issue is that you are experiencing life in a human body and so are confined within its functional limitations in this physical world. You have to grow your intuitive abilities from your spirit to your physical body. By doing so, you will enhance your body's functionality, and this will allow better harmony between you and it.

Growing this ability takes time and effort of course and comes with successes and failures. Both the successes and the failures each teach you and your body along the way. Keep in mind, failure isn't a bad thing. It's a lesson that must be learned, just as the successes are.

Society tends to focus on success as being complete and good, while treating failure as empty and bad. But the failures teach us at least equally as much as the successes do, arguably more overall since we generally experience more failures than successes.

You can try something one hundred times, with ninety-nine being failures and one being a success. The ninety-nine failures were simply you learning ninety-nine ways to do it. The success was you learning another way to do it. The success or failure was determined by the goal, but ultimately all one hundred attempts each equally achieved something. What each achieved was based on the perceived goal. So success or failure ultimately is just a perception. All one hundred attempts were simply lessons. More often than not, you can't find the perceptual success without first going through the perceptual failures. As the old saying goes, the only way around it is through it.

Noodles, Don't Noodles

All of this talk of energy flow, resistance, acceptance, trust, thoughts of the brain versus feelings of your spirit, perception, learning, etcetera, makes me think of a scene from one of my favorite animated movies. Yes again with the movies and TV show examples. I'm very serious when I say that the universe speaks through creativity. So many great lessons are out there to be learned when you set aside the concept that a movie is just a movie and open your mind to what the universe is trying to tell you.

The movie I have in mind in this case is *Kung Fu Panda*®.[13] It's such a great movie on so many levels! It's funny, has action and suspense, is heartwarming, and has great life lessons hidden beneath the surface. Lessons that quietly whisper to you in a way that's easy to absorb and understand.

In case you're not familiar with the movie, *Kung Fu Panda*®[13] is about a panda by the name of Po, who is fascinated with kung fu and often daydreams of becoming the legendary dragon warrior, a mythical kung fu master. Po is a chubby and insecure panda, though, and nobody sees him as being able to practice kung fu, let alone be the dragon warrior. Po doesn't even believe it himself. He just fantasizes about kung fu and fighting alongside his idols, the Furious Five.

The Furious Five are a group of five kung fu warriors, comprised of a tigress, viper, monkey, crane, and praying mantis, who are all highly trained and skilled warriors. The Furious Five are led by a kung fu master by the name of Shifu, who is a tiny red panda with a dedicated and stern mentality toward kung fu. The Furious Five and Master Shifu all live at the Jade Palace with Master Oogway, a very wise and elderly tortoise, who is the creator of kung fu and is Master Shifu's mentor.

The Jade Palace is a sacred kung fu training facility, which is situated atop Jade Mountain and overlooks the Valley of Peace. The Jade Palace and its surrounding grounds contain many ancient relics of kung fu history. The palace grounds also contain a variety of mystical locations that Master Oogway utilized in the process of creating kung fu and attaining enlightenment.

One day, Master Oogway has a vision that the snow leopard, Tai Lung, the story's antagonist and former kung fu prodigy of Master Shifu, will break free from prison and return to wreak havoc on the Valley of Peace. Tai Lung had been imprisoned some years before because he had gone on a rampage after Master Oogway saw darkness in him and refused to declare him as the mythical dragon warrior. After this vision of Tai Lung escaping, Master Oogway tells Shifu it's time to finally choose the true dragon warrior and that they will stop Tai Lung and save the Valley of Peace. He also tells Shifu that not only will the dragon warrior bring peace to the valley but also to Shifu himself.

With Oogway's announcement to Shifu that it's time to choose the Dragon Warrior, Shifu arranges for a tournament to be held at the palace, where Master Oogway will purportedly make his selection. Master Shifu assumes the dragon warrior will be one of the Furious Five, since they have been training all of their lives to become the ultimate kung fu warrior. That proves to be an incorrect assumption, however.

As the tournament begins, Po rushes to the palace to catch a glimpse of who the dragon warrior will be. He ends up running late because his father, who owns a local noodle shop, wants him to sell noodles at the event. As Po hurries over with a noodle cart, he arrives to find the palace doors closed. Being the diehard kung fu and Furious Five fan, he is determined to get in.

After hilariously trying and failing numerous ways to get into the tournament, Po comes upon a box of fireworks, which gives him an idea. He ties the fireworks to a chair in an effort to shoot himself over the walls. That of course doesn't go as planned. He ends up shooting himself high into the air, over the walls, and smack into the middle of the palace grounds, where Master Oogway is about to choose the dragon warrior. After he crashes into the middle of the arena, he opens his eyes to find the Furious Five all glaring at him. He then turns his head and sees Master Oogway pointing his finger at him. Master Oogway has chosen Po to be the dragon warrior.

Po being selected as the dragon warrior sends Master Shifu into a tizzy. He tries to convince Master Oogway that this flabby panda can't possibly be the answer to their problems. Shifu goes on to explain to Oogway that he had been about to point to Tigress when the panda landed in front of her. He pleads that it was just an accident to which Oogway replies, "There are no accidents."[13] This unfortunately doesn't satisfy Shifu, and he starts coming up with ways to make Po's life so difficult that he'll quit by morning. What proceeds is exactly that. Shifu does everything he can to force Po out. Po doesn't give up, though, and keeps powering through, failing over and over again. No matter what Shifu does, Po just won't give up and quit, which only further frustrates Master Shifu.

After an evening where Po tries and fails to befriend the Furious Five, he winds up below a peach tree stuffing his face with as many peaches as will fit in his mouth. Just then Master Oogway walks up and says, "I see you found the sacred peach tree of heavenly wisdom."[13] Po panics, not realizing the tree is sacred and begins spitting out all the peaches. He apologizes profusely to Master Oogway, who replies, "I understand. You eat when you are upset."[13] Po tries to deny it, but the wise Oogway sees beyond his words.

Master Oogway proceeds to ask Po why he's so upset. Po breaks down and vents to Oogway how he had sucked more that day than anyone has ever sucked in the history of kung fu, in the history of China, in the history of sucking. To which Oogway replies, "Probably."[13] Po goes on to vent how the Furious Five hate him and how could Shifu ever turn him into the Dragon Warrior. Oogway agrees with him along the way. Po then tells Oogway that maybe he should go back to making noodles. Oogway then replies, "Quit, don't quit, noodles, don't noodles. You are too concerned with what was and what will be. There's a saying…yesterday is history, tomorrow is a mystery, but today is a gift; that is why it's called the present."[13]

The next morning Master Shifu and the Furious Five awake to find Po not in his room. Shifu proudly announces his conclusion that Po has finally quit. As they proceed outside, they find that Po hasn't actually quit but is instead stuck in one of the training apparatuses. Master Oogway's wise words had inspired Po not give up, and he had enthusiastically gotten up before everyone else to start training early. Master Shifu sees Po's renewed determination and gets even more determined himself to force Po out. He tells Po that he's been taking it easy on him but no more. As Shifu literally beats the crap out of the panda, Po optimistically promises Shifu and the Furious Five that he will never quit. This determination and the official news that Tai Lung has indeed escaped prison triggers Shifu to find Master Oogway and appeal to him about the situation.

Shifu finds Oogway at the sacred peach tree of heavenly wisdom and, in a fit of frustration, tells him of Tai Lung's escape and how the panda is not fit to defeat him. Oogway calmly responds by saying, "My old friend, the panda will never fulfill his destiny, nor you yours, until you let go of the illusion of control."[13] Shifu replies, "Illusion?"[13] Oogway then says, "Yes, look at this tree, Shifu. I cannot make it blossom when it suits me, nor make it bear fruit before its time."[13] Shifu responds with clear frustration, "But there are things we can control."[13] Shifu then hits the peach tree, knocking down numerous peaches. He continues on by saying, "I can control when the fruit will fall. And I can control where to plant the seed. That is no illusion master."[13] Oogway giggles a bit during Shifu's rant and once again calmly responds by saying, "Ah yes, but no matter what you do, that seed will grow to be a peach tree. You may wish for an apple or an orange...but you will get a peach."[13]

The conversation and movie continue on of course, and I will indeed leave you at a cliff-hanger with it. I stopped there because that wisdom that Oogway shares with Po and Shifu is spot on to what I am discussing in this lesson. There are things we can control and cannot control. There are things we control spiritually and things we control physically. We have influence over our physical lives, but we cannot physically force life to go where our spirit and the universe do not want it to go. We cannot force things to be what our minds think they should be. We must respect and trust our higher selves, the universe, and the path that we spiritually have chosen. There is a balance in accepting what is, what can be, and what will be. You must feel for that balance. You must accept that you are not physically in control of the bigger picture; you never have been and never will be. You must flow with life by riding the energy that moves around and through you.

Ugh! Stop Being So Grabby

Sometimes I think to myself how balancing control in life is like placing an open hand in a river or stream. If you allow your hand to calmly rest in the water, then it will flow over and around your hand with ease. You'll be able to feel and enjoy the water as long as you allow it to flow. If you try to grab the water, however, then you'll find yourself empty-handed and frustrated.

Think about this for a moment: imagine placing your hand in a flowing river. Imagine the water flowing over it. Close your eyes and imagine the feel of the water and the energy moving it. Now imagine grabbing it. When you grab it, all the water and energy squish out of your hand, and you end up holding nothing. The harder you grasp, the less water and energy remain. Now imagine releasing your grip and again allow the water and energy to flow in your hand. You are able to hold them with an open hand. This is much like the energy of life. Allow it to flow, but don't try to control it. Flow with it, move with it, and be one with it.

It's Getting Deep in Here

As I end this lesson, I want to leave you with a task. Ask yourself this on a daily basis: What is life trying to teach me with my current circumstances? Regardless of whether you are facing challenges or not, no matter if things seem easy or hard, or if they appear positive or negative. Ask yourself this: What am I trying to teach myself, what am I trying to learn, why has the energy of life presented this situation to me? When you do this, you'll begin to remove the obstacles in your physical mind that lead you to believe that what happens in your life is random or in your physical control. As you relinquish that concept of physical control, you begin to gain access to the true spiritual control that always has been and always will be within you.

Once you reach this level of spiritual consciousness, you become hyperaware that you and your body are partners, that you and the universe are partners, that you and the energy of life are partners, that you are on a journey that you chose to take, that you chose this path for a reason, that control is in you but isn't just you, that individual control is an illusion and true control is really about harmony and balance with everyone and everything that exists. As these truths becomes clear, you begin to understand that physical life is simply a school; it can be enjoyable, but it's not all fun and games.

Sometimes the lessons are easy, and sometimes they're hard. Either way, you're learning, and that's the point of it all. Once you achieve this awareness and knowledge, only then will you truly flow with life like a leaf in the wind.

LESSON 4:

Beauty Is in the Eyes of the Beholder

Me, Me, Me, and Me

Beauty is in the eyes of the beholder...

If you think about that phrase—really break it down and fully digest what it might mean in its truest sense—you'll start to understand the depth of how much it says in such few and simple words.

If you were to google this phrase, you'd undoubtedly see a general consensus that it means, essentially, that physical beauty is subjective, that what one person sees as beautiful another may see as the opposite. To me that definition barely taps into the spectrum of what it actually covers. That definition implies that it's only relevant to physical beauty. I see it as being so much further-reaching than that. I see it really being about our perception as a whole and how any given circumstance in life can be beautiful depending on how you look at it, including the perceptually negative aspects of life.

So *beauty is in the eyes of the beholder* isn't just about physical beauty by any means; it's literally about how you perceive your entire life, the people in it, the situations you face day in and day out, the world overall, and even the entire freakin' universe. This one phrase really taps into some deep and profound shit!

Perception. That's really what the phrase *beauty is in the eyes of the beholder* is about. I've let the concept behind this word and all that it potentially could mean simmer in my spiritual and physical consciousness for countless hours. There are so many implications to perception that I doubt it's even remotely possible to scratch the surface of what it can potentially expand into. I will try to cover some basics in this lesson, though, or at least what seem like basics from my own perception.

I'm going to get into some deep stuff, but I'll start off on the lighter side by thinking about a song I mentioned in lesson one. I'm thinking once again of the song "Beautiful,"[1] by Carly Rae Jepsen and Justin Bieber. "What makes you so beautiful is you don't know how beautiful you are...to me." This is such a beautiful lyric and message. More importantly it's such a beautiful thing to feel on both the giving and receiving side. As beautiful as the entire lyric is, I'd like to focus on just one part for this moment. I'd like to focus on the *to me* part.

Me, me, me, and me. Perception is all about you, yourself, and nobody else. With that in mind, what I love about it is that nobody can tell you what your perception is. Your perception belongs to you and only you. Others can certainly tell you what their perception is or what they think your perception should be. People can even influence your perception if you allow them to. But nobody can actually define your perception other than you. With that power comes another aspect that nobody can control besides you, which is that nobody can change your perception other than you. I can scream at the top of my lungs, shower you with money, or beat the crap out of you in an effort to change your perception, but none of it will work. Nothing will change your perception until you decide to change it.

As much of a relief as it is to know that your perception belongs exclusively to you, that relief quickly slips away when you eventually realize that it comes along with the responsibility of recognizing when to change it. It's also strictly on you if your perception is not serving you well. You created your perception after all, or you allowed someone else to influence your perception. So yep...it's all on you, baby! Still I think it's absolutely amazing that we have this ability, this power to control our reality simply through tuning our own perception. I don't know any other way to say it other than... well...it's beautiful.

The Prison Experience

I've often pondered the realization that two people can experience the exact same circumstance, but each of their perceptions will be different. They may be quite similar or very different, but either way, they're still unique to each person.

For example, I once saw a meme where two people were in prison, and each was painting a picture of the view from their cell. The first prisoner painted a picture of a drab window with bars on it. The second prisoner painted the same window but painted the outside beyond the bars. As a matter of fact, that second prisoner didn't even include the bars at all in their picture, so all you saw was the appealing outdoor scene through the window. Two people in the same situation, looking at the same window with two different perceptions.

The moral of that meme was that what you focus on, you create. It's a beautiful idea and very true in many situations. It's kind of the glass-half-empty-versus-half-full concept. However, that's a somewhat limited view for the most part. True, there are situations you may face where if you choose to not focus on the negative and, in turn, focus only on the positive, your experience will likely be much better.

For instance the second prisoner chose to not focus on the bars and instead only painted the outdoor scene. They presumably are having a better prison experience and a better life experience overall since they focused on the perceptively positive aspect. The first prisoner, on the other hand, was focused on the perceptively negative aspect, which is why they painted the bars on the window and no outdoor scene. Presumably the first prisoner would have a harder time in prison and in life since they were focused on the restricting bars on the window rather than the beautiful outdoor scene.

The reality is, though, that yes, you do need to see the positive side of things, but you can't hide the negative side either (i.e., the bars on the window). Otherwise, you'd just be living a lie. And that in itself is negative. A paradox maybe? Nah, I don't think so. It's really just about balance.

No matter the situation we face, it's so important to see the truth in it, regardless of what that truth is–and regardless of whether that truth is typically perceived as positive, negative, or somewhere in between. Let me repeat that: a truth can be perceived as positive or negative; it really depends on each person's individual perception.

If you can't accept the truth, regardless of its perception, then you're headed down a very dark and unpleasant path. Seriously! You can't go around pretending that the negative doesn't exist; otherwise you'll miss the truth far too often to have a healthy and balanced life experience.

The reality is that you need to be aware of the truth, no matter what your perception of it is. Once you acknowledge and accept the truth, regardless of your individual perception of it, then you can certainly choose what to focus on in that truth to create a perception that's more palatable for you. But ignoring or pretending that a perceptively negative truth doesn't exist simply will not get you anywhere you want to be.

I mention this because I have seen far too many *positive* people going around burying their head in the sand in an effort to stay positive. Some examples would be white people in the United States who genuinely see and treat people of color as equals yet don't believe racism really exists. Or a person who is utterly shocked when their partner unexpectedly ends a long relationship. You know... the ones who had no clue their partner was unhappy. These people can't handle the truth because they perceive it as negative, so they just ignore or bury it. The reality is that those folks are actually very negative; they just can't see it because they have their blinders on.

On the flip side, I've seen many people be perceived as *negative*, when in reality they're not at all. They're simply aware of the truth and aren't afraid to call it as it is. I have seen some folks like this focus too much on the negative, which only magnifies its intensity, but they aren't really negative themselves. They're actually very positive since they're open to the full truth.

Let me give you an example of acknowledging the whole truth, regardless of the negative or positive perception, and then altering your focus so you create the perception you choose. Let's go simple here and use the aforementioned prisoner painting scenario.

Assume for a moment that both prisoners are consciously aware of what it is that they're not painting. So the first prisoner is consciously aware that there's an appealing view of the outdoors beyond the bars, and the second prisoner is consciously aware that there are bars blocking the view of the outside and keeping them trapped inside the cell. In this scenario both prisoners have equal awareness of the full truth. However, the first prisoner has made a choice to focus on the perceptually negative aspect of the situation, and the second prisoner has made a choice to focus on the perceptually positive aspect of the situation. Neither are hiding or missing any part of the truth of their reality, which is truly amazing actually. They are both simply choosing a different aspect to focus on, which is each of their prerogatives and isn't for anyone else to judge.

I intentionally note above that each aspect is perceptually negative or positive because the reality is that neither one is negative nor positive. They are both simply facts of the situation. Each person has a perception of what they find positive or negative and then chooses what to focus on. Again, it's all each person's prerogative, and it's not for me, you, or anyone else to judge that decision. We must respect it.

However, the view of the second prisoner is generally perceived by most people as positive, as most people would get a better feel off of the vibe of that outdoor view than they would off of the view of the bars. It's a reasonable conclusion then that most people would prefer to focus on the vibe that makes them feel better. After all, everyone wants to feel good, right?

The key thing here, though, is it's a choice as long as you are aware of the whole truth. With that choice you get to choose your perception. You get to choose if you focus on what makes you feel good or what makes you feel bad. Again, what makes you feel good or feel bad is not for anyone to judge other than yourself. Heck, someone may look at the bars on the window and see them as comforting and see the outdoors as scary. Hey, it could happen! In that case the bars are perceived as positive, and the outdoors are perceived as negative. You must feel that for yourself, though, and then define your perception as *you* choose.

Now let me pose a different scenario. It's the same prisoner painting situation but this time assume both prisoners are not consciously aware of the whole truth. So the first prisoner is not aware of the outdoor view, and the second prisoner is not aware of the bars in the window. Now this may seem silly because, duh, who wouldn't see the bars on the windows, right? Roll with me on this, though, because it plays into a bigger picture.

In this scenario both prisoners are trapped into perceiving one perception because they aren't aware of the whole truth of the situation. So both prisoners are actually in the same boat. Neither one of them is making a choice, so both are in equally negative situations. Yes, you read that correctly. They are both in equally negative situations. Why? Simply because neither is consciously aware of the whole truth–they're only seeing part of it. So both are living a lie. Now the lie of the first prisoner may be perceived by you and me as more negative than that of the second prisoner, but both are actually equally negative. Just like the prior scenario when I noted that both prisoners' perceptions were neither negative nor positive because it was their decision to make. In this scenario, though, neither is making a choice, so both are truly prisoners of their limited awareness. This type of situation is always negative, and that's not my perception. It's simply a fact.

The Poisoned Apple

Anytime there's a situation where the full truth is either not known or is being withheld, whether it be intentionally or unintentionally withheld, it really isn't a good thing. It's a really bad thing actually. Really, really bad.

Imagine for a moment that you were holding a poisoned apple in front of you and you're superhungry. If you know the apple is poisoned, logically you won't eat it, despite your hunger. If you don't know the apple is poisoned, then you probably will eat it and will most likely get deathly sick, fall into some wicked trance, or even die. Yuck! Sad, isn't it?

Now imagine that someone gives you that poisoned apple, someone who knows the apple is poisoned, and they are intentionally hiding the truth from you. This is a very bad situation indeed. This person is manipulating your perception of the situation. They have taken away your freedom to choose your perception. Superyuck!

Throughout human existence there have been far too many occasions where the truth has been hidden from people, and in turn, their perceptions have been manipulated. Take for instance something on a grand scale, like being told by your political, religious, or military leaders that a certain country is an enemy. This is quite ridiculous actually. Is an entire country of people truly your enemy? Fuck no! The political, religious, or military leaders of one country may be an enemy to the political, religious, or military leaders of another country, but the people themselves, as a whole, are not an enemy...and never will be.

A crazy thing about a situation like this is that oftentimes the political, religious, or military leaders of a country may never directly say that another country is an enemy. They may simply imply it in a speech by providing limited information or use the media to do the same thing. Once again someone creates a situation where you don't have all the information, yet you don't know that you don't have all the information. Because you don't know the whole truth, your perception is manipulated without your conscious awareness.

Now let's throw into the mix that such situations can occur not just from political, religious, or military leaders, but also from powerful corporations or individuals. Think about all the news you watch or read, TV commercials you see, social media advertisements, etcetera. Is your perception affected by those? You bet your ass it is!

The key to preventing this manipulation is quite simple, which is why it ultimately falls on you to ensure your perception isn't being manipulated. This is so simple it's laughable. You must question your perception of everything until you know the whole truth yourself, or at least a reasonable assessment of it. And question it often, even revisiting perceptions repeatedly. Over time you will inevitably gain new information, so it's important to regularly revisit your perceptions to determine if they need to change or not. If you do this then it makes it very difficult, and ultimately impossible, for anyone to manipulate your perception for any significant length of time. Manipulators rely on people not questioning their perceptions; it's their secret weapon against you. Questioning your perception disarms them and returns your power to you.

The Mind Fuck

A big part of experiencing a perceptually enjoyable and successful life is being able to see the bigger picture, to look at your experiences from different angles and opening yourself to knowledge that may not be staring you right in the face. This makes me think of a conversation I once had with a coworker friend—a conversation that highlighted exactly how our perceptions can be manipulated in ways that impact the very core of who we are and how we perceive our lives.

One day this coworker friend was venting to me about how it sucked always living paycheck to paycheck, as we both had been doing all our lives, and how wealthy people seem to have it right, but we have it wrong. She had it in her mind that wealthy people are successes, and those who are not wealthy are failures.

This coworker friend was someone I genuinely liked as a person. You know–just one of those people you feel an undefined connection with–like a soul friend or something. We both came from backgrounds where we had to be street-smart to make it through. We both were handed nothing and had to fight for everything we had. With us both living in the United States I clearly had it easier than her since I was a white man of Irish and English heritage, and she was a brown woman of Mexican heritage. Despite our different heritage, though, we had a special kind of kinship. We were like family...vibe family.

My friend had worked for the company that employed us for over twenty years. She had started out as a temporary employee and had worked her way through several positions before hitting a ceiling in a peon role. She was paid less than most other people, despite her tenure with the company and performing the exact same job. This was presumably because she was both a woman and of Mexican descent, and nobody really even noticed her for the most part. She was just a worker, sitting in a cubicle, in a sea of hundreds of other cubicles, all lined up in a drab and lifeless corporate office.

What I saw in my friend, though, was a bright and powerful old soul, someone who cared about what she did and busted her ass to get the job done to the best of her ability. She wasn't perfect by any means–nobody in her role could be, given the lack of support from the powers that be–but she worked hard and went above and beyond with every single thing she worked on. She was beyond awesome in my perception.

In this conversation, my friend had this vibe about her that came through so clearly to me. She was physically communicating that she was frustrated by her financial situation, but her vibe, which she didn't express physically, told me that she felt down about herself over it. She of course had her typical joking tone going on, kind of a fuck-my-life type of thing. But I saw deeper than that. I saw sadness, disappointment, and deep feelings of failure, the same feelings I had felt so many times in my life.

The vibes I was picking up from her in this conversation were so opposite of what I saw her as. So...I don't know...I had to do something to help her see her own beauty and success. What ended up coming out of my mouth was unrehearsed and unplanned. It actually shocked me that I said it because it was pretty deep and spot on, and I said it with such ease, confidence, and passion. It was like I had been divinely inspired to say what I said, almost like it wasn't even me speaking.

What I said to my friend opened her mind and changed her vibe. After I said it, I felt something click in her and in me as well. For her those feelings of sadness, disappointment, and failure faded away and were replaced with feelings of pure pride, confidence, and success. For me I realized right then and there that I could potentially help someone break free from the mind fuck that so many of us get caught up in.

My response to my friend was this: I said that I used to feel the same way, that somehow people with excess money were better than me, smarter, luckier, or more evolved in some way–that they had won gold at the Olympics, but I didn't even place. I'd ask myself what I was doing wrong and how could I fix it. I told her I was always so frustrated about it until one day I had an epiphany, a realization that it was all bullshit.

I went on to explain to her that I had spent countless amounts of time trying to understand life, learning different philosophies on spirituality, personal growth, and success. I told her how I had read self-help books on manifesting wealth and abundance but found them for the most part to be totally wrong. They felt wrong, deep in my soul. Sure, there were key pieces of information that were helpful or motivating, but mostly they fed into the same bullshit that society had already fed me, which was that I was doing something wrong, that I was failing and needed to learn to do it right, that those with money were the winners, and I was the loser.

I explained to my friend that at some point I finally came to the realization that all of those feelings of failure and inadequacy were being fed to me. Within all of my life lessons, meditations, inner philosophical journeys, and teachings by some truly wise teachers, what I had learned from it all was that we spiritually manifest everything in our lives. And that, as we evolve both spiritually and physically, we learn to need less and in turn manifest less. I told her that I noticed something consistent about the wisest and most humble people throughout time. They all have or had very few physical possessions in life. It wasn't because they were stupid or foolish, but because they were wise and that was what they chose to manifest.

I continued by telling my friend that my philosophy now is that those who are old souls—who are wise, who have evolved longer and further in life—are those who manifest only what they need. I then asked her if she was able to pay her bills. She said yes. I asked her if she had food and shelter. She again said yes. I asked her if she had a job and a car to drive to work in. She once again replied with a yes.

So I told her, from my perspective she was the one who was doing it right. She was wise to only manifest what she needed. She'd lived long and had learned that excess didn't serve a purpose—that those with so much excess had it simply because they had unresolved issues with selfishness—some more than others. Those with so much excess were those that still had much more to learn.

I described to my friend that I saw her as being a grad school student while the absurdly wealthy were like preschoolers still learning not to fight over and hoard all the toys for themselves. I begged her, "Don't be ashamed of what you manifest. Be proud of it. You are a beautiful and wise old soul who has learned to not be selfish, who has learned to not be wasteful, and learned to only manifest what you need." I emphasized that she was the one who was truly successful.

The moral of this story is so simple to understand yet so complex to implement in your life: we must break apart the perceptions that society hands us by questioning everything and searching for the true answers within ourselves. The complexity is that it is often easier said than done.

Even the most basic constructs of our society—like being wealthy is strong and successful while anything less is weak and a failure—can be challenging to unwind from our perceptions. Every single day in one way or another, the world is subliminally mind-fucking us and telling us what is beautiful, what is successful, what is right, what is wrong, and who we are. We are persistently lied to, so we must question everything, learn the truth, and define our perceptions ourselves.

When you watch a popular dating show on TV, you must resist being subliminally told what an attractive person should look like. You must have confidence in yourself when you step into a classroom or office space and see that the vast majority of the people are not like you, and you feel the pressure to change or hide yourself to fit in. You must build a protective wall in your mind when you're scrolling through social media and see advertisements for products that will fix all your supposed physical flaws or help you become successful like this person or that person.

All of this can be very challenging to prevent, especially when there so many other ways your perceptions can be influenced, like if you go to church and are told what is and what isn't good, when you go to work and are constantly evaluated for how productive or successful you are, or when you're at home, and your parents tell you that you should be a certain way. People may whisper and giggle as you walk through the mall because you are different than everyone else. Or when you read news headlines and people's opinions or suggestions are presented as facts. This is truly the hard part–to have strength to withstand the pressure, to hold tightly onto the true reality that you are beautiful just the way you are, and to always know that you, and you alone, are in control of your perception.

I could go on and on about all the different perceptions that we're force-fed on a daily basis by TV, news, advertising, political leaders, religions, employers, schools, friends, family, or by society as a whole. But I can't. You must dig into all of that yourself, open your awareness, accept that outside forces can influence you in ways that aren't obvious, feel for your own truth, and redefine your perceptions as you see fit. And do it over and over again. Over time you will evolve to be able to recognize a forced perception right when it starts to occur, and you'll learn how to prevent it from hijacking your perception before it can influence your outlook on life. Once you get to this point, then you'll truly alter your life for the better, because you'll be in full control of your perception, and you will choose how you want it to be.

The Clarification

Before I proceed further, I need to include a clarification. My comments to my coworker friend about wealthy people being immature and selfish aren't intended to imply that it applies to all wealthy people. Again, it's about balance. I know of some people who have lots of money, use it to do many good things in the world, and didn't step on anyone to get it. And obviously financial wealth is on a spectrum, with some people being slightly wealthy and others being filthy fucking rich. Regardless of where someone may fall on that spectrum, the definition of whether they're immature and selfish is defined by their actions or lack thereof.

A person can certainly be financially wealthy and not be immature and selfish. However, I have personally spent a significant amount of time around many very financially wealthy people and can say firsthand that a large percentage of them attain their financial wealth through immaturity and selfishness.

The reality is that people who are highly evolved very rarely manifest extreme financial wealth or an excess of anything else, for that matter. They're much too selfless, generous, and harmonious to do that. They may manifest comfortable abundance, but they rarely manifest anything in massive excess. The only time I've seen a highly evolved person manifest excessive financial wealth is because they needed it to achieve something extraordinary that primarily benefited others, not themselves. I will clarify this with an example to ensure that some selfish shit face out there doesn't use my words to wrongly create a notion that they're everyone's fucking hero or something.

A great example would be Oprah Winfrey, who is extremely wealthy but didn't create her wealth by stepping on or taking advantage of anyone along the way. She has dedicated a significant amount of her time and money to benefiting other people, mainly in the form of teaching. She operates by the principle that if you give a person a fish, they eat for a day, but if teach a person to fish, they eat for lifetime. Oprah has been an inspiration to countless people through her teaching, financial funding and donations, kindness, and generosity. She is truly a gift to society and needed to be extremely wealthy to achieve that.

In addition life is complicated, and there are so many paths and things going on that it's impossible to define someone's level of spiritual and physical evolution by just their level of wealth, or by anything else, for that matter. My personal belief is that we all learn from one another, and we all teach one another…for better or for worse. Some people may have lives that appear easier or better than others, but that is likely just an inaccurate perception based on limited knowledge of that person's life. Sometimes a person may be filthy rich but horribly miserable. Another person may be horribly poor but very happy overall. A person's level of evolution cannot be easily defined from a physical perspective, and it probably doesn't even serve a purpose to try to define it in such a way.

My comments to my coworker friend were about breaking down false yet common perceptions that society puts on us, the perceptions that tell us that those who have less are less, and those who have more are more. My comments to her were intended to awaken her inner knowledge that this common perception is simply untrue.

The Mind Fuck Part Deux

All of this talk about misperceptions of financial wealth and success makes me think of a wonderful short story. I've seen many versions of this story and honestly don't believe anyone knows who originally wrote it; otherwise I would gladly give them their due credit. The story is typically titled "The Fisherman and the Businessman," and the version I'm familiar with goes something like this...

A rich businessman is horrified to find a fisherman lying beside his boat smoking a pipe. The businessman asks the fisherman, "Why aren't you out fishing?" The fisherman replies, "Because I've caught enough fish for the day." The businessman then asks, "Why don't you catch more?" The fisherman replies, "What would I do with them?" The businessman then says, "You could earn more money. Then you could have a motor fitted to your boat to go into deeper waters and catch more fish. Then you would have enough money to buy nylon nets. These would bring you more fish and more money. Soon you would have enough money to own two boats...maybe even a fleet of boats. Then you would be a rich man like me." The fisherman replies, "What would I do then?" The businessman says, "Well, you could then sit back and enjoy life." The fisherman replies to the businessman, "What do you think I'm doing right now?"

Obviously, the moral of this story is similar to what I mentioned to my coworker friend. The perception that excessive wealth is the pinnacle of success is simply not true. That one must do more, be more, consume more, have more, more, more, and more. *No*...more is not better! The world ingrains in us that the financially wealthiest people in the world are these amazing and phenomenal success stories that we should admire and emulate. We're led to believe that the biggest and wealthiest companies around the globe are what every company should be like. Are they really successful though? I personally consider them a cancer of society, clear failures, and a result of flawed societal perceptions of success.

Now don't get me wrong, some of these companies have done great things, but overall, they have taken too much. Overall they don't benefit the world in a truly meaningful way. They haven't made a positive impact in society overall. With all their profits, they could easily have a fairly paid, happy, and healthy staff. They could stop polluting the environment, they could stop making environmentally hazardous packaging, they could make their products with the health of all life in mind. But they don't. They're selfish and immature, are run by selfish and immature executives, and are owned by even more selfish and immature shareholders. They just take, and take, and take. Sure, they give a little back, but overall they just take. They take from us financially, environmentally, and from our health and well-being. That is how they have so much excess–by taking as much as they can and giving the bare minimum back. They're nothing more than pirates. That is not success. That is total and complete failure on their part and failure by global society.

The only way to change this situation with excessively wealthy individuals and companies is to change ourselves and our perceptions of success. We need to redefine for ourselves what success truly is. After all, their success is because of us. So if we change ourselves, then we will inevitably change them.

Yellow Butterflies

Now that I've beaten that perception to death, which I hope you realize I am doing on purpose since it's such an important aspect to learn and change, I will move on to another very important aspect... choosing what to focus on.

With your physical mind and spiritual awareness open, your energetic radar cranking, and with facts in hand, you will have everything you need to choose what to focus on to create the perception of your choice. Just like the story of the prisoners earlier in this lesson, you can decide if you want to focus on the fact that there are bars on the windows, and you're stuck inside a cell (presuming you perceive that as negative), or if you want to focus on the fact that there's a beautiful outdoor scene beyond those bars (presuming you perceive that as positive)–a scene you'll gain access to one day if you don't give up. Out there where the sun is shining, a soft breeze is blowing, flowers are in bloom, and yellow butterflies are flittering about.

Yellow butterflies make me think of a song that I love and listen to on special occasions. It's an old song from 1993 by a little-known band by the name of The Party. The name of the song is of course titled "Yellow Butterfly."[14] The first verse goes like this, "I saw a yellow butterfly. This pretty butterfly just passed me by. She flew above me to say hello. Waved her wings at me to let me know. That today I stay away from all my worries. And my tears and fears will dry from the sun. I can't be afraid to face tomorrow. 'Cause I'll finally be free. Free to be with me."[14]

So often in life when I've faced a challenge, I'll see a yellow butterfly flitter across my path. It's one of those things that is so easily missed or dismissed. But with an open mind and awareness it can be so much more than it appears. When I see a yellow butterfly, I always think of this song and take it as a sign or an omen from the universe that everything will be ok. No matter how difficult things may be or how dark life may seem, there's always something beautiful to focus on. Even if it's just a yellow butterfly flittering by to remind me that the darkness will pass. To remind me that, yes, there are challenges in life, but there's also beauty in many different forms. And that if I focus on the beauty of life then those dark times will be illuminated and turn out much brighter.

Everyone faces challenges; this is simply a fact of life. How you perceive those challenges will define your perception of your life.

As a self-proclaimed realist, who is hyperaware of both the positive and negative facts of every situation I face, I can tell you firsthand that accepting the full truth for what it is and then focusing on what you perceive as the beautiful side of it will permanently alter your perception of your life for the better.

Right now, as I type these very words, it's April of 2021, and I'm facing one of the most challenging times of my life. The COVID-19 pandemic has been raging for a year, and I've been unemployed the entire time. In the midst of the pandemic, I finalized a long, drawn-out divorce where I walked away with nothing financially other than a ton of debt, went bankrupt, lost my car in the process, and worst of all…I've had to sleep on my ex-wife's sofa the entire time because I simply can't afford to even rent a room somewhere else and still provide financial support for my son.

Trust me when I say this: I'm hyperaware of the challenges I face at this particular time in my life. I'm not burying my head in the sand and pretending they don't exist by any means. There isn't a moment that goes by where I'm not keenly aware of how I despise living with my ex-wife, of the difficulty of my financial situation, and what the odds are of me getting a good paying corporate job in the midst of this pandemic. I'm clearly aware that I'm forty-three, unemployed, bankrupt, technically homeless, and in the middle of a really shitty time. Those are all facts of my situation at this moment, but they are not all the facts.

Because I'm living in my ex-wife's home, I get to see my son every single day. I get to have dinner with him, watch TV with him, tuck him in at night, and do so many other things that I wouldn't get to do if I wasn't in this situation. The divorce is also finally complete, and my future path will no longer be influenced by my ex or the negativity that relationship brought me.

In addition, I haven't had to work in almost a year. I'm so fortunate to have had all this time off to heal from all the toxicity that I eliminated from my life. I'm very fortunate that when I lost my corporate job, I was given a severance package where my health insurance was covered for a significant amount of time. With that insurance and all my free time, I was able to go to a therapist every week to amplify my healing.

Last but not least, I've had the opportunity to write this book. A book I've wanted to write for so long but lacked the confidence, time, and a clear path to do it. This book has been a lifelong evolution for me, and this challenging time has been the catalyst to bring it out of the darkness and into the light. As a matter of fact, had I not faced the challenges I faced throughout my life, then I wouldn't have learned what I'm sharing with you in this book. So all those perceptively negative experiences I faced have turned out to be perceptively positive experiences in the big picture.

I mention my current situation not to evoke pity or as an opportunity for me to vent about some shitty stuff I've faced. Frankly, my brain is telling me that I should be embarrassed to admit much of that, especially in such a public way. I mention it, though, despite what I've determined to be invalid fears from my brain, to highlight that we all face challenges in our lives. We all have bad shit going on in one way or another, and we all have to find a way to get through it. If you open your awareness to all the facts, acknowledge and accept them, and choose to focus on the facts that make you feel good–that excite and inspire you, that are the light in the darkness of your life, then you will start to experience a life that truly is beautiful.

Another example of this concept is the daughter of my coworker friend who I mentioned in lesson 1 as battling cancer. At this moment in time she's nineteen and has been battling leukemia for almost two years. In the midst of it and the barrage of chemotherapy treatments, she graduated high school and began attending college. Seriously! What a fucking trouper she is! She went to her high school graduation completely bald and layered in protective coverings because her immune system was so beaten down that her body needed the extra protection. Despite being frail, weak, bald, and ravaged by cancer and chemotherapy treatments, she went to her graduation, stood proudly and courageously in front of the cheering crowd, and received her diploma.

After graduating she began attending college online, despite being sick a significant portion of the time. She had weekly appointments where she had to drive forty miles to the hospital to wait for up to eight hours to have her chest port accessed–which was often very painful–and be injected with chemotherapy treatments that slowly sucked the life out of her. She did it, though, and she focused on what made her feel good to get through it.

My friend's daughter didn't pretend she didn't have cancer, and she didn't refuse to go to treatments. No, she was always aware of it and felt every fucking moment of it. She just chose to focus on the other facts of her situation that made her hopeful and feel good. She was being treated by one of the best hospitals and staff in the world to treat leukemia. She also chose to focus on the fact that she had a wonderful, loving, and supportive family who were with her every step of the way, driving her to treatments, taking care of her when she felt horrible, and making any type of food she felt she could hold down. She chose to focus on her friends who were there to lift her mood when she was feeling down. She chose to focus on the fact that she was going to defeat cancer and would come away from it wiser, stronger, and ready to continue on with her young life that would be full of many more challenges but also many more beautiful experiences.

Set Yourself Free

The moral of this lesson is simply this: being aware of your perceptions, questioning the truth behind them, and accepting the fact that you ultimately are in control of them are all key factors in tuning your perceptions to be whatever you decide you want them to be. Outside forces may attempt to tell you what your perceptions should be; they may try to manipulate you into making your perceptions what they want them to be, but ultimately it is on you to define them. Nobody can really control them unless you allow them to. Accept that, appreciate it, love it, and enjoy it. This is your true freedom.

This life we live is nothing less than a school. School isn't always easy, especially as you progress to higher levels. Sure, preschool is pretty cakey; kindergarten isn't too bad either. But as you elevate your learning, the lessons get harder and harder. Eventually, though, you learn enough to where it starts to get easier again. You run into some tough lessons and tests on a regular basis, but you get through them. If you don't pass, then you try again and go into it better prepared the next time. Life is about learning and teaching.

Those with lots of money aren't better than those with less money. Excessive amounts of anything don't make someone smarter or better than anyone else. In many cases, it means they simply haven't learned yet that hoarding doesn't benefit anyone in the big picture, not even themselves. They haven't learned yet that everything is connected and that if one creature is suffering, then we all suffer. They haven't learned that the energy of everyone and everything runs together and affects everything else. They haven't yet learned that those with less are often the ones who have evolved further, learned to be balanced, and only manifest what they need. They are unaware that those who have the least, those who live in impoverished nations, those who are starving, living on the streets, or fleeing their war-stricken homelands with nothing other than hope are often the ones who have sacrificed the most to be our greatest teachers. It takes the most evolved, selfless, and bravest of souls to take on such challenging roles in life.

When you're in school, you can choose to focus on the fact that you're trapped in a classroom and learning some really hard shit if you want. That won't make it any better though; you still have to learn, and you still have to take the tests. Such a limited perception can actually make it worse because it will simply slow your progress and drag out the most challenging parts, delaying your completion and progression to the next level.

With a focus on the big picture and the light in the darkness, you can choose to recognize that, for whatever reason, we have all chosen to live the lives we live. We have chosen our majors, the classes we need to take, and our paths to graduation. When you accept that you choose your path for a reason and don't put that control in anyone else's hands...not even your God's hands, you set yourself free to experience life with peace, happiness, and harmony. You learn that despite the challenges, no matter the wars, famine, genocide, or disease, that life is beautiful, and that beauty truly lies in the eyes of the beholder.

LESSON 5:

Everyone Is Weird

Ew, Gross!

A few days ago, my son was preparing for bed when he asked me if I would set the alarm on his phone and place it on the nightstand in his room. He asked this of me because he's a total germaphobe and had just freshly washed and lotioned up his hands. He's been a germaphobe since he was a little kid, which he probably inherited from me as I'm hyperaware of literally everything, including germs. But the COVID-19 pandemic certainly ratcheted up his germ fear several notches.

Understanding and respecting his predicament, I said, "Sure, no problem, Bub." (Bub is a nickname I use for him.) Before proceeding, though, I gently reminded him that I had already wiped down his phone after he had been out and about earlier in the day, so it was clean enough for him to do it himself if he preferred. He nervously replied, saying he'd still like it if I did it for him. It was clear to me that his discomfort with the idea was intense enough that there was no point in me pushing him any further. So I went ahead and set the alarm and took the phone upstairs to his room.

Upon my return to the front room, where he had been while I took his phone upstairs, he thanked me for doing that for him with his typical genuine and polite vibe. He immediately followed up his thank-you with an apology for not feeling comfortable enough to take it to his room himself. Before I could respond, his tone changed, and he added that he knew he was weird and that it must be annoying to deal with.

This sentiment caught me by surprise as it was the first time he had openly recognized how his phobia might be perceived by someone else. It made sense though; he was fourteen at that moment, and it was about the time when teenagers become more aware of what other people think of them. I could sense the insecurity behind his comments and wanted to make him feel at ease about it. I didn't want to lie to him, though, and say it's not weird, because the reality is that most people likely find his germ phobia weird. I personally didn't find it weird…I totally got it. It was April 2021, we were in the midst of the COVID-19 global pandemic, and I knew how his very active mind worked. I absolutely believed in that moment his brain-based fear was overriding his spiritual wisdom, and I wanted to help him with that in any way I could, but I definitely didn't think he was weird.

Most people wouldn't be so understanding of my son's phobia, though, and I didn't want to lie to him about that. At that moment an answer came to mind, an answer that wouldn't lie about the situation and would hopefully help ease his insecurity as well. I very simply and truthfully said, "No worries, Bub…everyone is weird."

After my reply a smile awakened on his face, and a clear and deep sense of relief washed over him. I was relieved myself as well since the comment had apparently achieved my objective even more than I had thought possible, given the little time I'd had to contemplate my response.

Along with his smile and relief came a wonderful and sincere comment back to me. He said, "Wow, Dude [Dude is his nickname for me]. You're really wise. You should write a book to share your wisdom." I felt a ping from the universe in that moment, as I hadn't yet told him that I was already writing such a book. I didn't want to explain the book in that moment so just lightheartedly giggled and said, "Yeah, that's a great idea...I could even name one of the chapters 'Everyone Is Weird.'" He smiled and said, "You know what? That's a great idea actually."

I knew right then and there that this situation was a sign that there was something that needed to be said on the subject. The universe was highlighting this for me and pointing me in this direction. I've learned to recognize and trust such a clear nudge from the universe so decided that it would be the next lesson I would write.

I'm Sooo Weird!

Before my son headed upstairs to finish getting ready for bed, I seized the opportunity to elaborate a bit on the subject. I briefly explained to him that everyone is weird in one way or another. Most people hide their weirdness, but some people don't. Regardless, we all have some trait or traits that someone somewhere will inevitably find weird.

For example, some people are germaphobes, some think of germs as their best friends, and others are somewhere in between. Some people walk differently than others, and some don't walk at all. Some hold a pen in their left hand, some in their right, some both, and some are incapable of holding a pen. Some people put their left legs into their pants first, some put their right legs in first, and some people don't even have legs. Some people wear makeup to add flare to their natural beauty, some are insecure about their beauty and wear makeup to hide it, and some don't wear any makeup at all to display their natural beauty with pride. Some spend thousands of dollars purchasing professional-grade bicycles and gear so they can join cycling groups and ride through towns with other amateur cyclists they long to fit in with. Some hop on Harley-Davison motorcycles fully decked out in their leather biker gear, aggressively pursuing attention as they loudly and proudly parade through the city streets. And some simply like to be alone and don't want to fit in anywhere or desire any attention at all.

Everyone is different from each other, and those differences make each person weird to everyone else. Weirdness is a spectrum, where some people are at a similar place on the spectrum as another and thus perceive that person as being less weird than another. The reality is, though, we're all different, so we're all weirdos to each other in one way or another.

The perception of weirdness is simply insecurity in most cases. An insecure person might think they're perceived as weird, or it could be they're perceiving someone else as weird. Either way it's just an insecurity that the differences we all have from each other somehow keep us from fitting in.

When someone thinks they themselves are weird, they are comparing themselves to everyone else on one or multiple points, recognizing their uniqueness, then fearing that those points will be perceived by others as weird. On the flip side, when someone perceives someone else as being weird, they're insecure in the reality that we're all different, and they're struggling to accept the beauty in those differences. They may also be fearing that those differences will become the norm and, in turn, make them the perceived weird ones.

Oftentimes the latter stems from something else that the person isn't dealing with in a balanced and healthy manner, so they try to compensate by deflecting and calling someone else out as being weird in an effort to hide their own insecurities. That, in turn, drives the insecurities of the people who think they're being perceived as weird. Two completely different perspectives feed each other and boil down to the same things: insecurity and lacking a healthy and balanced view of themselves and others.

Many people openly find me weird, and I've learned to be cool with that. I don't find myself weird...I'm just me. Don't get me wrong—it's natural for your brain to compare you to others. That's all part of its normal analytical process of observing and adapting itself to the world. I've just learned to understand that and prevent it from having a negative impact on me.

I now recognize that I'm different and appreciate that uniqueness as a beautiful thing. I recognize that I'm different than everyone else, so of course I'm weird from their perspective. I also recognize that if other people perceive my differences, or weirdness, as a negative, then that's their negativity, not mine. That's their insecurity, not mine.

I don't live my life in the constructs of other people's lives, nor do I want to. So their conclusion that I'm weird is simply a reflection of their own insecurity and negativity. It's a reflection of their own lack of confidence, knowledge, and acceptance—a reflection of their unbalanced and unhealthy view of themselves and others.

Frankly speaking I'd rather be perceived as *weird* rather than *normal*. After all, some of the most inspirational, creative, intelligent, and intuitive people are defined by society as weird. I take it as a compliment to be regarded in such company. I take it as a truth that I am different, because I am definitely different than everyone else. So I am definitely weird, but weird in a good way, weird in a beautiful way.

Whoa, Nelly!

Insecurity is most often thought of as a negative thing, but it's actually a really good thing when it's managed in a healthy and balanced way. Think about it from a functional perspective; insecurity, as it's relates to the feeling of weirdness, is the result of your brain analyzing its physical self within the world and determining whether there's something about it that isn't matching the socially accepted standard. If it determines that some aspect is substandard, then that creates a logical desire to evolve to match that standard.

For example, let's say you're a budding professional artist, and your brain is comparing your drawing skills to other professional artists or some sort of drawing standard in an effort to determine what techniques or skills you need to improve upon to produce a professional grade drawing. This is a really good thing. And a necessary one for that matter. Without that self-analysis and comparison to others, you wouldn't have the awareness about what skills need development and improvement.

This self-analysis occurs across an infinite and constantly evolving number of appropriate reflection points in one's life. The analysis can be more on the technical side, like an artist evaluating their drawing skills, a singer evaluating their vocal range, or a business analyst evaluating their report development skills. It can also be more on the social or emotional side, like a person evaluating their approach to communicating with friends, or a person evaluating if the outfit they're wearing is appropriate for work, a night out with friends, or a romantic date. This self-analysis is beautifully designed and is a required function to exist in society.

The commonly recognized negative aspect of insecurity, again it relates to the feeling of weirdness, arises when the functionality runs unchecked, and it's allowed to analyze the physical self in ways that aren't directly intended by design. This is where your spiritual self must step in to prevent the beneficial self-analysis from turning into a negative one.

For example, when your brain strays too far and begins analyzing if your height, the thickness of your hair, or the size of your nose meet social standards, you don't have any control over those things, so there is no benefit to analyzing such subject matter. This is when your spiritual self must step in and say, "Whoa, Nelly—no access granted, sucka!" In all seriousness, an internal line must be drawn to prevent such negative self-analysis.

Let's remember lesson 2 and the discussion over you not being your thoughts. You are energy—otherwise known as your spirit—inhabiting an organic machine made of a solid form of energy—otherwise known as your physical body—and your brain is the central processor for this organic machine/body. In other words your body is the avatar, and you are the player controlling that avatar.

Sure, there are automatic, or involuntary, functions that the avatar, or body, will process on its own that you don't have any control over, such as your heart beating, blood pumping, or hair growing. But the voluntary functions are in your control, such as when you move your hand, cross your legs, or analyze a particular subject. You have some power to control that analysis, and you must be on guard to make sure your brain doesn't run wild with it.

Again, your brain is doing its job by analyzing. So it's not broken or anything. It might need some training, but it's basically doing what it's designed to. You just need to guide it at times, keep it on task and going in the right direction. When it does stray, then you must stop it and remind yourself that you are beautifully weird just the way you are. Distract your brain with another task if you must, even something as simple as a mantra. Just don't allow it to analyze in a negative way.

Fuckin' Perfect

One of the things I love to do and find very helpful when my brain's analysis of my physical self has crossed a line into negative self-analysis—which inevitably happens on a regular basis—is to listen to music that reminds me just how beautiful and perfect it is. One of my favorites is the song "F**kin' Perfect,"[15] by P!nk.

I'm not sure if this was intended by the writers of the song or not, but when I'm listening to it, I don't think of it as something being sung to someone else. I think of the song as me singing it to me. The spiritual me singing the song to the physical me. My favorite part is the chorus, "Pretty, pretty please, don't you ever, ever feel like you're less than fuckin' perfect. Pretty, pretty please, if you ever, ever feel like you're nothing, you're fuckin' perfect to me."[15]

Sometimes if that negative self-analysis goes too far and puts me in a funk, I'll set this song to repeat and listen to it over and over again until I'm able to unfuck myself. Listening to a song on repeat like this and thinking about it as a message to yourself might seem silly, but it actually helps, at least for me anyway. This is one of the best tools I use to keep myself tuned, balanced, and free of negative self-analysis. The nice thing, too, is that any number of songs can be used to achieve this, and the song choice can vary depending on the subject matter of the negative self-analysis. The key thing is to ensure the song of choice evokes a positive and balancing reaction within yourself, your mind, and your vibe.

If a song doesn't evoke a positive and balancing reaction within you, then it shouldn't be used for unwinding negative self-analysis. Actually any song that doesn't meet the positive and balancing criteria should be avoided, as it can potentially evoke different reactions that you may not intend, and you may not realize it until after the damage is done. Then you end up having to unfuck yourself from both your internal negative self-analysis and the negativity that was evoked from the song, which is obviously a situation to avoid.

Let's take, for example, the song "Loser,"[16] by Beck, with its dark undertone and lyrics that say, "I'm a loser baby, so why don't you kill me."[16] Don't get me wrong; "Loser"[16] is a great song and has been very successful. However, it's not the type of song to use when trying to unwind negative self-analysis. Now this song could theoretically evoke a positive reaction within someone depending on their perception of it, so I'm certainly not passing judgment on that. That's just not likely a common reaction, though, especially when you're in the mindset of negative self-analysis.

To listen to such a song like "Loser,"[16] you have to be in a balanced place to withstand the heavy and depressing vibes. If you're in a balanced place, then sure, you can listen to the song without issue. If you're not in a balanced place, however, you should definitely steer clear of it until you are and can understand and appreciate the dark path in which it was written. Or if you're listening to it and start to transition into a negative mind frame, then you need to recognize that, stop listening to it, and unwind any potential damage that has been created.

The same concept can be applied beyond music; it can be TV shows, movies, books, or even people, like friends and family, for example. If you're in a state of negative self-analysis and find someone or something other than music can bring you into a balanced and a positive mindset, then that's awesome! Go for it! The decision on what to use is ultimately up to you and will be influenced by your life experiences and your existing perceptions. So go for whatever achieves the results you are looking for and need. Again, as long as it's positive and balancing for you, then it's a good thing.

Just be aware of the opposite reactions as well. If you find that someone or something influences you negatively, then limit your exposure to only times when you are in a balanced place and can handle its energy and subsequent effects.

The Gigantic Shithole of Despair

The concept of intentionally exposing yourself to positive influences and intentionally limiting your exposure to negative influences may seem simple or trivial, but I can assure you that it really has a big impact on your life and how you perceive your physical self in the world. And it may have a bigger impact than you realize if you aren't giving it enough of your awareness.

If the negative influences in your life outweigh the positive influences for too long, then your negative self-analysis can run completely amok and slowly lead you down a dark path that eventually grows into depression. Persistent negative self-analysis–I'm not smart enough, I'm too fat or too thin, my boobs are too small, my nose is too big, my ass is too flat, I'm too old, I'm not sexy, nobody likes me, etcetera–can all lead to such an imbalance that you get persistently depressed.

That depression can cause other negative influences in your life and put you in one gigantic shithole of despair. Just as powerful as positive influences can be at setting a beautiful tone to your life, negative influences can be equally powerful and can set a depressing tone. I've experienced this myself so can speak to it firsthand. It can be the absolute shits to be so out of balance. I'm talking burning-butthole-diarrhea type of shits.

Throughout my life I've experienced deep states of depression, and there was a consistency about them that took me most of my life to identify, understand, and effectively neutralize. The consistency was that the depression occurred at times when negative self-analysis and/or negative influences were so out of control that I dug myself into the depths of literal hell. I just wasn't consciously aware of it, let alone of my power to change it.

In those times I wasn't consciously aware of negative self-analysis, negative influence of people and things in my life, or the subsequent insecurities they created. When I say I was depressed, I mean I was fucking depressed…nearly all of the damn time! Sometimes it was worse than others, and sometimes I'd snap out of it awhile, but depression was like the proverbial monkey on my back. No matter what I did, I couldn't set that monkey free.

Not until I finally learned the key, the key that unlocked the door of balance, wisdom, happiness, and beauty. This key didn't arrive to me in a flash of a moment though; it slowly manifested over time. Piece by piece this key was built by my experiences in life, the knowledge I gained through them, and the universe providing me a road map to finding each piece and putting them all together. This key is what I'm attempting to bring your awareness to in this lesson and throughout the entire book.

Fuck My Life

As crazy as this may sound, I can look back at my life and realize that I experienced depression from a very early age. I'm talking like at five years old. I'm very serious when I say that. None of this was in my control, but I was born into kind of a fucked-up family, as I'm sure many people are. My early childhood was full of negative influences and had the bare minimum of positive influences.

As a child, I felt my mother certainly loved me, but she had her own issues that consumed a majority of her capacity to care for me in a way a child really needs to be cared for. My father was nothing but a negative, cold, and empty presence in my life. I had two siblings who lived in the same house as I did. My full-blooded sister was similar to my father in her self-centered, egotistical, and manipulative ways. And my half sister was a storm of chaos, was believed by some to be a drug addict, got pregnant by age sixteen, and spent a decent amount of time in juvenile hall.

I also had other, much older half siblings who didn't live with us, so I rarely had any interactions with them, and they never made any efforts to be involved with me in any way. As far as friends went... well...I had some I guess, technically speaking anyway. There were neighborhood kids who were more bullies than friends, but I hung out with them because there was nobody else around. I vaguely remember having one genuine friend for a few months in kindergarten, but he moved away, and I was left with only the neighborhood bullies. This was the foundation I grew up on. My best description of it was negative, empty, and forgettable.

As I grew older, things didn't get much better. Actually they got worse in the sense that the heavy presence of negative influences and the devastating lack of positive influences eventually became too much, and it started manifesting even more negativity—not just to me, but through me as well.

When I was in the middle of the third grade, we moved to a retirement neighborhood where there were literally no other kids around (did I forget to mention that my dad was old as fuck?). I started at a new school midyear but clearly didn't fit in. Shortly thereafter I was suspended for two weeks for ditching one day. In the fourth grade, I was expelled for an entire year and nearly wound up in juvenile hall for my supposed involvement with a bully friend who brought a large, serrated, and retractable knife to school.

After being expelled, I was sent to a school for troubled kids, which only made my issues worse. All negative, no positive. After that experience I swore off friends as they, for the most part, were either bullies or troublemakers. That didn't stop the negativity though. In the sixth grade, I was being bullied and harassed by a teacher, who seemed to take pleasure in making my life miserable. Things were so bad at school that, by the end of that year, my mother decided to homeschool me. Here I was, an eleven-year-old kid, living a life of just simple yuck. No friends, terrible school experiences, and a cold, empty, and chaotic family life.

Starting in the seventh grade, my mother did indeed attempt to homeschool me for a few weeks. But just like everything else with her, she didn't have the psychological capacity to follow through with it. Over the course of the next six years, through all of middle and high school, I was supposedly homeschooled. That wasn't the truth though; it was just a facade. Truth is my mother never actually homeschooled me at all after those first few weeks. She just told people she was homeschooling me, but she never did the actual work associated with it.

Back then homeschooling wasn't common where I lived, and there were few regulations around it. So somehow my mother got away with completely neglecting my education. (Sorry, Mom...just being honest!) Instead of doing schoolwork, she had me do chores around the house and help take care of my chaotic half sister's children, one of whom was born fourteen weeks premature and had countless health issues as a result, including two holes in his heart, underdeveloped lungs and intestines, and brain damage. That child spent four months in the hospital after he was born, and my half sister abandoned him and her two other kids shortly thereafter. She took off and wasn't seen or heard from for a significant period of time.

Throughout my teen years, I became a caretaker to three young children...well, actually two of them for most of the time. My half sister eventually returned and took custody of the middle child. The other two, including the one born prematurely, were eventually legally adopted by my mother, and I became like an older brother to them, oftentimes more like a father in some ways, as my father was not involved with them on any meaningful level.

At age twelve I also took on a newspaper route delivering sixty newspapers a day starting at 3:00 a.m., 365 days a year–rain, shine, fog, or ice. Eventually that route grew to three hundred papers per day. I took on such a large paper route because my father, in all his infinite selflessness, refused to allow my mother to buy me any clothes or take me to a doctor or dentist, despite the fact that he had money to cover such things. He didn't have a lot by any means, but he definitely could have swung it had anyone outside of himself been a priority to him.

Nobody had ever taught me about dental hygiene, and I hadn't been to a dentist since I was five years old. So my teeth were literally rotting at this point. Not surprisingly as I reflect back, my mother clearly hadn't been taught about dental hygiene, either, as she was on the verge of losing all her teeth at the ripe old age of forty.

For clothing I scrounged up anything my sister no longer wore that was more gender neutral (T-shirts, flip-flops, sweats, etcetera). Taking on the larger route allowed me to buy some basic clothes for myself and begin to repair the damage to my rotting teeth.

I still remember the day, at age sixteen, when I walked myself two miles to a dentist's office to begin the work. Both the office staff and the dentist had a vibe of disbelief and pity when I said I was alone and paying cash. The dentist was kind enough to grant me a cash discount for the work, which after numerous visits, came to a whopping $2,300. And that was just to get the basics repaired. What money I didn't spend on clothes or the dentist, inevitably I lent and eventually gave to my mother, who struggled to get money from my father to even pay utility bills. She used my money to fill in the gaps.

By the time I turned eighteen, I had no friends, hadn't been to school in six years, and was loaded down with responsibilities that were way beyond my years. I grew up hard, I grew up fast, and I grew up alone. True, I was surrounded by people the entire time, but underneath that facade I was alone, longing for something I never truly knew or had...love and happiness.

I was empty though–bone dry. I hadn't experienced enough positivity in my life, so my scales were tipped way over to the wrong side. And I didn't understand how to protect myself from the negativity I experienced or prevent negative self-analysis from taking hold and getting out of control. Looking back I realize I had become terribly insecure and miserably depressed. I really didn't realize it in that moment though. I was just focused on trying to make things better. I didn't really know what better was though.

The Cold and Empty House

Later that year I finally had saved up enough money to move out and start a life on my own. This was truly exciting! When I moved out, I decided to move to San Diego. I don't know why I chose San Diego; I was just always drawn to Southern California, and San Diego somehow came up as an option I could afford. So I literally walked away from my life and started over.

There was a huge problem though. As I mentioned I didn't know how to protect myself from negative influences and negative self-analysis. And I didn't have enough positive experience and love in my life up to that point to use as a frame of reference for finding the love and happiness I desired in my new life. This proved to be a major issue for me.

Shortly after moving to San Diego, I met my future ex-wife. I was nineteen, and she was twenty-five. When we met, I knew she wasn't the one for me. I knew it deep down inside, in the energy I was feeling but hadn't yet learned to understand and trust. I doubted the energy I felt inside, and I clung to the brain-based insecurities that had developed over the course of my life. I thought I was weird, that I didn't fit in, and that I wasn't worthy of love. I hadn't experienced much positive anything to that point; it was all mostly negative, degrading, and empty.

The powerful feelings in the depths of my soul told me this woman wasn't right for me, yet here she was being nice, friendly, and caring…maybe she even liked me. Hmmm…this was new for me. And it was way better than anything I had experienced before. It was like a whole new world had opened up to me. We would go out to the movies, to dinner, take walks on the beach, and just overall enjoy each other's company. It was nice. We were friends and eventually more.

Before long I met her family, and we moved in together. Her family was way different than mine. Oh my God, so different! She had a mother, a brother, and two grandparents in her immediate life. And they were all nice, and they all liked each other…wait…what? Could this be real? Yup, it was indeed. And guess what? They seemed to like me, too, and appeared to welcome me into their family.

Wow, this was fantastic! For the first time in my life, I was experiencing what appeared to be positive and healthy relationships. Not perfect relationships by any means, but positive. Yet something still told me that we weren't right for each other. Once I had experienced what I thought were positive relationships, I was fearful of going back to anything else, especially to what I grew up in. As you can imagine, I pushed those warning signs down and buried them deep inside me. And I kept up the relationship since it was so much better than what I had come from.

As time went by, I convinced myself that things were great. A serious problem was lurking, though, and it was growing: Was I happy? Truly happy? The answer was no. Though she and I technically got along well, we really didn't love each other. You know–in that special or magical kind of way. We were drawn together by negative energy; I just didn't consciously realize it.

You see, I had spent a good portion of my life being a caregiver, and she had spent a good portion of her life being cared for. We fit but for the wrong reasons. We were drawn to each other by negative forces. She showed a lonely, insecure, and depressed person a bit of attention and affection. In turn I cared for her in every way shape and form, just as she was used to. I had to pamper her in order to get any bit of affection back. The love I thought I was pampering for was just a facade though.

I liken our relationship to the idea of being outside in the freezing cold for a long period of time. Then you find a house, step inside, and immediately feel so much warmer and relieved. It's so much better than the outside! Once your body warms up and adjusts to the temperature, though, you then start to realize it's cold in there too. Not as cold as the outside, but cold nonetheless. You go to kick on the heater and find that there is no heater. It's just a cold and empty house.

What our relationship turned into for me was the exact same relationship my parents had but in reverse. And that all stemmed from subconsciously modeling the negativity I witnessed and experienced growing up. I'd had very limited positive experiences to counterbalance that.

Because my future ex-wife needed to be cared for in every way shape and form, and I was now her caregiver, the relationship grew out of balance. She was taking far more than she was giving, and I was giving far more than I was taking. She turned out to be very controlling and a master manipulator. She truly missed her calling and should have been a lawyer. She was a master at recognizing someone's vulnerability and using it against them to get what she needed.

These behaviors of hers all stemmed from her own insecurity. She felt like she couldn't take care of herself and needed someone to do it for her, even if she had to manipulate them to get them to do it. She didn't realize it, nor did I, but she was a hunter, and I was her prey. Two people who were desperately insecure, both feeding off each other's negative energy. A bad combination indeed.

The reality was that she was a very strong person who was more than capable of taking care of herself. She just needed to believe it and open herself to it. I was indeed a great caregiver, but I really just needed someone to care for me in a true and pure way. I didn't believe I was capable of getting such love, though, so settled for something that was a little better than what I had growing up. She was my cold house without a heater.

The Awakening

It took eleven years (1999–2010) of this toxic relationship for me to finally start to awaken to all of this and put an end to it. By that time, though, we had our son, who was three years old at the time, and splitting wasn't so easy without negatively impacting him in a life-altering way. So even though I ended the relationship with her, I stuck around to continue providing for our son. I foolishly didn't proceed with the divorce for many years. She was exceptionally good at manipulating me into believing a divorce would be bad for our son. She knew he was my soft spot, and I wouldn't do anything to negatively impact him. She used him as a pawn to get me to do what she wanted; I just didn't realize that until much later.

Over the course of the following eight years (2010–2018), I learned about myself, my insecurities, my depression, and how toxic our relationship was to me. I learned where I made mistakes and how I could prevent them from occurring again. However, my now ex and I were still legally married at that point and living under the same roof, so I was really still in the same boat. And guess what? I was still insecure and horribly depressed.

I was so depressed that the desire to not live this life anymore crept into my mind daily. My anthem was a song by Flogging Molly named "The Worst Day Since Yesterday."[17] Oh my...the title of that songs says it all. Despite everything I had learned thus far, the negative self-analysis and depression were still out of control, and I was finally hitting rock bottom.

One evening in 2018, I experienced one of the worst moods I had ever been in. It was a night where I was overwhelmed with the reality that I was sad, beaten down, and completely frustrated with the situation I was in. I feared I wasn't worthy or capable of experiencing anything better. Lost in my own misery, I wrapped my T-shirt tightly around my neck to test if I could just go to sleep and not wake up again. I had a hefty life insurance policy that covered suicide, which I had researched extensively would actually pay out in such a case, and I feared that death might be the only way out of the mess I was in. Sure, my son would be taken care of financially, but I wouldn't be around to support him in life. I would finally be free, though, and what kind of a father would I be to him if I stuck around and unintentionally taught him how to be unhappy? That weighed heavily on me.

While I was lying there with this T-shirt wrapped around my neck, struggling to breathe, I kept hearing the chorus from the song "Don't Let Go,"[18] by Sarah McLachlan and Bryan Adams, play in my mind. The angelic yet haunting words Sarah sings of "Don't let go"[18] kept playing over and over again inside me. I knew in my heart that I needed to take that T-shirt off and not give up. I knew that the problem wasn't that I wanted to die; it was that I already felt dead. And I desperately wanted to live. But I didn't know how to do that though. I ended up angrily removing the T-shirt from my neck and prayed to the universe and my spirit guides for help. I then quickly drifted off to sleep.

The next morning I awoke to something different. Something happened to me that night that I honestly can't define with any certainty. I have no physical recollection of having any dreams or any profound experience. I simply went to sleep angry, frustrated, and desperate for change. I slept straight through the night, which never happens for me. I always wake up several times a night, even to just turn over. But not that night. That night I slept without waking once and then awoke in the morning to something I'll never forget.

For a very brief moment as I awoke, I felt my spiritual consciousness awaken while my physical body was still asleep. In that flash of a moment, I felt an overwhelming feeling of happiness and love. It was an indescribably powerful feeling that I still remember clearly to this day. My body's eyes were closed, and I was present in it, yet I was somehow disconnected from it. In that moment of pure happiness and love, a voice spoke to me. Not a physical voice though. It was more like the voice of the universe/God or spirit guide or something. It was an infusion of knowledge directly into the essence of me. It very clearly said, "Don't give up; just take it one step at a time. Don't look too far forward and get overwhelmed at the path in front of you… just take one step at a time and only focus on that step."

In the next moment, my physical eyes began to open, and my body was now waking up. I lay there for probably fifteen minutes and held onto that warm feeling, contemplating what had happened. The happiness and love stayed with me, and there was another feeling as well. I was excited…genuinely excited! This energy had me fully charged, and I couldn't wait to get up and get started. Get started on what though? I couldn't specifically remember…but it was good, really, really good. No, wait…it was beautiful. I knew it in the depths of my soul, and I knew I would find my way to it, whatever it was.

That morning set into motion a steep climb out of the deep pit of despair I had found myself in. All of the lessons I received throughout my life, inner reflections I had made, and subsequent knowledge I had gained had all accumulated into this moment. I now knew that I needed to start by cleaning out all the shit in my life that I no longer needed or wanted. And I was nothing but willing and excited to do so. I felt a divine guidance walking with me and helping me pick that shit up and throw it all out. As a result I finally filed for divorce despite the strong resistance, manipulation, and threats from my now ex. And I did it with excitement for the beautiful unknowns that lay ahead and without any fear whatsoever. I was finally, and permanently, unfucking myself.

Unfucked

It's now been two and a half years since that day (as of the time of writing this), and I've not had one bit of depression in me since then. And I've not taken a single pill to achieve it. I only have excitement since then and still do to this day.

With the help of the universe and my loving, trusted, and dedicated spirit guides, I've cleaned everything out of my life except for my son, who was the only thing within it at that time that was true and pure to me. And when I say everything…I mean everything. My toxic corporate job, friends that weren't really friends, possessions that were only burdens to me, debts, and most of all I threw out all that led me to those things. I threw out all of the negative energy that controlled me, the negative self-analysis, and the depression.

Today I'm free from all of that, and I can genuinely say I'm happy. Yes I still do have challenges, and there are things I'm experiencing that I don't enjoy one bit. There's no doubt about that, and I don't hide it. Despite that I'm happy, and no challenge I face will take that from me. For I now see the beauty in those challenges, I see the lessons I'm learning, I see the perceptually bad things as good things in disguise, and I see so many wonderful things in my future. For that is the future I choose to focus on.

In an effort to be completely transparent with you and to highlight the separation between you and your brain, right now my brain is sounding the fear and insecurity alarm because of the story I just shared. My brain has analyzed the situation and is recognizing that my experiences aren't typically considered positive, successful, strong, or manly. And the data it's giving me is that I should hide my story to avoid a large number of people creating negative perceptions of me. But that's just my brain doing what it's programmed to do: warn me of risks and dangers. It uses the feelings of fear and insecurity to do that. Like I mentioned in lesson 3, our brains perceive the risk and danger of touching a hot pan the same as they perceive the risk and danger of exposing your perceptually negative truth for the world to see. So my brain is doing exactly what it's supposed to be doing, and I'm so thankful to it for that.

However, it's my job, the real me…the spiritual me, to take in that data and decide if it's valid to move forward with. Just like it's my job to take in the experiences my avatar has had and decide if I myself perceive them as positive or negative, embarrassing and depressing, or lessons and pathways that taught me so much and led me to exactly where I'm at right now, sharing my story in an effort to help someone else break free from negative self-analysis, negative circumstances they were either born into or created themselves, and the subsequent depression they may face.

The Elaboration

Before I proceed, I have two subjects in mind that I feel necessary to elaborate on. First off my comments about depression are based on my experience and my experience alone. I'm in no way saying the depression I faced is the same as anyone else's. And I'm certainly not saying nobody needs medication for depression, nor am I passing any judgment on doing so. I'm not a medical doctor or a mental health professional so am in no way offering medical advice. I merely wrote, and will continue to write, of my experience with depression and how I was able to successfully, and permanently, overcome it.

Everybody's life is different, and you should follow your own path to freedom from negativity. If you find the lights of my path helpful for you, then that's beautiful. It's your decision though. Do what you feel is best for you.

In addition, just because I've conquered my depression doesn't mean I don't get down or in a bad mood. Trust me–I do feel down sometimes and do get in moods. It simply means that I have found the way to not allow those down moments and moods to get out of control. After all, downer moods are ok...they're actually very important and beneficial as long as they don't get out of control.

Downer moods are a form of information and communication from yourself, both your spirit and your physical body, and sometimes even from the universe. You definitely should never ignore or bury those feelings, because as I mentioned in lesson 4, you would be living a lie. And that in itself can lead to depression. You must be open and honest with yourself to feel those feelings and hear the communication that something needs your awareness and attention. Feel it, acknowledge it, accept it, address it the best you can, and then move on. What I've found is that the very act of doing so actually prevents it from spinning out of control.

For example, two days ago I wrote my story that I shared in this lesson and was planning on moving on to the next subject. After I wrote it, though, I began feeling like something was missing or off, so I spent all yesterday editing and writing in an attempt to rectify those feelings. I didn't know exactly what the issue was though. I had to feel for it.

The morning was spent editing and went very well. I felt so much better afterward with regards to that portion of the lesson. What you read earlier is the result of that effort. The afternoon was spent starting to write the next part of this lesson, and it didn't go quite as well. I was struggling with finding what I needed to say. I wrote a couple of pages' worth of content, which was all good stuff, but it just didn't feel right. It felt like it wasn't flowing as it should, and I was getting frustrated and down because of that.

At this point my confidence started getting shaken, and I started questioning my goal for the content. As that occurred I began consciously recognizing how I was feeling. I decided to stop writing as I was just wasting time and energy. I've learned that in situations such as that I need to just step away and commune with myself, the universe, and my spirit guides. I need to let the issue marinate in me and allow all the feelings to come to the surface.

As I let the issue marinate, I started feeling even more down, which was ok actually. There was information in that, and I needed to explore it. Now had I not accepted this and understood that there was information for me in this, then the mood could have gotten out of control. That negative self-analysis could have run amok and potentially led me to stop writing altogether. Instead I was compassionate toward myself and defused the negative self-analysis. I reminded myself to flow with it and just allow the knowledge to emerge when it was ready.

I ended up not writing in the evening at all, and I just took a long walk, listened to some music, and watched a movie instead. Throughout the evening I would think and feel about the situation and see what would come up. Each time I did, new information would come to my awareness. By the time I went to bed, I had an idea of what the issue might be and a possible path to resolve it.

After waking up this morning, I continued with the same process while eating breakfast and showering. By the time I sat down to write this morning, I was clear on what the issue was, and the downer mood had completely disappeared. After I opened my laptop, I simply deleted the couple pages of content I had written for the next section and started fresh.

Yesterday I had indeed gone off on the wrong path. That's what was bothering me and bringing my mood down. That was ok though; had I not experienced that, then I wouldn't have gotten to the clarity I have this morning and wouldn't be writing the words I'm writing in this moment. So it all serves a purpose, even the wasted time and the downer mood. You just need to be open and honest with yourself, allow your feelings to flow like a leaf in the wind. Listen and feel for the knowledge your spiritual self, the universe, and your spirit guides are communicating to you.

The second subject I would like to elaborate on is about the experience I had that night/morning in 2018. As I noted, I'm not sure exactly what happened that evening/morning as I have no physical recollection other than what I noted. I certainly have an idea of what happened though.

I'm inclined to believe I was gifted with a reminder of what was still to come in this life. The experience itself was not something my body and brain experienced though; only the spiritual me experienced it, so I don't have a physical memory of it. That spirit-based knowledge is embedded somewhere I don't have physical access to at this point in time. I suspect those specific memories are intentionally locked away, for they might affect the future in ways that are not intended to occur.

Despite the fact that I couldn't physically recall what exactly happened that evening/morning, I was left with the energy that spiritual knowledge created within me. That energy then transferred to my body/brain, creating the feelings I noted. That energy was enough to give me the boost I desperately needed. It was simply a jump start or an infusion of energy. It by itself, though, wasn't what pulled me out of the hole I was wallowing in. It was me that pulled me out. And I used all of the knowledge I had gained from all of my life lessons to know how to actually climb out.

That infusion of energy that night/morning got me off the ground and standing up. It was a reminder why I needed to climb out of that shithole. It was a reminder of the fact that not only could I climb out, but there was something beautiful waiting for me beyond it. Something so powerful and meaningful to me that it would be worth every bit of effort necessary to climb out and get to it.

In this book I'm attempting to give you both the knowledge I gained throughout my life and that boost of energy you may need to stand up and start climbing out of your own shithole, should you be stuck in one of course. And hopefully teach you a few tips to gain access to your own divine knowledge in the process.

I Love Me

One of the most powerful elements in one's journey to stop negative self-analysis in its tracks and to prevent negative insecurities and depression is learning to be compassionate with yourself. Compassion for yourself is often overlooked yet is such an important piece in the puzzle of life.

When you have a bad day at school or work, wouldn't it be wonderful if someone gave you a big hug and told you that they loved you and were there to support you in any way they could? You're damn straight that would be wonderful! That doesn't always happen in this physical life though. Even if you do have it in your physical life, you don't have it available to you at any given moment. So you must rely on yourself to provide it. Having compassion for yourself is really the foundation to the house of you.

You are around yourself 24 hours a day, 7 days a week, and 365 days a year. So it makes so much sense that you need to be compassionate with and love yourself. But so many of us don't give ourselves the compassion and love we so desperately need. And if we aren't compassionate with ourselves, then how are we to be compassionate and loving with others in a healthy and balanced way?

When I learned about self-compassion and love...man...it changed my life. It's those little words of encouragement I give myself, the love songs I listen to and think about, and the guiltless permission I give myself to take breaks when I'm overwhelmed or feeling down that help me so much. They make the difference between having insecurities or not, being depressed or not, and feeling happy or not. That positive self-feedback counteracts the negative energy in the world and negative thoughts in my brain. When the world kicks my ass, I'm always there to lift me up. So I encourage you to take the time to give yourself the love and compassion you deserve. Love yourself the way you want someone else to love you. In turn you'll be able to love your life and the world you live in.

Awareness and understanding of negative self-analysis, depression, and compassion is such an important issue in the world today, yet it barely gets the attention it deserves. It's such an important and fundamental piece of our overall health that it truly should be taught throughout elementary, middle, and high school, as we call it here in the United States. Everyone should understand this subject in the same way we all understand that our hearts beat to pump blood throughout our bodies. It's that fundamental. The reality is, though, that we're more likely to learn of this subject through memes on social media, which we only learn one inconsistent fragment at a time.

Imagine for a moment if this were taught as a fundamental subject in school. Wow, I can say wholeheartedly that my life leading up to this moment would have been so much happier and productive had it been taught to me when I was young. And I'm confident that the majority of the world would benefit from it similarly in one way or another. That's powerful shit right there! Imagine how much bullying would be reduced because potential bullies would learn about and address their own insecurities. They'd learn how to have compassion for both themselves and others, preventing the bullying from ever occurring in the first place. Imagine if all the kids who got bullied were taught the same, preventing all the depression and feelings of weirdness that stem from not having that awareness and knowledge. Again...wow...wow, wow, wow, and wow!

Now here's an even bigger wow...imagine all those kids growing up and not being the assholes we all work with or have worked with at some point in our lives. Imagine all the crime, abuse, and greed that would be prevented simply by people learning from an early age how to love and take care of themselves, especially when that love either doesn't exist or is lacking from their own families. Imagine all the sexist, racist, and hateful behaviors that would be reduced, and maybe even eliminated. This would be truly life-altering and utterly profound. This would be a world where everyone would accept each other's weirdness without prejudice, judgment, and fear. It would be a world of pure love and compassion. That may seem far-fetched or even weird, but it's very much achievable.

It all starts with you though–you loving and having compassion for yourself. Once you achieve that, then it will inevitably spread from you to your family, friends, coworkers, neighbors, and so on. They will in turn spread it as well. Before you know it, you will be influencing the world in an enormously impactful and positive way. The generational wounds we all carry within us will eventually heal and then we, as a global society, will finally find the peace and harmony we all desire. We all will finally understand, appreciate, and love the fact that everyone is weird.

LESSON 6:

Let It Go

The Calm before the Storm

Everything in our lives teaches us something, whether we recognize it in the midst of a lesson or not. The people around us, the situations we're in, and even our thoughts, emotions, and vibes all teach us important lessons. Some of those lessons are simple and short in duration, and others are complex and can take months, years, decades, or even an entire lifetime to learn. And it all happens no matter if those lessons are perceptively enjoyable, difficult, or somewhere in between. More often than not, the level of enjoyment or difficulty is part of the lesson to be learned. The beauty of it all is that, within a lesson, we're often the teachers as well as the students. From an operational perspective, I personally find it fascinating to understand and observe such mastery at work. It truly is divinely ingenious.

After the in-depth discussion of insecurities in the last lesson, I couldn't help but feel drawn to focusing this lesson on another challenging situation that many, if not all, of us experience to at least a certain degree at some point in our lives. Ooh…it's such a frightening word I almost hesitate to even say it. Ok, I'm just going to bite the bullet (deep breath)...anxiety. Aaaah (another deep breath). So much better to just spit it out.

Anxiety and all that comes along with such chaotic energy is something that can be terribly and quite literally, frightening. Never fear though. As with anything else in life, there's always something to learn when this manifestation of our powerful minds comes for a visit.

Anxiety was a very long and challenging lesson I learned–one that I'm honestly still working on to this day in one way or another and probably will until the day I graduate this life. I have conquered the most severe forms of it, though, which I will share more details about a little bit later in the lesson. The lessons I learned through anxiety have been some of the most impactful when it comes to the art of remaining calm. After all, you can't achieve a true state of peace and calm without having experienced the opposite, a true state of anxiety and all-out panic.

Throughout our lives we inevitably experience at least a small level of anxiety on a regular basis. Whether it be before getting up on stage in a play, preparing for a date, or walking into a job interview. Similar to insecurities, anxiety actually serves a necessary function from an operational perspective, which is exactly why our bodies and brains are designed and programmed to experience it. Let's dig into that functionality a bit...

At its core anxiety is basically your brain anticipating a negative situation and then placing your body into an elevated state so that it can react most effectively to however you decide to address the situation.

For example, let's say you're in the wilds of Africa, and your ears hear the roar of a lion far off in the distance. Your brain immediately goes into a state of anxiety as it anticipates a potentially dangerous situation. Once your brain goes into an anxiety state, then it immediately triggers your body into that heightened state as well. Your heart starts pumping blood faster, adrenaline and other hormones start flowing throughout your body, your ears perk up to hear more subtle or distant sounds, your eyes dilate to receive more light, muscles tense in preparation of physical activity, and countless other functions go into high alert. All in preparation for potentially having to flee from that situation.

With your body now being in a heightened state, new information starts pouring into your brain for analysis. In turn it processes and pushes the data to you in mere fractions of a second from the time it's received, all so you can make a decision as quickly as possible. This time of heightened awareness and preparedness is the designed state of anxiety.

Now imagine for a moment that, during this state of anxiety, your body continues listening for that lion but no longer hears it. You wait five, ten, fifteen minutes and never hear it again. Your body has been in this anxious state of anticipation the entire time, with your brain quickly processing and pushing you data until you finally conclude that the lion is gone and you're safe. Your brain then comes out of the anxiety state and directs your body to do the same. Your muscles start relaxing, heart rate slows, adrenaline stops pumping, etcetera. You slowly come down into your normal and comfortable state.

Now imagine the opposite for a moment. In this heightened state of anxiety, your body continues listening for that lion, and your ears eventually hear it again. This time the roar is louder, and you can hear the brush being stepped on and pushed away as the lion moves closer to you. Your brain is running at high capacity to push the incoming data to you in fractions of a second so you can quickly make a decision on how to react. As soon as you give the command to get the hell out of there, your brain elevates its state from anxiety to panic as the danger is now imminent.

As soon as your brain goes into panic mode, it directs your body to do the same. Your body immediately starts running at full capacity. All functions and resources that support that run are cranked up to the highest priority level, such as blood flow, oxygen, and energy. At the same time, your brain is reducing or even shutting down low priority functions, such as digestion or blood flow to the skin. All of those involuntary actions are executed based on the coding that was done when the human body was designed. That state of panic will stay in effect until the data your brain is receiving from your body indicates you're safe. Once you're satisfied that you're safe, your brain will slowly bring your body back down to a lowered state of alert where your muscles begin to relax, heart rate slows, and so on.

As you can see, anxiety and panic are very important and necessary functions of your brain and body. They serve to protect you and keep you safe and secure. It's clear why your brain and body would be designed to function in the way they do. It's ingenious of course!

The example I gave, though, is based on a far less common state of human existence in current times–one where you would be in the wild and have to be hyperaware of potential animals attacking. Those of us who live in cities and towns don't typically have to be concerned about wild animals attacking. However, the functionality is still useful and very much necessary, as there are still predators lurking about...they're just not lions, tigers, and bears. They could be rapists, human traffickers, murders, muggers, or even the po-po. No matter if you live in the wilds of the earth or in an urban setting, threats to our safety are all around, and the role of anxiety and panic have a very real and necessary place within that life.

Pucker Up, Buttercup

In modern times the trigger for anxiety isn't always an animal or a person about to attack. The same benefits still apply even though you're not being physically threatened. Your brain has become aware of a potentially negative situation ahead and is preparing your body to react in a way that optimizes success.

Let's take the going on stage, a first date, and a job interview I noted earlier as examples. Your brain is aware of an expectation going into each of these situations; they're likely your own expectations but certainly could be someone else's as well. Let's say the expectations are completing the play successfully with everyone enjoying your performance, impressing the person you're out on a date with, and landing that new job. Your brain is also aware of what might happen if you fail to meet those expectations–you lose your role in the play, the person you're on the date with doesn't like you and never wants to see you again, and you don't get the job.

The possibility of failure to meet these expectations is what your brain has analyzed as a potential negative situation ahead. Based on the expectations, your brain will try to prepare and find solutions to prevent the potential failure. It can't do that, though, without knowing what exactly could potentially go wrong. So your brain starts analyzing possibilities that could cause an expectation failure, such as forgetting your lines in the play, saying something stupid to your date, or farting during the interview. All of this is in an effort to prepare for avoiding such failures. This is a really good thing obviously. Your brain is analyzing possible failure points so you can avoid actually failing. It's trying to help you be successful. Simply lovely, I must say.

During this process of your brain analyzing potential failure points, it passes the data to you, and you decide if any of it is legitimate. If you don't accept any of the potential failing points as legitimate, then your brain will not elevate to an anxious state, and you go about your business in a comfortable way. If you do accept any of the potential failing scenarios as legitimate, then your brain will take the necessary actions to prevent it from occurring. Part of that reaction is to go into a mild state of anxiety. Your heart starts pumping blood mildly faster, hormones that will help your body react start flowing, your physical awareness increases, your muscles tense, etcetera. These are all good things that will help you avoid the potential failure.

With your body in an elevated state, more resources are made available to key areas. More blood flow and oxygen to your brain where memory is stored so you more easily access your memorized lines for the play. The same thing occurs for the date, except it's used to remember things your date enjoys so you can bring up engaging conversation. For the job interview, your bunghole puckers up tensely, so you don't blow a stinker in the middle of it.

So yeah, you do get a bit anxious before situations that have expectations, but it's all to help you avoid failing to meet whatever the expectations are, regardless of who set them. That mild anxiety is a good thing in the big picture.

Where anxiety potentially turns into a bad thing is when the possible failing points your brain is analyzing starts dipping into the area of negative self-analysis that I mentioned in lesson 5. In such a scenario it's going too far and comes up with too many unrealistic and self-critical possibilities. If you don't shut them down as illegitimate right off the bat, then they can quickly get out of control, especially if you have underlying and unresolved insecurities. If those potential failing points are accepted as legitimate, then your brain will proceed into anxiety mode, but it will potentially be more intense since there are likely more of them, and they're more self-critical and feeding on those potentially unaddressed insecurities. This is where it starts to get really yucky.

In a situation such as this, your brain is pushing you all kinds of overly negative possibilities, and without the awareness to shut it down, you spin into a tizzy of anxiousness. The number of negative possibilities it's pushing you alone can be anxiety-inducing, let alone already being in an anxious state by just one getting through.

Imagine preparing to go on stage for a play, and your mind is full of thoughts or worries, like what if I trip going on stage, forget my lines, get nauseous and puke, my pants fall down, pass gas, the audience *boos* me–oh my God...what if I panic!

These kinds of thoughts are downright overwhelming and if you don't get them under control yet still try to power through...oh my...it could easily trigger your brain into an all-out panic. Except you don't have an animal to run from so all of that energy is building up in your body with no outlet to release it. *Bam!* You're now panicking as if you're running for your life, but you're not running anywhere. Your heart is pumping as fast as it would if you were running, adrenaline is flooding into your body, your muscles are tense, and your skin is pale from the blood flow being rerouted to support running away from a nonexistent danger. This is bad. If you can't calm yourself down and get your brain and body out of panic mode then you could potentially, and inadvertently, hyperventilate and pass out.

Sounds fun, eh? Nah it's definitely not. It sucks badly, can exacerbate feelings of insecurity, and further dwindle your self-confidence. Sadly, though, it's not the worst thing that intense false anxiety can trigger. Bear with me as I will explain what that is after I explain another trigger for intense false anxiety.

Stressorrhea

Again in modern times and more often in urban lifestyles, a new trigger for anxiety and panic has evolved outside of the traditional direct threat of physical harm or supporting normal social integration. As urban life has evolved to move faster and faster, and with perpetually increased levels of psychological stimuli, it has brought about elevated levels of physical and psychological stress along with it. Turns out that with enough stimulation, stress, and anticipation of potential negative situations, anxiety and panic can be triggered in a similar way to it being triggered by the awareness of a lion being nearby or by excessive negative self-analysis type thoughts/worries.

Yes, the fact that so many of us work forty, fifty, or sixty or more hours per week, sitting lethargically in front of a computer screen nearly the entire time, all while our brains are running at full capacity as if we are running a marathon, fucks with things a bit. Throw in there a lack of sleep and a barrage of constant future-based stressors like bills that need to be paid, kids that need to be picked up from school, grocery shopping that needs to be done, homes or cars that need to be purchased or repaired, family members that need help, etcetera, and you get a great big pile of steaming stressorrhea.

To compound that all, we live in a digital world where we carry our phones with us at all times and are constantly bombarded with information and stimuli, like social media alerts, emails, texts, voicemails, or even watching trending videos or playing a quick round on a popular game app.

With all of this lack of sleep and constant bombardment of psychological stress and stimulation, we inevitably get physically tired yet have to somehow keep going. So we ingest caffeine and sugar to stimulate our brains and bodies to stay awake and power through. The reality is, though, that we're stimulating ourselves into an all-out nervous stupor. Overall urbanites live psychologically chaotic lives, and most of us have become so accustomed to it that we have no idea of exactly how stressed our bodies and brains truly are. Well... until we hit the red line and the shit hits the fan.

When we're in situations where we're tired, multitasking beyond function, and have numerous potential negative future events processing in our minds, we trigger our brains into an automatic state of anxiety. Your brain thinks there may be a negative situation on the horizon, so it triggers your body to react accordingly: your heart pumps blood faster, hormone flow goes into high gear, muscles tense, etcetera. This is exactly the same state you would be in if you heard a lion nearby or if negative self-analysis were to get out of control.

You are now in a state of anxiety, hyperaware and fearful of what's to come. Now add in a stimulant like caffeine, which alters the way your brain functions and compounds the chaos, and that state has now increased to an even higher level—one that potentially borders on all-out panic. All that needs to happen now is something...anything...to push you just a tad over the red line. This is not good at all.

Imagine living this way on a daily basis, day in and day out, living in a near constant state of anxiety, and walking the line of panic. Your brain and body attempt to adapt by creating habitual automatic reactions. Over time these reactions to the induced stress wreak havoc on both your brain and body. They were not designed to withstand constant states of anxiety. Inevitably things start becoming overused and breaking down, no different than a car that is driven at top speed for eight, ten, or twelve hours a day without a pit stop or repair...day after day. The car would quickly break down, and so do our brains and bodies. When that happens something has to give. You might get sick in one way or another, or you might inadvertently trigger your brain and body into a state of panic. As I promised a few paragraphs ago, here's where things can get much worse.

Imagine being an urbanite with all of those urban based stressors and overstimulations, which trigger you into a constant state of anxiety. Plus, you have out-of-control negative self-analysis going on, which serves to only amplify your anxiety to a point where panic attacks happen on a regular basis. And…yes, there is an *and*…you experience a true physical threat to your life. *Ho…ly…shit!*

All of this happening at the same time is just too much, and your brain triggers a full reboot of the system. Your blood pressure drops, your heart slows to a crawl, you inevitably pass out, and your brain, and your body fully resets. When your system comes fully back online a few minutes later, you're dazed, confused, and feel like absolute shit. Uh-oh…and now your body is going into safe mode and dumping everything that was in it before the reboot. In moments you're projectile vomiting, and highly liquefied diarrhea is shooting out your asshole. Now this is bad—really, really bad. Your body has been pushed way too far beyond what it could handle. It had to reboot to prevent a catastrophic failure.

Now you might be asking yourself how the hell I know that something like this can happen. Well, the answer is short and sweet. I know this because I experienced such an event—not just once, but multiple times.

Oh My!

Picture it: San Diego California, 2006. I was twenty-nine years old, and I was just starting to truly awaken to the reality of how unhappy I had been in my life thus far, especially in the relationship with my now ex-wife. All of this had created a buildup of energy in me that was destined to come out in one way or another. Little did I know exactly how much energy was already built up, how tense I was, the desperation I felt for change, and what that could cause over the long-term. I would find out soon enough though.

At this time my now ex-wife was pregnant with our son. We had been together for roughly eight years at this point, married for six, and had held off on having kids because of financial limitations. She was six years older than me, and her biological clock was ticking. With her being thirty-five, we were at a point where we were either going to do it now or not at all. The latter was not something either of us wanted, so we decided to bite the bullet and somehow figure out the finances.

The baby was something I had passionately looked forward to long before we decided to get pregnant. Looking back, I believe I could sense the strong connection he and I would have and the genuine joy he would bring to my world and the world overall, for that matter. I could sense the importance of bringing him into this world and how that would impact so many other paths.

She had always been adamant that she didn't want to deal with the stress of working a full-time job while pregnant, which was a huge factor in the financial limitations. I agreed and supported the idea. So we decided I was going to be the only income provider during the entire pregnancy and into at least the first year or more of his childhood.

The game plan I came up with to facilitate her not working was that I would maintain my low-level corporate job and increase my hobby of stock market trading to make up for her missing wages. We also decided to diversify our investments into the real estate market that had been booming up to that point. In the short term, we would tap into our life savings to make up for her missing income; in the long term, the investments would backfill what we had taken out.

This plan was risky, of course, but it was my top priority for our son to have a stable and loving life, as you can imagine, given my childhood experiences. Limiting stress on his mother and her being home with him when he started his life was the foundation of achieving that. So it was well worth the risk from my point of view. Besides…I had been trading in the stock market for a few years and had built up a nice little nest egg in the process. So I felt comfortable I could make money with it in the long term. I wasn't confident at all on the real estate side; actually I had all kinds of bad vibes over it, but my now ex-wife was excited about it and encouraged me to push aside those feelings. Worst-case scenario—I thought we would blow through all of our savings, but what we would have in return would be priceless.

The pregnancy had gone very well overall, but there were some challenges during labor. Basically, my son wasn't turning, and they didn't know why. The doctor gave it some time and nudging to see if he would turn on his own, but after twelve hours of labor and no progress, they decided intervention was required. It was decided that a caesarian section was necessary. Turns out my son's leg was wedged in a weird spot, and that was preventing him from turning. That proved to be a good thing, though, because they also found the umbilical cord loosely wrapped around his neck. Had his leg not been wedged then, the umbilical cord would have choked him on his way out.

Fortunately all of this was caught in time, and he was born safe and sound. Having not planned for a caesarian section, though, we were caught off guard with the challenges that caused. As you can imagine, having your stomach cut open requires quite a bit of recovery and limits mobility during that time, which clearly isn't optimal when you have your first baby to now care for. My then wife certainly had the tougher challenge to face in dealing with that, so I of course did everything I could to aid in her recovery over the coming weeks.

The first week was the toughest, for sure. We ended up only staying in the hospital for three days because of the hospital room situation. We kept getting moved from room to room for unknown reasons; they were all shared occupancy, which was a challenge all on its own. She got some sleep in between moves and feedings but not as much as she needed. Over those three days, I got maybe a couple of hours of cumulative sleep, as all I had was a very hard chair to sit in beside the bed, and I was the only one capable of baby care.

I made it through this challenge by increasing my caffeine intake. Looking back I realize what a fool I was for that. I never liked coffee or tea so would drink a couple of cans of Mountain Dew every day. I had now increased that to three cans. I know, I know...Mountain Dew? Seriously? I guess it's just one of those things you learn over time.

On the third day, the doctor could tell we were both over it with the changing of rooms and so took pity on us and authorized an early release. As we were leaving the hospital, I got a call from my boss asking me to return to work right away. I had saved up enough paid time off to cover two weeks, but three sleepless days in, I was being hassled about it. I explained the situation and how there was no way for me to come back right away. The disappointment from my boss was palatable, but fortunately they backed off. Once we got home from the hospital, I shouldered all of the daily responsibilities so my son's mother could rest and recover from the surgery. The only thing I didn't handle was the actual feeding since the plan was to breastfeed.

By the end of that first week, we were both exhausted–me from lack of sleep and her from recovering from surgery. That's when my boss called me again, this time with an ultimatum. I needed to return to work on Monday, or I would lose my position within the company. I wanted to fight them on the threat, but since I was providing the sole income and this job was providing the health insurance paying the hefty hospital bill, I couldn't risk losing it. Fortunately my mother-in-law was able to take a few days off from her job to help out when I returned to work and while my then wife transitioned out of recovery mode.

In addition to the challenges I just mentioned, our son wasn't gaining weight. Actually he was losing it. A couple of people who specialized in breastfeeding came by the house to evaluate and assist. Neither were able to achieve the desired results though. At the recommendation of the pediatrician, we decided to try formula instead. That did the trick, and he immediately gained weight and quickly got on track to where he should be.

As the days went on, though, it became clear that the formula wasn't totally agreeing with him. Long story short, he appeared to have a digestive issue that required a highly specialized formula that would be easier for him to digest. The doctor had a decent amount of samples on hand, so we were able to test it out at no cost. Thankfully that permanently solved the issue. However, that formula proved to not be the cheapest thing in the world: $600 per month to be precise. But you gotta do what you gotta do, you know what I'm sayin'? In all seriousness we had no hesitation to do that obviously; it was just throwing a monkey wrench into the financial game plan. We had planned on breastfeeding, not formula feeding, let alone $600 per month for formula. Ouch!

By this point I was back at work full time, coming home and immediately taking over baby duty, doing all the house chores and grocery shopping, which my son's mom wasn't up to doing yet, checking up on the stock portfolio and potential new investments, and working with a real estate agent/investor on potential property purchases. In addition my son's mom and I had agreed to split the nighttime feedings, with her taking the first two and me taking the last two.

As time went by, though, we were both still exhausted. On some days my son's mom would nearly have breakdowns over her challenges with recovery, not enough sleep, and nobody being around during the day to help her. It may have just been the situation, or she may have been suffering some postpartum depression. She wouldn't even remotely consider speaking with a professional about it, so I did the only thing I could think of to hopefully make things better. I opted to try to give her a few days of solid sleep by taking on all of the nighttime feedings myself, now possible since we switched him to bottle feeding.

I had hoped with a few days' rest she would feel better, and we could get some stability in the situation. She did indeed start feeling much better; however, those few days of extra sleep turned into regular occurrences to keep her sane while I was at work. I was trying to do the right thing and bear the burden of the sleep loss, but it was taking a slow and subtle toll on me. To keep up with it all, I foolishly increased my caffeine intake again. By this time I had switched from three twelve-ounce cans to three twenty-ounce bottles. Oh my! It got me through though—just barely, but it certainly helped.

The Storm

When our son was one month old, something changed in him. All the feeding issues had been resolved, but all of a sudden, he began vomiting up every bit of milk he took down. I remember it well; it was Christmas day when it started. By the following day, he had literally vomited every bottle he had taken down and was beginning to cry inconsolably. The vomit wasn't just a spit-up kind of thing though–it was like projectile vomiting. We knew something was wrong. Fortunately we were able to get ahold of his pediatrician, despite the holiday, and she agreed to see him that day.

We immediately drove to the doctor's office and anxiously waited to figure out what was going on with him. We ended up never going home that day, as the doctor concluded that he had something called pyloric stenosis, and it required immediate surgery. She told us we needed to take him to Rady Children's Hospital in San Diego, where another doctor was waiting for us.

We immediately headed over and were taken right in for him to have an ultrasound, which confirmed he indeed had pyloric stenosis. Pyloric stenosis is an issue where the sphincter muscle between the lower stomach and the small intestine, which normally opens and closes to allow food to pass into the intestines, becomes stuck in the closed position. Basically what was going in wasn't passing through so would back up and need to come out someway…thus the projectile vomiting. Nothing he was eating was making it to his intestines, so he was literally starving…thus the inconsolable crying.

After confirmation of the diagnosis, we were immediately checked in to the hospital, and preparations began for him to go into surgery. It was such a frightening time, as you can imagine. We ended up staying in the hospital for four days; unfortunately they only allowed one parent to stay with him. There was no way I was leaving, so I insisted on staying. They accepted us both being there but said they only had one chair that was suitable for sleeping, which I obviously gave to my son's mom. I ended up sleeping as much as I could in a metal folding chair. Thankfully, though, the surgery went very well, and our son was healthy and recovering. Of course my caffeine and sugar intake remained high throughout this ordeal.

Things definitely improved after the surgery. He was eating well and growing as he should be, and we were starting to get the hang of the sleeping situation. We both were still not getting the sleep we used to, but it was getting better. I was still trying to give my son's mom breaks from the nighttime feedings, though, which certainly was hard to handle and required heavy amounts of caffeine for me to maintain. I was also still shouldering a heavy load on the work front and trying to carry a heavy share of the home responsibilities. But I was hopeful things would improve even more as he got older and would sleep longer during the night.

Eventually his night sleeping did improve as well; however, the toll the lack of sleep, high caffeine, high sugar, and balancing too many things had taken on me was too much, and I was on the verge of breaking down. Little did I know that I had already been experiencing numerous issues with anxiety, and I had absolutely no awareness of the effects of the negative self-analysis that ran rampant inside my mind on a regular basis. This was all leading somewhere nobody would willingly choose. All that was missing was the straw that would break the camel's back.

Just before my son turned a year old, one of the stock investments I made went south as news hit that the company had been fraudulently reporting their earnings. Additionally we had purchased an investment property, and I was trying to fit in do-it-yourself repairs to save some cash. This house investment made me very nervous.

The home itself was more expensive than I felt comfortable investing in, but a business partner who my now ex-wife was friends with had insisted it was a great investment. I knew little of the intricacies of the real estate market, so considering the friendship between the business partner and my now ex, I went against my instincts and trusted in what we were being told.

The plan was to fix up this investment property and rent it out for a few years before selling. At the same time, this business partner also had hooked us up with a group of investors buying up homes in Texas that were being purchased at a negotiated bulk price. We agreed to purchase three of them. We honestly didn't have the money to purchase them, which was one of the things that made me so nervous. We were leveraging our own condo and the investment home we had just purchased in order to finance these new homes. The vibe of the situation was eating away at me; I intensely felt something was off and just was starting to understand and trust those types of feelings.

After we had owned this investment property for a few months and were just starting to get into the purchase of the Texas properties, my vibes grew to the point I could no longer ignore them. I ended up putting my foot down and told our business partner I wanted us out of the Texas deals, and I wanted to sell the investment property we already owned. This business partner was pissed and told me we would lose a ton of money and threatened to sue us. I didn't care at that point though; everything in me was telling me to get out of it.

I pulled the plug in the nick of time, because doing so revealed that our business partner was a swindler and had been accused of numerous counts of fraud. We got out in time to lose only $10,000 and a lot of time and energy. Had we stayed in longer, we would have lost everything, as the housing market began crashing just months later, and this shady business partner screwed a lot of other investors over to save their own ass. The whole situation had my nerves rattled to their core.

The Shit Hits the Fan

While all of these investments were in the midst of crashing, my employer was doing some remodeling of their headquarters and was giving away some bookshelves they no longer needed. I thought one would go great in our garage, so I opted to take it. I had a large truck with an extended bed at the time so pulled it around to the side of the building to load it. I found a guy who worked in facilities and asked him if he'd help me load this rather large and heavy solid wood shelf. He kindly agreed, and we both carried it out a side door where I had pulled up my truck.

I had already measured the bed of my truck, and the shelf should have just fit. But I failed to realize that the wheel wells weren't straight, so the shelf got stuck between them when we slid it in. It was only off a tiny bit, though, and the shelf was just for my garage, so I didn't care if it got scratched. I figured, if we gave it a good shove, then that would get it in enough where I could close the tailgate.

With the shelf now stuck, I asked the guy who was helping me to give it a big push on the count of three. I counted one…two…three…

We both had backed up a bit and charged at the shelf with our shoulders. I unfortunately didn't hit the shelf with my shoulder, however. I mistakenly made contact with my elbow first. I had hit it with quite a bit of force, though, more than my elbow could take without moving out of place. As my elbow hit the shelf, the impact pushed it into my ribs where I immediately felt something snap.

The wind was instantly knocked out of me, and all of a sudden, I couldn't breathe. The shelf moved in this process but not enough to close the tailgate, so the guy that was helping me went in for another push. I, however, hunched over in pain and lack of air. I knew something was wrong, but I hadn't grasped the severity of the issue. I thought maybe I just hit wrong and knocked the wind out of myself.

I was trying to keep my composure despite starting to feel woozy. I didn't want to make a big deal of my injury, so I simply told the guy that I think I hurt myself a bit and said we should just leave the shelf as it was with the tailgate left open. He clearly couldn't tell how injured I was because he responded saying that he thought we could get it in more and wanted to give it another go. Barely breathing, I just told him, "Nah…let's just leave it." He agreed and headed back into the building.

Looking back I realize now that I was probably in a bit of shock at this point. The pain was fading, and I was a bit out of it. I needed to move my truck, though, so I foolishly, yet carefully, got in and drove it over to a parking spot a short bit away. After parking the truck, I slowly walked into the building and over to my desk to sit down and rest. It was a large building, though, so it took me a solid five labored minutes to get to my desk. Not a long distance in normal circumstances, but in this case, it seemed twice as long.

Reality started to hit me when I sat down at my desk. My mind was now racing, wondering what I had done to myself. I didn't understand it at the time, but I was starting to have a panic attack. This incident had pushed my body too far. With the lack of sleep, overcaffeination, excess sugar, stress over investments, a mind racing a million miles an hour, and being physically hurt and fearing it maybe something worse…I was finally cracking.

I felt like absolute shit at this point. The only thing I could think of doing was to call my then wife and ask her to take me to the hospital. She picked up, and being short of breath and not wanting my coworkers to hear, I quietly told her that I think I broke my ribs and asked her to come get me. She was caught off guard and asked what happened. I couldn't even respond to her question. I said, "Please... just come get me."

My heart was racing at this point. I could barely breathe, yet my body felt like it was running a marathon. My mind just kept thinking, *What if I seriously hurt myself?* So many thoughts were rushing through my brain that I couldn't rationalize anything. I was feeling so woozy, the only thing I could think of doing was going to the bathroom where nobody would see me. Somehow–and I really don't know how–I got up and walked over to the nearby bathroom.

By the time I got inside the one-person bathroom and closed the door, every thought in my mind was pure fear. *Had I broken my ribs? Why did my chest hurt so badly? Maybe I'm having a heart attack? What if I die and leave my son without a father?* By this point the panic had taken control, and I just wanted to lie down and make it all go away. Pain overwhelmed me as I attempted to lie down on the cold tiles of this public bathroom (yuck!). As I got to the ground and set my head on the tiles, I lost consciousness.

After blacking out an unknown amount of time, I began to come to. Everything was blurry for a moment, and I wasn't sure where I was. I remember hearing the overhead fan running and feeling cold... freezing cold. Wait no–I was extremely hot–so hot I was drenched with sweat. I was freezing cold and sweating profusely all at the same time. The next thing I knew I started feeling nauseous and knew I was going to puke. I tried to get up, but the pain on the right side of my ribs was intense. So I leaned more to my left side and got on my knees as quickly as possible. Just then, as I was reaching the toilet, I began violently vomiting up everything in my stomach, painfully heaving with each convulsion.

Just as I stopped puking and was trying to assess if I was finished, I felt a gurgling in my intestines. I'm not sure how but I stood up, pulled my pants down, and sat on the toilet I had just vomited into. The most liquefied and foul-smelling diarrhea I had ever experienced began shooting straight out of my ass. As I sat there spewing this nasty smelling shit that seemed to go on forever, I felt my stomach clenching. I tried to hold it in but couldn't. I puckered up, stood up, and pressed the flusher as I began dry heaving into the foul toilet. The heaving stopped after a minute or two. I wasn't sure if more still needed to come out the other side so sat down again to make sure there were no surprises. Thankfully it had stopped.

Now that the puking and diarrhea had stopped, I somehow cleaned myself up, washed my hands, and laid down on the ground once more. I felt light-headed but didn't pass out. I was tired, though, so tired I couldn't stay awake. I ended up falling in and out of sleep. Maybe I was in and out of consciousness; I'm not sure.

I stayed on the floor in the bathroom for what seemed like forever–freezing cold and drenched in sweat. Eventually all of those racing thoughts and panic were beginning to slow. They were still there for sure, but it wasn't as bad. I began focusing on just trying to feel better. I prayed to the universe to please help me. I must have been in that state for thirty minutes at least when my front pocket began buzzing. It was my then wife calling my cell; she was parked outside the building and asking me where I was. I told her I was in the bathroom and would be out in a few minutes.

I didn't know how I was going to get up but knew I needed to. Otherwise someone would have to come in to help me, and that started me panicking again. So I told myself, *No, I can do this*. I began repeating to myself over and over, *Everything is going to be all right. I can do this.* Over and over again, I thought that to myself as I stood up, got myself and the bathroom presentable, washed up, and opened the door.

As I walked out of the bathroom, a coworker happened to be walking by and saw me. She immediately asked me if I was ok. I simply replied, "Been better." She told me that I was superpale and asked if I needed some help. I told her, "No, my wife is here to pick me up." I asked her to please let everyone know I wasn't feeling well and was leaving for the day. Without going back to my desk to get my belongings, I headed straight out the lobby doors and to the car, where my then-wife was waiting.

After carefully getting into the passenger seat of the car, I explained to my then-wife what had happened. She told me I looked like death warmed over and drove me to the hospital. What happened next was hours of waiting–dazed and confused–in the emergency waiting room. My now ex-wife couldn't stay with me, as her mother had come over to watch our son and needed to get back to work. So shortly after arriving at the emergency room, she left to care for our son.

I'm confident I was in some type of shock because I barely remember anything from that time waiting in the emergency room. All I remember is how cold I was and the uncontrollable shivering that accompanied it. I'm guessing I had been there an hour or two when the triage nurse walked past me slumped over in a chair. As she passed me she paused, turned back, and came closer to me. She asked if anyone had seen me yet. I tried to tell her no, but I couldn't get any words out. She then placed her hands on both sides of my head and lifted it up to flash a light into my eyes. She immediately called for two paramedics to come over and help her get me onto a gurney.

The paramedics took me straight back beyond the double doors to a bed where the two gentlemen lifted me up and placed me in it. I remember this part so clearly: the triage nurse who had found me in the waiting room went over to a cabinet, pulled out some blankets, and placed them on me. They were heated and felt soooo good! After several hours when I had felt like absolute shit, the warmth of the blankets and her care were like a breath of fresh air. Up to this point in my life, I don't think I had ever felt as cared for as I did by that nurse. That's pretty fucking sad actually.

As I lay there in the emergency room bed, the nurse never left my side. As I warmed up, she hooked me up to an IV and asked me what had happened. I was starting to feel a bit better and was able to explain what had occurred. Over the coming hours, various tests, x-rays, and blood work were done. In the end they confirmed I had indeed broken my ribs. No other abnormalities were found, and nobody explained anything else beyond the broken ribs. About midnight the nurse told me they were going to release me and called for my then wife to pick me up. I was given instructions on how to care for the broken ribs and told I should schedule a follow up with my primary doctor. I was then discharged.

Everything Changed

After that day nothing was the same. Yes, my ribs hurt and all that, but that wasn't the issue. Something had changed in me. After a few days of rest, I attempted to go with my son and his mom to our local Target to do some weekly shopping. This was the first time I had been out of the house since coming home from the hospital. I was, of course, taking it easy getting in and out of the car and such, but I was feeling weird, and I didn't know what it was or why. I blew it off, though, and decided to go into the store anyway.

While walking through the store, I was nervous for some reason. I had to keep reminding myself to breath and had to keep repeating to myself that everything was ok. In an attempt to distract myself, I reached to look at a kid's shirt hanging on a rack beside me. Unfortunately, I reached just the wrong way and felt a strong twinge of pain where the break was in my ribs. All of a sudden, fear engulfed me. I started breathing heavily and struggling to keep my composure. The thoughts in my mind were racing out of control. Every fear my brain could think of was swirling around and clogging my awareness. Then it hit: I began fearing I had seriously hurt myself again, and I couldn't breathe anymore. I was starting to hyperventilate.

I tried to take deep breaths, but it hurt too badly. I was feeling light-headed and sweating profusely, so right there in between racks of clothing in the children's section, I lay down on the floor. My then-wife snapped at me out of embarrassment and told me to get up. I couldn't though. I didn't understand it at the time, but I was having another panic attack. From my perspective, though, I was dying.

Fortunately the store was pretty quiet at that point, and nobody noticed me on the floor. After a couple of minutes of my then-wife barking at me to get up, I was able to stand without passing out. I immediately walked outside so I could breathe better while my son and his mom continued with the shopping. The cool air helped, though the difficulty in taking a deep breath certainly hindered my ability to calm down. One of the instructions I was given was to take deep breaths despite the pain to prevent my lungs from collapsing, so I pushed through the pain. I ended up going back to the car and waiting for my son and his mom to finish shopping. Once in the car, I was able to slowly calm down.

Over the following few months, I had numerous panic attacks, each in different situations but similar as far as the overload of racing thoughts, heavy sweating, feeling of passing out, and sometimes actually losing consciousness. Working was difficult, and I had to take frequent breaks to the bathroom or to go outside to calm down. There were even two incidents where I went back to the emergency room because I literally thought I had further damaged my ribs and feared more serious damage. Each time I was quickly released, as they could find no issues.

During this time I also had been to my primary doctor several times and explained in detail all that was happening. He of course blew it all off each time and simply told me I was fine. Never once did he or anyone else ever tell me I was experiencing anxiety or having panic attacks. Not once. They all just said that nothing was wrong with me and huffily sent me on my way. I could tell they were frustrated with me, but I truly felt horrible and knew that something was wrong.

Over the following year, I did everything I could to keep the anxiety and panic at bay with limited intervention or treatment. All of the same responsibilities were still on me–working long hours, not enough sleep, too much stimulation, etcetera–plus our son was being evaluated for autism because of some developmental delays. So I was still in the exact same situation. Despite the many doctor's office and emergency room visits, nobody had diagnosed me with anxiety, let alone panic attacks, and I honestly didn't even know what they were. I had heard of anxiety before, but I didn't really know what it actually was, so I never even considered I might be suffering from it.

That all changed, though, maybe a year after the broken rib event when I experienced another major panic attack with puking and the whole bit. This time I was at an outpatient medical facility, waiting to have a minor, unrelated procedure. I was being hooked up to some monitors, and I got triggered. Next thing I knew, I awoke freezing cold and drenched in sweat with a group of doctors and nurses hovering over me trying to bring me back to consciousness.

After this event my primary doctor told me I needed to see a cardiologist since I had repeated fainting events. He said if I didn't get cleared from the cardiologist, then my driver's license would likely be revoked. That was just the comment I needed to make me feel better. The idea of losing my driver's license didn't drive my already sky-high levels of stress higher or anything. Nah, it was a supercomforting feeling to not only be blown off by the doctor repeatedly but also to be threatened with having my license taken away. *Not!* OMG! What an incompetent douche that guy was!

The cardiologist I ended up seeing was young, which was refreshing, and ran a ton of tests on me. At the end he told me he was confident I didn't have any heart issues. I had explained to him all that had happened over the past year, and he kindly told me what his thoughts were. He explained that he had recently graduated from medical school and experienced something similar when he was working numerous long shifts, cramming for tests, and drinking too much caffeine. He told me it was anxiety and panic attacks, and he thought what I was experiencing was the same. It all made sense now. This is why everyone else blew me off. They basically thought I was nuts. What assholes!

After the cardiologist told me I likely was suffering anxiety and panic attacks, I did my own research to learn more about it. There wasn't much I could do with the stress in my life at that point, but I did stop drinking caffeine and sodas. I immediately noticed a huge difference just from that. I attempted to reintroduce caffeine sometime later, but within days, I noticed the panicky feelings returning. It was clear to me that I could no longer handle caffeine the same way I did before. My body seemed permanently altered. So I gave it up indefinitely.

Caffeine wasn't the only issue that triggered my anxiety and panic attacks though. The biggest culprit was stress. What's funny to me, looking back on all that happened is that, before this had all occurred, I had been to an acupuncturist, and she had told me my stress levels were off the charts. I thought she was nuts at the time because I didn't feel stressed at all. Despite my insistence that I wasn't stressed, she told me I needed to find a way to unwind myself; otherwise, I would eventually snap. I clearly didn't get it at the time, but I did after finally realizing that I had been experiencing anxiety and panic and what all of that truly meant.

The acupuncturist was totally right, and I get that now. I eventually learned that I had spent my entire life trying to be everything to everyone. I had been so highly stressed for so long that it felt normal to me. The very suggestion that I was overstressed made no sense to me because that's all I knew. I had no frame of reference to anything different. It took me years to fully grasp the severity of my stress and to learn how to recover from it.

Staying Safe

The point of the story I shared, and the detail I provided, was to show how normal life stresses can escalate over time and compound into a full-on breakdown. Your brain and body have limitations, and they need your awareness and care to avoid being damaged. Just like how you need to be aware of how hot something is to avoid being burned, you also need to be aware of your stress to avoid cracking up. And just like how you need to know what to do when you get burned, you also need to know what to do when you get overstressed. I didn't have that knowledge and awareness, and as a result, I got pushed too far, and I will never be able to completely wipe away the effects of that experience.

To this day I still have to contend with what happened to me so many years ago as my brain and body remember it clearly. In overly stressful situations, they can easily snap backward and have a panic attack. I've learned how to stop that from occurring, but I have to be aware of it at all times. I have to manage my stress and know my triggers.

The last panic attack I experienced was ten years ago (not including the marijuana event I noted in lesson 2 since that was a unique situation), and nobody knew it had occurred because I recognized what was happening, and I knew how to stop it (just as I did with the marijuana event). Learning how to successfully do that gave me the tools and confidence I needed to protect myself from going through it again. I will share what that actually looks like for me in a short bit. For now, though, I want to be clear of the risks of too much unrelieved stress and too much caffeine and other stimulants and the need take care of your mind and body, because nobody else lives in it besides you.

You're the only one who knows what is stressful to your brain and body, what triggers them, and how they feel. So listen to your body and brain; be aware and observe how they are feeling and reacting. Trust them when they're telling you something. Your body, including your brain, is your vessel for moving around this world. If you treat it as such and care for it as it needs to be cared for, then you will find yourself experiencing this thing called life in a much more enjoyable way.

Let's face it, life can be overwhelming, and that's just the way it is. Just like how you can't control a hurricane, tornado, or earthquake from happening, you also can't control life outside of your body and its overwhelming aspects. What you can do, though, just as you would in a storm or natural disaster, is protect yourself as it passes. Keep yourself safe while that storm rages.

There's an old saying that says a boat can't sink, no matter how bad the storm is, as long as the water doesn't get inside. The same goes for the overwhelming aspects of life. It can't sink you if it doesn't get in. The greatest tool I use to prevent it from getting in is to be prepared for the storm. Because the reality is that storms come and go all of the time, so you have to be prepared for them.

Back Off, Buddy...I Got the Feels

First and foremost what I've found to be a key element is taking time to listen to my mind and body. I've learned to separate my awareness of the spiritual me and the physical me, and then I pay close attention to how the physical me is feeling and what energy it's emitting. Quite often my body will feel something that is off. In the past I didn't pay one bit of attention to that but have learned that it always means something. If I'm physically feeling tired, I ask my brain to analyze that and where it may be coming from. I also focus in on the energy that I am picking up from my body and try to feel what its saying.

For example, just before I wrote this very paragraph, I took a day off from writing because I was feeling tired in an unusual way. I wasn't tired because I hadn't had enough sleep or anything like that. I was simply feeling drained, and it happened very quickly after finishing the paragraph before this one. In that moment I didn't know exactly why I was feeling drained of energy, but I knew there was a good reason for it. I immediately recognized it, appreciated it as a message, and took the action of stopping.

Once I stopped writing, I had to remind myself that breaks are needed. Naturally my brain started to analyze all over the place, and some of those places were things like, *If I take a break, then I'll get behind schedule*. I shut that analysis down immediately though. My brain didn't mean anything negative by that analysis; it was just providing data to me, and it could have been totally valid in a different scenario. However, I took that data and compared it with the vibes I was getting. I decided that data wasn't valid because I wasn't just being lazy or avoiding something. I legitimately was drained. I had been writing for five days straight so reminded myself about self-compassion and that a break was warranted and reasonable. Maybe I just needed some downtime, or maybe there was something bothering me at a really deep level. Time would allow me to figure that out.

Sure enough, throughout my day off, I realized that the paragraph I had started to write was going in the wrong direction. What I realized was that if I kept going with what I had written, then I would go completely astray from what I'm trying to achieve here, and it would have been very difficult to fix down the line. Basically, I had taken the wrong road, and I needed to get off it right away.

When I started writing a short bit ago, I deleted the entire paragraph I had written previously and started with my new perspective. What you see here is a result of that and I feel energized over it. You see–the physical body can manifest sensations based on the vibes that are running through it. Maybe it was coming from my own spiritual knowledge that I don't have complete logical access to, maybe it was from the universe, or maybe it was from my spirit guides. Whichever it was my body was manifesting feelings because of it. And there was knowledge in those feelings. Had I not stopped and listened, then that energy would have stayed in me, persistently knocking at my door asking to be let out, building up and turning into physical stress or depression.

Let me provide another example but from a different perspective. Let's take the story I shared of my anxiety and panic attacks. Over the course of years, my body had been screaming at me that I was unhappy, depressed, overstressed, mired in bad situations, etcetera. I ignored those feelings over and over again. The energy of each one built up over time, compounding over and over again, and adding to the other physical stresses of not sleeping and being overstimulated. Eventually it all became too much, and my brain and body couldn't handle it anymore. Had I listened to my body over those years and dug into what it was feeling, then those stresses wouldn't have built up, and I wouldn't have cracked. Listening to how your body, including your brain, is feeling is a fundamental element in stress prevention and management.

I Love Me More

I briefly mentioned self-compassion moments ago, which is a big element in the prevention and addressing of stress. I find that stress can build up in my physical body if I don't cut myself some slack. I'm the type of person who pushes myself hard, which is a great thing to a certain degree. If I don't give myself enough self-compassion, though, then I can quickly run myself down.

Just like how I mentioned that I allowed myself to guiltlessly take a day off, granting yourself time off to unwind, digest knowledge and vibes, and commune with your whole self, the universe, and your spirit guides is so important. When you goof up, don't look at it as a bad thing and stress out over it. It just ends up being stress on top of stress, which doesn't serve you well. Instead focus on the message and the knowledge that you are gaining. Appreciate that for what it is and allow yourself to accept it. By doing so, you end up relieving the stress. Obviously you don't want to go too far and become a total slacker or anything. Again it's all about balance. Allow your brain to analyze the situation with all its infinite glory but be sure to add in compassion for yourself and shut down negative self-analysis as soon as it starts.

I Don't Need That Shit

Another key element to managing stress, and ultimately anxiety and panic, is managing expectations—both your own as well as others'. This weaves tightly into self-compassion and is a cornerstone for many elements of stress prevention.

For example, I would love to finish this book today or even this month, but that's simply not possible. I frequently catch my brain analyzing that if I were to complete one lesson in *X* amount of time, then I'll have it finished by this or that date. I have to shut that down every time and remind myself that I'll finish the book when I finish it. I have to remind myself that I'm not a slacker, so I don't need to be concerned about that at all. On the contrary actually, I remind myself that I'm more likely to push myself too hard and run myself down, so I need to be more focused on that over potential slacking. I remind myself to flow, don't force. I feel the energy flowing through me and around me...I go with it. It takes me where I need to go and when I need to go there. I remind myself to trust that flow and believe in it.

The same thing basically applies to managing expectations from others as well, with one subtle yet important difference. With managing self-expectations, I need to convince myself of what is realistic and what isn't. When managing others' expectations, however, I don't need to convince them of anything. I still need that beautiful self-compassion. I just need to communicate, in the most positive yet honest way possible, if their expectations are not matching what I feel I have capacity to achieve. They can then take it or leave it. At that point it's up to me to be aware and accept whatever the potential ramifications are of that.

For example, let's say my boss says I need to finish a project in one day that I don't feel I can do in that time frame. I allow my brain to analyze the situation and potential scenarios, which provides me the data I need to make sure there are no other avenues to meet my boss's expectation. If I don't find any, then I politely and professionally communicate that. My job from there is to accept that and not beat myself up over it. Again think about self-compassion. My boss's reaction is their choice and whether they accept my position or not is completely up to them. I have no power over what goes on in their brain. If they accept it or are willing to negotiate, then fantastic. If not and they want to scold or punish me, then so be it. That's their karma to deal with, it's their own insecurities manifesting, and it's their own lesson to be learned. If they fire me, then that's my destiny.

When I think back to when my boss had the expectation that I would return to work right away after my son was born, if I was in that situation today, I would have simply said no. I would have said, "I'm taking two weeks off as planned, and that's that." The reality is that my boss wouldn't have fired me. I could have been moved to a different position, of course, but they wouldn't have fired me. Even if they did fire me...whatevs, bruh! I neither need nor want that kind of shit in my life. In all honesty...the reason I pushed myself too hard to meet my boss's expectations back then was because I wasn't managing my own expectations properly. So by managing your own expectations, you end up managing the expectations of others at the same time. That's the flow of life right there, baby!

All the Little Things

Besides listening to your mind and body, having self-compassion, and managing expectations, I have a variety of things I've learned to do that help me clear out stress and built-up energy. I consider all of these things to be very grounding. The term grounding for me means that it harmonizes my mind, body, energy, and spirit. These activities bring all of me into one place and help me release stress.

Duh, Don't Forget to Breathe

One of those things is the most basic task of breathing. Just the simple act of making sure to take deep breaths, hold them for a moment, and then breath it all out makes a subtle yet impactful difference. Breathing is of vital importance to your body, so if you don't breathe effectively, then your body won't perform at optimal capacity, which makes it more challenging for it to manage stress. I also find that taking a deep breath helps my mind let go of unwanted thoughts and overanalysis. It's kind of like a polite smack in the face to my brain so it'll chill the fuck out. So if you're not in the habit of doing this very easy and simple task, then I highly recommend you give it a try.

Oooohmmm

Along with the focused breathing I noted, I sometimes even do a mini-meditation at the same time. I imagine my energy as being roots reaching out of my feet and stretching all the way to the core of the earth, tapping into the powerful energy flow of the earth itself. At the same time, I imagine my energy roots coming out of the top of my head and stretching out into the universe, connecting to the infinite energy that exists out there. I energetically connect myself to the earth and universe...and I just breathe and let that energy flow. As the energy of the earth and universe flows through me, I allow it to carry away any stress with it.

It doesn't take long to do this; you can do it in the shower, while at work, or on the subway. Nobody needs to know you're doing it either. You don't even have to close your eyes to do it. This mini-meditation is something I love to do and perform anytime I feel stress or energy building up in me.

Move Your Ass, You Lazy Bastard

I also find movement of your body to be very beneficial and helpful in managing stress, especially if you live a rather sedentary lifestyle. I used to not like admitting I lived a sedentary lifestyle because...well, I don't know...I guess it was just an ego thing. The reality was for me, though, that I sat in front of a computer eight to twelve hours a day. Sure, I was exhausted at the end of those hours, but physically the only thing I had done was eat and go to the bathroom. If that isn't the definition of sedentary, then I don't know what is.

Adding more movement into your day can change that sedentary lifestyle, get energy flowing, and relieve stress. If that scares the shit out of you because you don't have time, then think baby steps. One of the things I used to do at my last corporate job was use the restroom on the opposite side of the building. I worked on the second floor on the west side of the building, so I'd walk to the east side and down the stairs to take a leak in a first-floor bathroom. It took me an extra five minutes in total but do that a few times a day, and hot damn! You're quite a bit more active, and the energy and stress are moving along with it.

If you can fit in some long-term movements, then that's fantastic too! It doesn't have to be fancy or anything. My personal favorite is either walking up and down the stairs in the condo I live in at the moment or walking around the inside of the house. Yeah, you heard that correctly. Don't judge now! I literally walk around my house. This condo is open concept, and the downstairs area is roughly 1,100 square feet and rectangular in shape. So I'll put in my earbuds and just walk around the perimeter over and over again for ten minutes to an hour. It becomes like a moving meditation for me. I would walk outside, but there's a lot of traffic in the neighborhood and that shit stresses me out, so I just walk inside. Ok, go ahead and laugh now… it's fine. Seriously though—do whatever works for you and feel that stress melt away.

Just Chillin'

Another thing I've learned to do to relieve stress is set time aside for myself to unwind. I really like it at nighttime when everyone in my house is asleep. The neighborhood is quiet at that time, so I can just chill. I also love watching movies and listening to music during this time. Man, that stuff is sooo good at unwinding me. Maybe throw in a glass of wine or a beer to really make it special. Just don't go overboard on the booze or anything. Nobody likes to hear it, but that shit is literally toxic to your body, so moderation is definitely key.

Taking time for yourself doesn't have to be just when you're home either. When you're at work, take advantage of breaks and go outside to take a few deep breaths. You end up getting movement in there, too, so it's a triple whammy! If you're an introvert or empath like me, then you can even do something like that when out and about in crowds as well. I live in Southern California at this moment and love going to Disneyland®. It's one of the toughest places for me, though, since the crowds can be overwhelming. When I feel the stress building up, I will tell anyone I'm with that I need to take a break. I'll then grab a snack or an herbal tea and head over to one of the quieter spots in the park to chill for ten or fifteen minutes. Or I'll even throw in my earbuds for a short bit just for a break. After that I'm recharged and ready to power on.

I'll be honest: some people think I'm weird because I do that stuff, but I don't give a flying fuck. I think they're weird because they don't–so there!

Speaking of introversion and empaths, I've always been both, and that has certainly gotten stronger as I've evolved. My ability to pick up on and understand vibes has grown to a point where my ability to go out in public can be limiting at times, especially if the folks I come across have chaotic vibes. And guess what? That's ok. Society tells us that we're all supposed to be jolly and social, but as I noted in lesson 4, that's just a perception. And it's one that doesn't fit for everyone. If you're a social butterfly and/or not affected by people's vibes, then that's fantastic for you. If you're like me, though, or somewhere in between and find those situations stressful then give yourself a break, breathe, mini-meditate, have a cup of tea or a snack, monitor your own expectations, and communicate honestly with people so you don't burn out or stress out.

Would You Like a Cup of Tea...or a Mint Maybe?

Just a few more things that I find very grounding and stress relieving are peppermints, various herbal teas, and eating unprocessed and nutritionally balanced foods.

I don't know exactly what it is about peppermints for me, but I pop a couple anytime I feel myself becoming ungrounded, and it quickly pulls me back into place. I definitely recommend organic peppermints so you don't get some fake crap that's gonna make you feel shitty. For me popping a few in stressful situations can be the difference between stressing out and not. That's how impactful it is for me.

Herbal teas can work in a similar way. I also definitely recommend going the organic route with them. I don't want to recommend specific teas because everyone has their own tastes and needs. Do some research, though, and try some out. You can even mix and match by using multiple tea bags to create your own flavors. I often will mix lemongrass or peppermint into other teas to give them a little extra kick. Herbal teas definitely can take some getting used to, but it's well worth the effort. Maybe even add some raw honey in to make it a sweet treat. I personally have a cup of herbal tea with raw honey every night shortly after dinner. It's just a nice little night cap.

What the Fuck Are You Eating?

Processed foods are loaded with shit that your body will struggle to digest, which will only add stress to your body. Keeping it as natural as possible is something I've done for years now, and it has made a big difference for me in how I feel and manage stress.

Having balanced nutrition in my meals has made a big difference as well. At each meal I make sure there are carbs, fat, protein, and fiber. Contrary to what the diet industry tries to manipulate your perception to be, carbs and fat are good for you as long as they are the healthy kind (i.e., not the processed shit). Protein is good for you too, obviously, but too much of it–just like anything else–isn't good. So keep it balanced to keep yourself balanced.

Too Relieved to Grieve

Before I wrap up this lesson, which to be honest has been a bit triggering for me to write, I'd like to share the lyrics from a song that embodies the essence of letting go of stress. It's a song the world fell in love with back in 2013/2014. If you haven't already guessed, the name of the song is "Let It Go"[19] from the Disney® movie *Frozen*.[20] I don't think it's relevant to give a full recap of the movie, so instead I will summarize only what leads to the song being sung.

At the beginning of the movie you witness a young Princess Elsa–who has been born with magical powers that allow her to summon and manipulate snow and ice at will–and her younger sister, Princess Anna, playing in their family's castle. Anna has mischievously awoken Elsa from her sleep and infamously asks her if she wants to build a snowman. The two then frolic about the castle using Elsa's powers to build one, along with making it snow, also creating an ice rink, a snow slide, and a series of ice pillars that Anna uses to jump higher and higher into the air.

The situation quickly gets out of control as Anna jumps between the pillars too fast and Elsa is left struggling to keep up with her in building a new pillar before Anna jumps. In Elsa's panic to build a new pillar quickly enough, she slips on the ice, and the magic she had shot to create a new ice pillar inadvertently hits Anna in the head instead. Anna falls to the ground and Elsa screams for their parents. While this is taking place, the ice they have been playing with quickly begins growing and consuming the castle. Clearly Elsa being upset over the accident has triggered her magic to spread the ice, despite the fact that she isn't logically telling it to.

Elsa and Anna's parents, King Agnarr and Queen Iduna, come rushing into the room where Anna lies unconscious in Elsa's arms. King Agnarr immediately loses his cool at seeing Anna unconscious and frustratingly asks Elsa what she has done. He then comments about how her magic has gotten out of hand. As a viewer you can't help but see the guilt and stress that comment places on Elsa. She clearly already feels terrible about what has happened as she is crying and trying to explain that it was an accident.

Fortunately, King Agnarr knows where they could take Anna to be cured of her ice injury. All three of them rush off to the nearby forest where they meet up with a group of trolls. The leader of the trolls, Pabbie, heals Anna but recommends that all magic be removed from her, including her memories of it. Pabbie then warns Elsa, saying, "Listen to me, Elsa. Your power will only grow. There is beauty in it but also great danger! You must learn to control it...fear will be your enemy!"[20]

King Agnarr responds to Pabbie's comments by saying that they will find a way to control Elsa's power. They'll start with locking the gates of the castle, reducing the staff, limiting her contact with people, and keeping her power hidden from everyone–including Anna–until she can learn to control it.

What follows is years of Elsa hiding away in her room. Anna frequently tries to engage with Elsa and get her to come out and play, but the fear of losing control of her power and potentially hurting Anna again keeps her locked away. During this time her father gives her a pair of gloves to help her control her power. He teaches her to "conceal it, don't feel it," [20] which she repeats to herself on a regular basis.

Over the years Elsa's power gets stronger, and she has a harder and harder time keeping it concealed. At one point she tells her parents, "I'm scared…it's getting stronger!"[20] Her father replies, "Getting upset only makes it worse…calm down."[20] That doesn't work, though, and she ends up refusing to touch even them out of fear of hurting them.

By the time the girls are young adults, their parents take a trip over the ocean. While on this voyage, their ship sinks in a terrible storm, and they pass away. The next thing you see is Anna emotionally knocking on Elsa's door, trying again to connect with her. Their parents have just passed away, and now all they have is each other. But Elsa still won't come out. The fear inside her is so strong that she not only is locked away in her room but also locked away within herself. She's trapped by her fear. Sad, lonely, and afraid.

Three years later the day has arrived that Elsa has dreaded. She has come of age, and the gates of the castle are being opened to celebrate her coronation, where she will become queen of Arendelle. The town is excited for this event, as the gates of the castle have been closed for so many years. Even visitors from other kingdoms have come to join in the celebration. Of course, Anna is excited as well, as this is an opportunity to no longer be alone. Not only has Elsa been alone all of these years, but so has Anna. Elsa's situation has left them both terribly alone, even though they've lived together in the same castle the entire time.

As the coronation ceremony comes closer, Elsa is locked in her room preparing, practicing keeping her power under control. During the coronation she must remove her gloves to hold a scepter and another object. When she takes the gloves off, she could potentially freeze them. She repeats to herself, "Don't let them in, don't let them see, be the good girl you always have to be. Conceal, don't feel. Put on a show. Make one wrong move, and everyone will know."[20]

As the ceremony begins, Elsa is asked to remove her gloves. She's so anxious and is shaking as she removes them. She's bordering on panicking. She removes the gloves, grabs hold of the objects, and turns around for everyone to see her. As the official announces her as Queen Elsa in front of the crowd, the objects she's holding begin to freeze. She panics and quickly puts them down and puts her gloves back on. She did it! She made it through, and the crowd cheers.

During the afterparty Elsa and Anna speak for the first time in years. They quickly get comfortable with each other and almost appear as if they might be able to have a relationship again. Anna even comments about how nice it is for them to be talking again. She wishes out loud that it could be this way all of the time. Elsa replies back, wishing for that as well. But her face turns sad, and she immediately snaps at Anna and tells her that it can't be...it just can't. She then turns away to avoid touching her. Anna then walks away upset.

As Anna is walking away, she trips, and Prince Hans of the Southern Isles, who Anna has met earlier that day and developed a crush on, catches her. They end up dancing and roaming around the castle getting to know each other better. In the process they start falling for each other...and on an abrupt whim, they end up getting engaged.

After the engagement, Anna takes Hans to meet Elsa so they can announce the good news. They both proceed to ask Elsa for her blessing. Elsa is understandably confused but Anna continues on by rambling off a bunch of details, and Elsa can barely get a word in edgewise. She quickly gets frustrated and cuts Anna off, telling her that no one is getting married. Anna and Elsa proceed to get in an argument right there in front of everyone at the party.

Elsa has done a fantastic job keeping her composure all day, but she's holding so much in, and this revelation has clearly rattled her even more. She walks off and announces that the party is over and to close the gates. Anna then loses her cool and tries to stop Elsa from leaving. She ends up inadvertently pulling one of Elsa's gloves off in the process. The argument then escalates, and Anna confronts Elsa over why she has shut her out for so long. Elsa is noticeably cracking. All of the energy she's had built up in her for so long is beginning to bubble over.

As Anna continues challenging Elsa and specifically asks her what she's so afraid of, the frustrated energy within Elsa finally hits a boiling point, and she snaps. She turns around aggressively, with her one glove still missing, and says, "I said enough!"[20] Just then, magic bursts out of her and builds a protective barrier of ice spears around her. Everyone is in shock, and one of the visitors from one of the other kingdoms comments out loud that this is sorcery. Elsa panics and runs out the doors. She begins running through the crowd outside the castle and gets blocked. One of the townspeople asks her if she's all right. She panics again and turns the nearby water fountain into ice. Just then the man from inside who has said this was sorcery yells, "There she is–stop her."[20] She begs, "Please, just stay away from me...stay away."[20] And she shoots ice toward the man. Everyone in the town witnesses this and begins fearing her.

Elsa is now having a full-on panic attack and is running for her life. Anna follows behind trying to stop her. She wants to help her sister but can't catch up to her. Elsa then begins to discover the full extent of her power by turning the fjord in front of her to ice as she begins to run on it. Anna wants to follow, but Hans stops her. As Elsa runs away, it begins snowing in Arendelle and the entire fjord freezes. Moments later you see Elsa running in the nearby frozen and desolate forest, heading toward an ice-covered mountain. She then begins to sing the following lyrics from the song "Let It Go":[19]

> The snow glows bright on the mountain tonight, not a footprint to be seen. A kingdom of isolation, and it looks like I'm the queen. The wind is howling like this swirling storm inside. Couldn't keep it in, heaven knows I've tried. Don't let them in, don't let them see, be the good girl you always have to be. Conceal, don't feel, don't let them know. Well, now they know. Let it go, let it go. Can't hold it back anymore. Let it go, let it go. Turn away and slam the door. I don't care what they're going to say. Let the storm rage on. The cold never bothered me anyway. It's funny how some distance makes everything seem small. And the fears that once controlled me can't get to me at all. It's time to see what I can do, to test the limits and break through. No right, no wrong, no rules for me. I'm free. Let it go, let it go. I am one with the wind and sky. Let it go, let it go. You'll never see me cry. Here I stand and here I'll stay. Let the storm rage on. My power flurries through the air into the ground. My soul is spiraling in frozen fractals all around. I'm never going back; the past is in

> the past. Let it go, let it go. When I'll rise like the break of dawn. Let it go, let it go. That perfect girl is gone. Here I stand in the light of day. Let the storm rage on. The cold never bothered me anyway.[19]

Such powerful lyrics, I must say. Absolutely beautiful! I remember hearing someone on TV once ask another person why that song was so popular with not just kids but also adults. The person never really answered the question and just talked about something else. I thought about it carefully at the time though. My personal take is that everyone feels stress and fear build up in them, they feel like those fears prevent them from being who they really are, and this song is all about letting that go and finally being free of it. So many people can relate to that in so many ways, and that's why people were drawn to it, in my humble opinion.

The lyrics I quoted above are from the movie version of "Let It Go,"[19] sung by Idina Menzel, but there's also a "Single Version,"[21] which was sung by Demi Lovato. In that, there's a slightly different lyric that I love and want to share. It goes, "Up here in the cold, thin air I finally can breathe. I know I left a life behind, but I'm too relieved to grieve."[21] I've always had a very powerful connection with the energy behind that lyric, and it touches me deeply. Probably because I myself left so much behind and am too relieved to grieve.

My hope with this lesson is that maybe me sharing my story, and the many things I learned along the way will somehow help you break free from your stress, fear, anxiety, and panic attacks. That you, too, will learn how to let it go.

LESSON 7:

Bad Words

Help Me...It's So Heavy

I saw a movie back in 2014 that has proven to be one of my favorite comedies of all time and is one that I watch at least a few times a year. Besides starring my absolute favorite comedic actor and the humor being dry, sarcastic, and pushing the boundaries of what society tells us is acceptable, there's also a powerful story behind it that carries a deeply emotional meaning. And it's one that I'm confident most people can relate to in one way or another. The movie ended up having such an influence on me, that I knew early in the conception of this book that I would not only use it as an intro to this lesson but also as the name of the lesson as well. That movie is *Bad Words*,[22] starring, directed, and produced by Jason Bateman.

The movie begins in a school gymnasium where Columbus Ohio's Fifteenth Annual Regional Spelling Bee is about to begin. The gymnasium is full of young and eager kids who are all preparing to compete for the title of regional spelling bee champion and a spot at the coveted Golden Quill National Spelling Bee. Along with the eager kids are, of course, excited parents and family all helping their children prepare by placing their contestant number lanyards around their necks, straightening their clothes, and helping them practice some words before the competition begins. As the camera pans through the crowd, you can't help but notice a sea of smiling faces, optimism, and the innocence of this competition. That's until the camera makes its way to the main character of the movie, a forty-year-old man by the name of Guy Trilby (Jason Bateman).

Guy is standing at the back of the gym with his earbuds in, listening to music and looking focused and unemotional. His voice begins to speak over the scene in what appears to be a message to you, the viewer. He explains, in the past tense, the motivation for what is about to happen. As he's speaking these words the camera zooms out, and you suddenly hear a muffled voice interrupt Guy's message. The muffled voice is a father of one of the young contestants, who's pouring himself a drink from a refreshment table that Guy is standing next to.

Guy proceeds to take the earbuds out of his ears so he can hear what this father is saying. The voice is now no longer muffled with the earbuds out. The father babbles on, attempting to make small talk with Guy and saying how Guy must be so proud, presumably of his child, who surely must be a competitor. This father continues by saying how he's proud of his own competing child and asks Guy which one is his. Guy's demeanor has now gone from focused and unemotional to annoyed and slightly agitated.

Guy interrupts this father's question by saying, "Buddy, no thank you. This chat...I'm all set. I'm just trying to get some food in my face before I get stuck up on that stage, ok?"[22] The father is in a bit of shock and disbelief with what he's just heard. Then all the sudden he gets an enlightened look on his face and says, "Right–my bad. You must be our host for today."[22] Guy interrupts him again and says,

"No, I'm not...I'm the winner."[22] Guy then abruptly walks off, heads up on stage, and has a seat with all the adolescent competitors.

After Guy has a seat on stage and places his contestant number lanyard around his neck, a large boy in the seat next to him begins awkwardly staring at him, which immediately catches Guy's attention. The boy then snottily asks, "What are you doing on stage, weirdo?"[22] Guy pauses for a moment and then replies with no emotion other than the ever-so-slight hint of a smirk, "Your chair called me for help. It was saying [in a whispering voice] help me...it's so heavy. [In a normal voice] You didn't hear it? I heard it."[22]

Before that conversation can proceed any further, a competition official smiles at Guy and tells him that the seats on stage are for competitors only. He answers her with a confident and sarcastic grin on his face and says, "Great. I'm in the right spot."[22] All the children seated in front of him turn around and begin looking at him with confusion. The competition official laughs at Guy's comment and clearly thinks he's joking. She's about to find out that he's very serious.

In the next scene, you find Guy standing outside the building, where both the competition official and the host are now lecturing him and saying he can't be part of the competition because it's for children only. He responds by saying he's well within the rules and quotes where on page 39 of the Golden Quill National Spelling Bee rule book, rule number twenty-four, subpoint B says, "The speller must not have passed beyond the eighth grade on or before February 1, 2011."[22] He continues by explaining that he unfortunately has not graduated from the eighth grade on or before that date and has never graduated the eighth grade at all.

This revelation starts an even more heated argument between them, where the official makes a derogatory remark about Guy's inability to graduate beyond the eighth grade, and the host accuses him of being a hijacker. In turn Guy and his sponsor, a reporter from an online news service, proceed to threaten them with a restraining order and injunction that will prevent the competition from continuing. Guy also dramatically threatens to sue them for defamation because of the derogatory comments. After some more heated and hilariously funny arguing, they allow Guy to continue in the competition to prevent it from being canceled for all the children waiting on stage.

What follows next is Guy wiping the floor with the competition. At one point after easily spelling the word *absquatulate* correctly, he even comments to the entire room, "Hey, moms, let's break out the rubber pillowcases tonight. Little pricks are going to be counting tears, not sheep."[22]

The scene then cuts to Guy running out of the building in slow motion while holding the competition trophy and anxiously looking back at a mob of angry parents chasing him. The reporter who has sponsored him quickly drives up, and Guy hops over the hood, jumps in the passenger seat, and prepares to drive off before the mob can reach them. Their efforts aren't quick enough, though, and as they begin to leave, a mother spits on the driver's side window, and a father, the same father who had chatted Guy up at the refreshment table, breaks the windshield by throwing a metal chair at it that he carried out of the gym while chasing Guy out of the building. Guy and the reporter then successfully make their getaway.

Reflecting back to the opening scene of the movie when the camera first pans over to Guy standing next to the refreshment table and just before the father that later broke the getaway car's windshield starts chatting him up, Guy's message over the scene say, "I'm not that good at a lot of stuff. Especially thinking things through. And that's why this plan was so shitty. But my feelings were hurt, and I'm glad I at least did something about it. Making bad decisions is nothing new to me. After all, I live alone at forty, and I make my living proofreading product warranties. A few weeks ago, I took a break from that, however, so I could do this whole thing. And it's pretty ironic that what I did was exactly what a child would do. I threw a tantrum just to get attention."[22]

I certainly don't want to spoil the whole movie in case you haven't seen it yet. Of course I highly recommend giving it a watch if you haven't already done so. I gotta tell you, though, I laugh my ass off every time I watch it! It never gets old for me!

What I will tell you is that Guy continues to compete in the Golden Quill National Spelling Bee, which is being televised for the first time that year. It becomes clear throughout the movie that Guy is an exceptionally intelligent person who is more than capable of winning the competition, no matter what word is placed before him. It also becomes clear that he's very frustrated about something, and competing in the spelling bee is his way of lashing out in an effort to expel the negative energy that this something has created in him. You get to see how unresolved emotional trauma builds up and manifests into putrid and toxic anger and how it creates unhealthy coping mechanisms along the way that have affected his life in deeply profound and long-lasting ways.

Finally at the end, you learn what the triggering offense was that led to all this anger, and you get to see the beginnings of healing. If you haven't figured it out yet, this is exactly why I was driven to make this movie the lead-in for this lesson. It's a lighthearted way to dive headfirst into the dark and ominous subject that is the basis of both the movie and this lesson. Frustration, anger, and all the foul shit that comes along with these powerful reactions.

It's That Fucking Lion Again

What thoughts and feelings come to you when you think about frustration and anger? Pause for a moment and really let this settle into you. Engage with it spiritually first, and then let what comes to you flow into your physical mind and be analyzed.

I've been persistently infused with these feelings throughout my life so have had the opportunity to invest a lot of time analyzing them in an effort to understand what exactly they are and their physical function in the human experience. I'll admit that in the past I thought of frustration and anger as simply bad things, and I didn't really dig any further into them than that. I didn't like them at all, and I had experienced far too much of them in my life. So I was actually quite fearful and even ashamed of them.

The truth is that these feelings, or energy actually, are no different than any other feeling/energy in that they serve a very legitimate and functional purpose. Just like how insecurity/depression and anxiety/panic serve a functional purpose...so does frustration and anger. And just like any of those other feelings, when they aren't addressed and managed, then overload occurs, and they can evolve into an unpleasant and a downright scary beast of destruction. The mind-blowing thing about that is...that's exactly what's supposed to happen.

Let's look at the functionality of frustration and anger by going back to the discussion about anxiety and panic from lesson 6 for a moment. Take the very same idea that you're out in the wilds of Africa and hear that lion off in the distance. Your body goes into a state of anxiety, then you hear the lion getting closer, so your brain elevates that state to panic. You're now running in all-out fear for your life. Your brain has altered the priorities of your body to optimize your chances of survival. Your body is essentially like a Transformer® from the movies, cartoons, and action figure toys. Your body has changed into this alternate form that will serve to protect you. This is where the situation ended in the discussion of anxiety and panic. And it's where it will begin for frustration and anger.

Imagine for a moment that you're in that exact same situation, but now the lion has caught up to you. You couldn't run away fast enough, and it now has you cornered...and you have nowhere to run to. Your body is still on full alert and in panic mode, while your brain is pushing data to you and awaiting a decision on what move to make. The energy of fear you are experiencing in this situation is building up in your body, which it will use as fuel to make a powerful move as soon as you make the decision on what move to make.

You don't have a move though; there are no viable options. You're cornered, and the lion is salivating as it prepares to attack. With no place to run, your body is now in a state of frustration on top of panic, as the buildup of fearful energy has become frustrated energy. This frustrated energy is designed to accumulate and be released in an explosive manner. Your body is now like a car with its rear wheels spinning, while your front wheels are frozen in place. This state of frustration is building to bring you to your maximum energetic charge for use in your last line of defense...attack.

Your eyes see a large stick on the ground, and your brain sends you that data. With nowhere to run, you make the decision to grab the stick and attack. Your brain and body are now elevated to a state of anger, flailing the stick and hitting the lion as hard as you can. This fucking lion isn't going to kill you...you're going to kill it!

The backbone of this attack is the pent-up frustrated energy. The front wheels of the proverbial car are no longer frozen in place, and the pent-up energy is propelling you forward. You've physically transformed into a fighting version of you to protect yourself from that lion. This state sets into motion a nearly complete automatic mode where your brain is making most of the functional decisions, and you're mostly only observing. Your body begins hitting the lion over and over again in a fit of rage. This expulsion of pent-up frustrated energy is the designed state of anger.

Let's play with this lion scenario for a moment just for some perspective. Imagine that you swing the large stick at the lion, and you hurt it. You swing again and again, hurting it each time. The lion now feels threatened so decides to retreat and runs away. You are now safe, at least for the moment. Your brain now transforms your body from attack mode back to panic so you can run away to safety. From there you descend to the state of anxiety and then finally to being calm.

The flip side of that scenario is obviously that the lion kills you, and it's game over for your avatar. Both you and your avatar's brain are hyperaware of that, which adds fuel to the fire of fighting off the lion in the first place. So the state of anger is a tool your brain and body can use to protect you from what they perceive as a life-threatening, or even life-ending, situation.

Mine, Mine, Mine

Let's look at another scenario where frustration and anger can be in play and serve a functional purpose, yet isn't an obviously life-threatening situation. Though your life isn't at risk, something of nearly equal importance is being threatened: your ego and your perception.

Imagine for a moment that you're a young male Neanderthal looking to mate with a young female. You've found a perspective mate and cornered her where she can't run away. Along comes your slightly older brother, who also wants to mate with this female. You immediately go into a state of anxiety as you feel threatened that your brother will attempt to steal your prospective mate.

As your body is in high alert and observing every move your brother makes, you see him turn toward her. The fearful/anxious energy is swelling into frustrated energy, priming you to defend what you perceive as your property. As the energy builds, you see your brother start to move toward the female. Your back wheels are spinning, while you and your brain try to find an effective solution. Your brother now makes a move on the female. You're now backed into a corner and have no other option but to attack.

You now shift into the state of anger where the frustrated energy comes lashing out. You punch him in the face, knocking him to the ground. He runs off crying, humiliated that you kicked his ass. As you turn around to claim your prize, you find the young female also has gone through her own states of anxiety, panic, frustration, and now anger as well. She wasn't interested in mating with either of you, and in her state of anger she has picked up a large stick and is now beating your ass with it, you little fucking pervert. You run off in humiliation, and she heads back to her cave, safe and sound.

Automatic Discharge

The ending of the previous scenario clearly had a twist of irony and humor to it, but it's very much a valid example of the functionality behind frustration and anger. At its core frustration is merely the state where energy is building up in your body with no outlet; your rear wheels are spinning, and your front wheels are locked. At its core anger is when that frustrated energy is expelled, and it comes bursting out; the front wheels unlock, and you propel forward nearly out of control. You need that energy to build up in your body so it can come bursting out to give you maximum power when you need to attack.

So anger is really about protecting, whether it be physically protecting your life or even protecting your possessions–loved ones, ego, state of mind, or anything else. Frustration and anger clearly serve an important operational function in the world we live in, no matter if you're a human or any other species. And just like insecurity, depression, anxiety, and panic, they can come out in any number of different situations, and they may not always be recognizable. Deep down, though, they're all the same energy and function...just showing up in different ways.

Keep in mind that your body is made up of matter, a solid form of energy. Your body also runs off of energy and can hold onto certain amounts of it in order to function, whether that be energy from food, emotions, nature, the universe, etcetera. Your body is flowing with various frequencies of energy, which is how it's possible to read a person's vibe. That's possible because the energy is flowing throughout the body, constantly being absorbed, processed, transformed, and discharged.

In any given situation, your brain and body will transform the energy they're absorbing, and/or have in reserves, to best suit the situation at hand. This is true regardless of whether the situation is laughing at a funny joke, crying because someone passed away, jumping for joy because you won the lottery, running away from a lion that's trying to eat you, or punching someone in the face that's threatening to take something you believe to be yours. Your body will transform the available energy to suit each situation. And in some cases, it will be a highly concentrated energy for defensive use. This is exactly what it's designed to do, and it works beautifully when used in the appropriate context.

As I mentioned, your body can hold onto certain amounts of energy. But there's a limit to what it can handle before your physical body literally overloads and is damaged from excess. Just as your cell phone or laptop computer can only hold so much energy before short-circuiting and becoming critically damaged, your body also can only contain so much. When your body gets close to overload, though, it will discharge whether you want it to or not. It will go into autopilot and discharge when needed if there's risk of a critical failure.

Think back to the story I shared in lesson 6 of when I had the panic attack, and my body went through a full reboot. I had reached a critical overload situation, so my body automatically shut down to reset into safe mode and prevent permanent damage. And it worked... it ultimately saved my avatar's life. That shutdown is an extreme example, though, since it wasn't just the buildup of one frequency of energy that led to it; it was a highly concentrated cocktail of sadness, fear, powerlessness, actual physical trauma in my avatar, and an overload of hyperaware analysis. But it goes to show how your body has automatic functionality to protect itself from damage, even if you aren't consciously aware of it or spiritually choose to activate it.

When frustrated energy hits the maximum level, the functionality to automatically discharge it will take place, though it doesn't need to do a full reboot in order to achieve it. All it needs to do is go into the state of anger where the energy will rapidly discharge. Sounds simple enough, however, the anger state is designed to be utilized in a situation when there's a threat and you need to attack. So it's naturally a hostile and destructive state that should only be used as a last line of defense.

If your body maxes out its capacity to hold frustrated energy, and you don't make a conscious decision on how to discharge it, then your brain will get to a point where it has to set into motion an automatic discharge. And without a legitimate need to attack, well... someone or something will bear the brunt of that destructive force. It could be you, your life partner, your kids, your best friend, a total stranger, your car, your job, or some inanimate object. Whichever it is...that energy will be discharged. And anything in its path will feel the destructive effects of it.

Losing Your Shit

Let's flip to a modern example of frustration and anger that's more relatable to the real world and interacts with energies we've discussed in previous lessons.

Imagine for a moment you're in New York City, and you're running to catch the subway after work. You're stressed after a long day at a high-pressure city job, and the streets are congested with thousands of other people in similar situations. Your body is already filled to half of its energy storage capacity from your day, yet you aren't consciously aware of it.

As you hustle through the streets and crowds to get to the subway, energy is building not just from what's happening inside you, but also from absorbing energy from the highly charged people around you. You look at your watch and realize that you've missed the 5:15 p.m. train you had planned to catch, and the next one is at 5:25 p.m. You know if you don't catch this one, then you're screwed and won't make it to your child's school in time to see the play they've rehearsed months for.

Anxiety has already set in as your hyperaware analysis is seeing all the potential failure points coming up. As you make your way to the subway entrance, down the stairs, and through the toll booth, you catch a glimpse of the train. It's already at the platform and people are loading. Your brain elevates to the state of panic out of fear of missing it, and you start running. Just as you get to the train, the doors close. The reality that you're going to miss your child's play hits you.

All that highly charged energy flowing inside of you now becomes frustrated energy as you're backed into a corner with no other options in sight. With no outlet and no options, the frustrated energy maxes out your body's storage capacity, and the anger state is automatically triggered. All the sudden your body begins pounding uncontrollably on the doors and desperately tries to pry them open, screaming profanities and making a scene on the platform. Meanwhile, someone inside the train notices you and sympathetically begins prying the doors open from their side. The doors then open, and you fall inside the train. The doors close shut, and the train departs to cheers from the crowd of other commuters around you.

This scenario seems like a happy ending, but truth be told, anger unnecessarily set in at the end, and you lost control. You didn't even think about it; you just reacted. It was the part when you were backed into a corner and had no other options that did it. The frustrated energy maxed out without an outlet, and you lost your shit.

You were so frustrated by missing the train and the likelihood that you would miss your child's play, that the frustrated energy shot through the roof, and you got fucking angry. It's understandable, to a certain degree, but it was still an uncontrolled situation that could have gone very badly under different circumstances. And you could have prevented it yet achieved the same result. You were just very fortunate that someone on the train heard you, and the whispers of their spirit guides to be compassionate. You were fortunate that your spirit guides were able to influence the situation to save your ass. Had that person not helped, then the situation could have been much different.

Let's rewind this missing the New York City subway train scenario and see what I mean when I say the situation could have ended much differently.

Imagine at the end when you're pounding on the doors and screaming profanities, nobody on the inside of the train sees you or is willing to help. The doors don't open, and the train leaves without you. You keep irrationally running along with the train in a fit of rage, pounding on it the whole way. As the train accelerates beyond your reach you keep pounding as if it's there, yet it's not. There's nothing there to pound on, so you lose your balance and fall off the platform, breaking your arm and collarbone in the process. A kind stranger must risk their life to jump onto the rat-shit-infested tracks to save your ass before another train rolls along. Great job, dipshit–now look what you got yourself into.

In that moment when your brain and body were in the angry state, you lost a lot of control over your physical self and could no longer easily influence your brain's decisions. Your brain basically went into autopilot and reverted to basic Neanderthal programming, which was that it treated the situation as a fighting scenario. You were just along for the ride at that point, for the most part, and had to watch as your brain made reflex decisions about how to physically react.

It didn't go well obviously and far too often doesn't when you're in such a situation. Your avatar's brain and body didn't do a bad job or anything. They did exactly what they were programmed to do… discharge and fight. The problem was that it happened in a scenario when it wasn't necessary or appropriate, and you lost control. Your avatar wasn't designed to run solo in this type of scenario, and it needed your influence.

You feel disappointed, I know; I do, too, but there's a bright side to all of this. There was an opportunity early in the situation where the anger state could have been prevented, and you could have remained in control to influence a better outcome. Learning to recognize and act on this opportunity is key to your evolution beyond frustration and anger.

Let's run that same scenario again but with a slight difference. This time you don't get angry and lose your shit.

In this scenario as you leave work and are en route to the subway station, you recognize that you had a stressful day and realize that you're heading into an even more stressful situation. As you're hustling to get to the subway station, you pop a couple of organic mints to ground yourself, and you take some deep breaths to discharge and transform some of that already existing highly charged energy into calm energy.

When you look at your watch and see that you've missed the 5:15 p.m. train, you start a mantra going in your brain repeating over and over again the simple words, "I have plenty of time, I am calm and relaxed, I will make it to the school safely."

As you make your way through the subway station and see the 5:25 p.m. train is already loading, your brain elevates to the state of mild anxiety but not the panic state. You hurry to the train, and the doors close just as you arrive. Your brain could take all its available resources to panic and get angry, but you stopped it. It's now focused exclusively on solutions.

The only solution it can find, though, is trying to pry the doors open. You give your brain the go-ahead, and it triggers your body into a mild and controlled state of panic to devote resources to opening that door. You're not freaking out or getting angry though. You are very rational and in full control.

You then start trying to open the doors. Your brain now shoots you a solution of pounding on the doors as well, in the hopes of getting someone inside the train to help. You give the go-ahead, and your body starts pounding on the doors. Someone hears you, their spirit guides whispers of compassion, and they help you pry the doors open. The doors open, and you fall in as the train begins to depart. The crowd on the train erupts in cheers that you made it.

Now you might be asking yourself, What the hell is the big difference between this last version versus the first one? Both ended exactly the same way, so what's the biggie? Well the biggie is that in the first version you lost your shit, and in this last version, you didn't. You remained calm and in control of your avatar.

In the first version, you were very fortunate that things didn't turn out as bad as the version where you fell off the platform. In the first version, your spirit guides were likely your savior, but your anger put that effort at risk. You weren't flowing; you were forcing. Any number of things could have affected that outcome since you were raging, as you saw in the version where nobody helped you open the doors, and you fell off the platform. By remaining calm you maintained control and flowed with the universe, optimizing your likelihood of success.

Let's run that scenario one more time exactly the same as the last, except this time nobody inside the train helps you. In this less charged state, you try to pry the doors open and begin pounding on them as well. Nobody responds, and the train departs without you. As the train moves along, your brain shoots you data indicating the risks of running along with it. You might trip, you might run into someone and hurt them or yourself, or you might fall off the platform. You recognize those as valid fears/concerns, so you give the go-ahead to stop and think for a moment.

You and your brain now start focusing on other solutions. A taxi quickly comes up as an option. You give the go-ahead, and your brain moves your body into a very mild and controlled state of panic where resources will be dedicated to a run to get you outside. You're calm, though, not out of control in any way. As you get to the surface, you see a taxi pulled over ahead of you. The thought of whistling comes to your awareness. You give the go-ahead and whistle louder than you've ever whistled before as you bolt for the taxi. Next thing you know, you're inside the vehicle explaining where you need to go and the urgency of the situation. Sure enough, traffic worked in your favor, and you get to the school safe and sound. You're fifteen minutes late, but that's ok; a lot of parents were running late, so they hadn't started yet. All is good.

See the difference now? Same exact situation as the version where you fell off the platform, but you didn't lose your shit this time. You were chill. You flowed with the universe and allowed it to move you where you needed to go. Do you think you caught that taxi by coincidence or that the traffic just happened to be light? Nah, you allowed it to flow to you. Your flowing gave your spirit guides the opportunity to make things happen.

In the version where you lost your shit, you were resisting so hard that your spirit guides were limited in what they could do. They were able to influence someone to jump on the tracks and pull your dumb ass up before you were killed, but you blocked them from helping you while you were raging. Remaining calm allows you to flow and make wise decisions. You remain in control of your avatar and optimize your human experience.

The art of remaining calm in stressful and energetically charged situations is a skill that is learned through awareness and practice, like how a professional runner remains calm in a race. They're well prepared when they line up at the starting line. They've practiced for years; they're warmed up, fueled up, hydrated, and are ready to run with all they have once the signal goes off. Their bodies go into a mild state of anxiety so they can pay close attention for when the signal goes off. Once it does their body goes into a mild and controlled state of panic, where all the resources in their bodies are dedicated to that run, to the strategy they've practiced over and over again. They don't panic and spaz out at all...they just run, breathe, and are very methodical with every move they make.

Can you imagine if the signal went off and the runner got angry, pushed competitors out of the way, and ran to the finish line flailing their arms while screaming like a maniac? Nah, that would be nuts! And they certainly wouldn't be highly trained professionals, if that were the case. They'd just be Neanderthals making fools of themselves. Might be an interesting watch on TV though!

My point here is this: your avatar has functionality to support your human experience. Being aware of that functionality, learning how it works, practicing how to use it most effectively, and thoughtfully engaging it at appropriate times is literally life-changing. Once you achieve this, you and your avatar's XP (experience points) increase exponentially. As you grow this ability, you start becoming a master of this educational and evolutionary game called life.

The Puppet Master

For a good portion of my adult life, I believed I had an anger issue. I remember back in 2010 sitting in a therapist's office, attempting to address my supposed anger issues, and explaining to him why I was there. After several sessions the therapist hit me with something profound that I wasn't expecting. He told me I didn't have an anger issue at all in his professional opinion. He said I was quite the opposite and that it was clear to him that I managed anger exceptionally well.

If you could have seen the look on my face when he said that, you'd probably laugh. I was literally dumbfounded by his assessment, as I truly believed I was an angry person. I ended up challenging him on it and asked if he was sure. He then asked me what made me think I was angry. I told him because I'm grumpy all the time; I'm verbally snippy toward my now ex-wife, I'm an aggressive driver, and I feel like my fuse is short. I also told him that my then wife would tell me on a regular basis that I was an angry and unpleasant person who needed mental help.

The therapist said that what he saw was someone who was terribly unhappy. A tremendous amount of frustration had built up inside me while I tried to maintain that unhappy life, yet I had no outlet for that frustration. He said that, given the amount of frustration in me, it was very impressive that I was able to manage it without serious outbursts. He added that in his assessment, I was a very grounded, emotionally intelligent, and calm person and that I didn't need to focus on addressing anger but should instead focus on eliminating what was making me so unhappy and, in turn, so frustrated.

I'll be honest with you; I left that session not fully grasping what the therapist told me. I totally understood what I needed to do in the context of what we were discussing, which is exactly why one week later, I ended the relationship with my now ex (I ended the relationship at that time in 2010 but sadly didn't pursue a legal divorce until 2018). What I didn't fully grasp, though, was that I needed to wake up to the reality that I had been mind fucked on the subject of anger.

I had blindly believed what I had been told by society and my now ex-wife without question. After years of inner reflection, analysis, and meditation, though, I've gained a deep understanding of what anger truly is and have come to a clear awareness that anger is not the beast that society leads us to believe. The beast is the frustrated energy that eventually turns into anger. Anger is merely the result of the frustrated energy lashing out when there's no more capacity to hold it. And without frustrated energy...there is no anger.

Think for a moment about all the things you define as anger. When someone takes the parking spot you've patiently been waiting for...is it anger you feel? Nope, it's frustration. Deep, festering energy within you that's being inherently suppressed so it can build up and later explode out. Anger is when that frustrated energy hits the red line, and you end up honking, rolling down your window, screaming creative profanities, and driving off with your middle finger flailing about.

How about when your neighbor is playing loud music late at night? Anger? Nope...it's frustration. Let's even consider something much more serious, like when you see a video on social media showing a law enforcement officer beat or kill an unarmed person who was peacefully protesting or had committed a nonviolent offense? Is it anger you feel when you see it? No...it's a potent buildup of frustration, which, depending on your life experiences, is likely comprised of sadness, fear, trauma, and feelings of powerlessness.

Of course each person will react differently to each of these scenarios based on a number of things, such as their current level of frustration, life experiences, the genetic predispositions of their avatar, and their ability or lack thereof to diffuse that energy and repurpose it for better use. Whatever the cause and whatever the reaction, it's frustration you're feeling, not anger. Frustration is the gun, and anger is the trigger being pulled. Without the gun there is no trigger to pull. So frustrated energy is the true beast. Frustration is the puppet master.

Excuse Me, Mr. Fuck Face

Now that we've clearly established that frustration is the real star of the show, not anger, let's dig into it and get a clearer picture of what creates it and how to diffuse it.

When you feel frustrated, what you're actually feeling is energy building up in your body that has no outlet for release. The very act of the energy being trapped and stagnating within you is the state of frustration.

One of the many questions I asked myself in my analysis of frustration was the following: What's the functionality that causes the energy behind it to build up versus release? I completely understood the operational function of the build up occurring, but I wasn't clear what the trigger was that resulted in it stagnating versus releasing.

For instance, let's say you win a $100 million jackpot in the lottery. Lots of energy is created when you find out you've won, but it doesn't stagnate and turn into frustration. Or you're at a comedy club, and the comedian on stage has you busting a gut in laughter along with all the people around you, for that matter. Yet that energy isn't building up into frustration. Flip those scenarios around, and instead of winning the lottery, you owe a bunch of money to the bank. Or instead of laughing your ass off, you have an argument with your partner. Totally different story now. In those situations, the energy quickly builds up and you get frustrated.

So what's the deal? Are there different types of energy being generated, and maybe the different types flow differently in our bodies? Or maybe our bodies somehow mutate the energy depending on our state of mind, and that mutation triggers our bodies to block the release?

I sat on this quandary for a an exceptionally long time before I could come to a clear understanding of what's actually happening to trigger frustration. And that clarity didn't come quickly or easily. It took many life challenges, countless hours of contemplation, and a ridiculous amount of frustration to get the clarification I needed to write the words I do now.

So here's the deal, kids: the energy we feel in frustration is not any different than the energy we feel in happiness. Energy is energy. The difference is in what we do with that energy based on how we feel and how we're conditioned to deal with those feelings that produce the energy. You see, when you feel happiness, love, and positive vibes. you quickly release that energy without hesitation. You release it through laughter, jumping around, hugging, or expressing those feelings in one way or another. But when you feel the opposite–when you're sad, fearful, or feeling some other negative vibes–then what do you do? You hold it in, you don't openly express it, and you keep it restricted within yourself as much as you can. Why? Because that's what we've been conditioned to do. And it's this response that causes the energy to stagnate and build.

In human society as we know it, expressing negative feelings is something we've been mind fucked not to do. We've been conditioned to believe that negative feelings should be kept to ourselves and only expressed in limited situations. We've been led to believe that we need to always be happy, follow the rules, do what we're told, or just not rock the boat. There's this unwritten rule that negative feelings are a bad thing.

Here's an example. Let's say you're in your fourth period class in high school, and your teacher assigns you three hours' worth of homework that must be turned in by midnight. How do you react? Do you say, "Excuse me, Mr. Fuck Face. I have three other classes with teachers who've all assigned me homework that's all due at midnight too"? Nope, you certainly can't say that. But you're feeling it, though, aren't you? You're damn straight you are! Heck, you can't even say that in the nicest and sweetest way possible. Nope! If you did you'd get scolded, ignored, written up, or maybe even assigned more homework. So you remain quiet and just roll with it, spending your evening stressed, exhausted, and overwhelmed. And all that energy is building in you the entire time, with no outlet for release because you don't have any fucking time to release it!

Here's another example. Let's say you and your partner had an argument right before you left for work. On your drive into the office, the reliving of the argument is bouncing around in your mind. You're offended, irritated, hurt, and are worried how things will smooth out. You want to vent to someone, but nobody you trust is available at that moment, or you don't have anyone in your life you feel comfortable venting to at all. You then get to the office and try to go about your day. But you can't; you're feeling depressed and fearful over the situation. You need to keep a smile on your face, though, so you don't look like the weak link in the chain and risk losing your annual pay raise that you desperately need, or worse yet, lose your job entirely. Your boss ends up swinging by and asks how you're doing. You say, "Good thanks, how about you?" They give you some equally bland response, and you both go about your day. So why didn't you tell your boss the truth? Obviously because it's personal, and you aren't best friends with your boss or anything, so it would be inappropriate to discuss such a thing in that situation. The result is that the energy sits in you, builds up, and becomes frustrated energy.

Let's quickly flip that last scenario around just for shits and giggles. In this scenario you didn't have an argument with your partner; this time around you got engaged instead. All that happened is bouncing around your mind as you drive into the office, and you're calling everyone you know en route to tell them every detail of the proposal. You're happy, excited, in love, and looking forward to your day. Once you get to the office, you're bubbling with smiles and telling everyone who will listen, including your boss. So what's the difference here? You felt completely comfortable sharing your feelings with everyone, including your boss. Why? Because it's all positive stuff that's considered good and appropriate to share. No risks! See...mind fuck!

This sad reality is due to society not being receptive to the expression of negative feelings. Some of that can be related to cultural, religious, or familial barriers that were built generations ago and have yet to be torn down. Other elements of it can be tied to ego, where we or our ancestors were punished by controlling egomaniacs for expressing anything that went against everything being all hunky-dory. Generally speaking, the majority of us have it embedded within us to hold in negative feelings until they magically go away. Spoiler alert: They never magically go away. They just build within us until that energy is released in one way or another. You know... the losing-your-shit kind of thing.

One Potent Little Bastard

One of the keys to reducing, and hopefully eliminating, frustration is to recognize the feelings that can cause the associated energy to stagnate in the first place. Yeah, yeah...we have to dig into those yucky feelings that we tend to bury and not deal with. From my perspective those feelings all boil down to a handful of core feelings. Those core feelings are sadness, fear, trauma, and powerlessness. Let's briefly dig into each of those so we can better understand what they actually are.

Sadness: In my opinion sadness is as close to the opposite of happiness as a feeling can get. What I mean by that is, happiness represents an energy frequency that is felt within your body. One might think that unhappiness is the opposite of happiness, but it actually isn't. Unhappiness doesn't represent an energy frequency at all; it's simply a statement that the energy frequency of happiness is not present within you. It doesn't represent something specifically; it represents the lack of something. So unhappiness isn't a feeling at all and doesn't really exist in the spectrum of feelings/energy. On the other hand, sadness represents an energy frequency just like happiness; it's just a frequency that's more on the opposite side of the overall energy spectrum. Many triggers fall under the umbrella of sadness, like missing someone you love, working a job you dislike, failing to achieve a goal, or feeling guilt/regret for hurting someone you care about. Most people probably wouldn't think of sadness as a source of frustration, but it's easily suppressed so, in turn, can certainly become frustration. It may not be as highly charged as the feeling of fear, but it will build up nonetheless and so can become frustration, and eventually anger.

Fear: Oh my...fear is an ugly one indeed. And fear is a highly charged feeling at that. It's an energy frequency that, even in small doses of suppression, can cause frustration to quickly max out and turn into anger. Fear may not always get triggered from a lion or a criminal chasing you though. Fear can also be triggered from having to engage with people you're not comfortable with, believing you're not worthy of love or friendship, or even having to touch a public restroom door handle that you're confident is covered in fecal bacteria. Fear is a large umbrella that even has anxiety, panic, and insecurities beneath it. Fear is a firecracker that can easily ignite and burst into an explosion of anger.

Trauma: You may not have thought of trauma as a feeling, but it is indeed. It represents an energy frequency that can be triggered by emotional and/or physical pain or a combination thereof. If you've ever endured the emotional and physical pain of being sexually assaulted, having a life-altering illness, or being in a major car accident, or if you've ever felt the emotional pain of a broken heart, being bullied, or being abandoned by a parent, then you know very well how trauma feels. Trauma isn't the sadness or fear that accompanies those experiences though. Trauma is the unhealed wounds that are often left behind, wounds that trigger energy no different than any other feeling. And that energy needs to be discharged. If not it will build up and become frustration.

Powerlessness: This is likely a feeling you haven't put much thought into, but it's an important feeling that often proves to be one potent little bastard. Powerlessness can be the feeling of being stuck and unable to change something you're sad about, fear, regret, or something that annoys you or is traumatic. Powerlessness can be the feeling you are being controlled and that you have limited or no choice in whatever the subject matter may be. As you can imagine, this feeling involves all manner of sins that can be committed against you or by you. Maybe you're living in an unpleasant situation but don't have enough money to move, maybe you hate your job but have to do it to afford the bare necessities of life, maybe you don't like the school you go to but you have to go because you don't have the freedom to choose another school, or maybe you can't openly express who you are because the government of the land you live upon restricts you from doing so without stiff penalties. Whatever it is that makes you feel powerless, stuck, or controlled, the energy it triggers will often sit within you, stagnate, and fester into a powerful cocktail of frustrated energy that will explode out if you don't find a way to release it.

This list of feelings that our avatars are capable of suppressing is certainly not a comprehensive one. Neither is it my intention nor is it even necessary to cover every single suppressible feeling that exists. My goal here is to narrow down the majority of potential feelings into a handful of top-level categories so I can get you thinking about them, how they make you feel, and how they can be suppressed. The truth is, many feelings can fall under multiple categories, which only amplifies their ability to frustrate you. Whichever feeling you feel, or whatever category/categories they fall under, the key thing to keep in mind is that all feelings, whether they be perceptively positive or negative, generate energy within you. And if that energy isn't discharged, then it will lead to frustration, which can eventually lead to an outburst of anger in one way or another. Knowing and understanding this will give you the ability to prevent frustration from occurring. It will remove the fuel from the equation, which is the tactic of choice in battling the forest fire that is anger.

Second Things Second

Now comes the hard work, my friend. It's time to discuss what to do about the fact that we hold in so much negative energy. And it's time to discuss how to reduce or eliminate frustrated energy from our bodies. We need to deal with and heal the beast within–within our physical bodies and within our society.

To be honest with you, some of what I'm about to say will be a bit redundant from what I've discussed in previous lessons, but it's important that we go over it from the perspective of frustration and anger. The truth is that all feelings interconnect, and so do the methodologies to manage them. And most often we must hear and experience the same things repetitively in order to learn from them. Over and over again, we will experience difficult situations, hard lessons, and traumatizing experiences–all so we can learn. Though many of these strategies will be similar in context to strategies discussed in other lessons, I promise to keep it real, interesting, and in perspective. Are you ready? Deep breath...ok, let's do this.

First things first...please remember to have compassion for yourself. The fact that you sometimes, or maybe all the time, feel frustrated and get angry is ok. It's ok. You're ok. There's nothing wrong with you. Your body is behaving exactly as it should, as it was designed to behave. Getting frustrated and angry is an important function of your avatar. It's designed to protect you and keep you alive in this literal MMO (massively multiplayer online) game and learning experience we call life. But we are evolving as avatars and as spirits, and part of that evolution is evolving beyond frustration and anger. The very fact that you're reading these words right now shows your progress on that path. You're learning, you're growing, and you're evolving. Be at peace with that, trust in this experience you have chosen to live, trust in God, the universe, or whatever it is you believe in. And most importantly...trust in yourself. You are doing a fantastic job, especially given the tough path you've courageously taken on this journey.

Second things second, please remember compassion for others. Just as your journey has been hard, so has it been for others as well. You're not alone, my friend. Not alone in this world, not alone in your insecurities, depression, anxiety, panic, sadness, fear, trauma, powerlessness, or your frustration and anger. You're not alone in that cold and dark forest. We're all here with you. You may not always see us, but we're here with you. We need you, and you need us. Together we are stronger, and together we will make this evolution a reality. We will evolve to that place where the warm sun shines and thaws our frozen souls. We're all on this journey together, and we all feel, we all hurt, and we all want to find happiness. The path to that happiness is through the challenges we face, it's through the frustration and anger we feel, and it's through the compassion we give. The compassion we give to ourselves, and the compassion we give to others. Hold that in your heart, and we will transcend frustration and anger together.

Did You Seriously Just Call Me a Demon?

With a full dose of compassion in hand, it's time to take a good look within yourself and ask some tough questions. If you were to put your feelings in a pie chart, how much of that pie is taken up by negative feelings like sadness, fear, trauma, and powerlessness? Like right here, right now...what comprises your feelings? Even the ones you don't want to think about but that you feel deep down. You may not be able to answer that question right away, and that's ok. Take your time to sit with it, meditate on it, and feel it all. Once you have an honest answer, come back and continue reading.

Hopefully the majority of your feelings are those that fall on the positive side of the energy spectrum, like love, happiness, calm, and empowerment. If not, that's ok. But if negative feelings are making up the majority, then you need to do something about that, as hard as that maybe, especially if there's consistency in that majority.

The way I think about this subject is this: I'm sure you've heard the terms *heaven* and *hell* before. Most people think of them as physical places existing outside of themselves. Like heaven is high in the clouds, and hell is deep underground. And some people think of that as being a load of bullshit. My philosophy is that they do exist but not outside our selves. They exist within us, within the energy that permeates our physical and spiritual selves. When our feelings/energy are on the positive side of the spectrum then we're in heaven. When they're on the negative side then we're in hell. There is no God or devil who controls where you reside; there's only you, and you're the only one who can influence where you take up roots.

Let's face it: bad shit happens to us. Bad shit that's caused by other people, proverbial demons of hell per se. And bad shit can make us feel those negative feelings that bury us squarely in the depths of hell itself. Good shit happens to us too. Good shit that's caused by other people, proverbial angels of heaven per se. And that good shit shoots us straight up to the sanctity of heaven itself. We can't always physically control what people do to us, good or bad. But what we can control is how we react to those things, what we choose to do with those feelings that were created through them, and how we manage the energy created by those feelings.

When it comes to negative feelings, we must focus on learning and healing from them. Because if you don't, then you will inevitably get frustrated and angry, and through that, you will cause bad shit to happen to others and likely yourself too. And when that happens, you become the proverbial demon, pushing people and yourself straight into the depths of hell. When you choose to face and heal negative feelings, regardless of who created them, you do the opposite. You inevitably create positive feelings in yourself and others. You end up becoming a proverbial angel, sending yourself and others into the beauty of heaven. Through our actions or lack thereof, we create heaven and hell within ourselves. And in that process, we choose where we will reside.

Getting back to the question I asked you about the pie chart of feelings, where do you land? Are you maybe 80 percent positive vibes and 20 percent negative? Or maybe 50 percent positive and 50 percent negative? Or...maybe you're 20 percent positive and 80 percent negative? No matter what your answer is, please know it's ok. There is no right or wrong answer here. There's only truth. And with that truth we decide our next steps, we decide our actions.

Where you land percentage-wise is simply a status indicator of your energetic state, and the work that must be done to maintain yourself. If you're at 100 percent positive vibes, then...fuck! Good for you! Sit back and enjoy it while you have it! If you're 80 percent positive and 20 percent negative, then you're feeling pretty darn good but have some work to do to monitor and heal/release those negative feelings/energy. If you're 50/50, then you're not feeling too bad. But you clearly have work to do and need to be on alert because, if any negative feelings/energy come at you, then you could end up in an area where your capacity to hold negative energy could head into the red zone. If you're 20 percent positive and 80 percent negative, then you're likely feeling pretty shitty, edgy, and cranky. You have a lot of work/healing to do, and you need to be on your highest alert. Because if anymore negative vibes come at you, then you may hit the red line and max out. You may be at risk of getting angry and losing your shit.

Just Haven't Met You Yet

You wanna know where I'm at right now percentage-wise? Honestly, I'm 50/50. And I've been at that level awhile. In my current situation, 50/50 is the best I can do, so I focus on making the best of it, and maintaining myself the best I can at that level. That level may seem concerning, but it's exceptionally good for me. I used to be at 100 percent negative and hovered at that point for a loooong period of time. Yeah, you heard that right...I lived in the depths of hell for a very long time, and boy, I know that place oh so well. So 50/50 is major progress for me! But I still have work to do for sure, and I must be on alert since shit happens sometimes, and I can't control that. What I can control, though, is being aware of my state, practice techniques to promote positive energy, and keep healing so that I can improve that state.

You might be wondering why I'm at 50/50, considering I have so much knowledge and experience to be able to write this book. Like why do I still have so much frustrated energy in me? Fair question. And I'll be totally open with you about the answer, despite the fear-based energy my own mind is creating while analyzing the implications of sharing such personal information. Personal information that some may consider foolish nonsense, naive, or pure fantasy. I'm going to proceed with sharing my truth with you, though, because I don't want to hold it in. I want to break the mind fuck of society and just be honest, let my truth out, and release that energy in the process.

I would have replied 90 percent positive and 10 percent negative to my question earlier except for one thing. One very big hole in my world that I'm still working on filling. You see, there's someone I miss terribly, so much so that I ache constantly for her. There's an emptiness inside my physical world that only she can fill, and that has resulted in me carrying around a lot of frustrated sadness. Sadness that keeps my overall frustration levels higher than I would have otherwise. The truth is, though, I don't have complete control over filling that void, not physically anyway. All I can do is heal myself and trust that the process of doing so will reunite me with her. In the meantime, I accept the frustration that comes along with the situation, as I know it's only temporary in the big picture, and ultimately well worth experiencing.

Who is this person, you might ask? This may sound silly, but she's my soulmate or *my girl* as I internally refer to her as. I have yet to meet her in this physical world, at least not that I can consciously validate anyway. I know her spiritually though; I feel her with me every moment of every day, and I've felt her with me my entire life. I remember her clearly, and I love her with all that I am. And I very much look forward to us being together one day soon. Me writing this book right now is part of my healing journey; it's the pathway that will lead to us being reunited. As crazy as that may sound, it's something I know without any doubt. I not only know it, but I also feel it. She is my truth.

Regardless of all that, I've made amazing progress in my healing and have been able to heal everything except that hole in my heart. And I don't pressure myself about it because I know that I left that hole there for a reason. For without that hole, I wouldn't have been able to experience all that I've experienced. And those experiences were the lessons I needed to learn so that I could pass that knowledge onto you now. So as painful as that hole has been to experience, I know it was necessary. And I trust that, I trust the path I chose, and I trust that the space I left reserved for her will be filled when the time is right. I don't physically know when that is, but I know it will be.

It's Time to Take the Trash Out

A key element in my own journey of healing and ratcheting down my levels of frustration has been to evaluate the culprits behind the frustrated energy that was embedded so deeply within me for so long. I had to identify what I needed to heal. Turns out that there was a lot. Much of that healing came in the form of elimination. What I mean by that is that I had shit in my life that repeatedly and consistently created negative energy within me. There were no ifs, ands, or buts about it; those things needed to be removed.

In some cases I was able to do surgical removal, and in others, I had to use a sledgehammer to do the deed. And there were even cases where I didn't know how to do the removal, so had to bring in the big guns. I had to ask the universe and my spirit guides for assistance and guidance. In those cases things happened that seemed scary in the moment, but I quickly reminded myself that I had asked for help, and that's exactly what I was getting. I wasn't in direct control, but I trusted those who were. And I knew it would all be ok in the end.

I unfortunately can't help you figure out specifically what needs removal from your life, but what I can do is offer you this: imagine holding onto a rope that is tightly wrapped around your hand. That rope is digging into your skin and causing so much pain and bleeding, but you hold on to it out of fear of what damage will occur if you let go. Consider this though: What if holding on is doing more damage than letting go? You can't keep holding onto a rope that's tearing at your hands. At some point you just have to weigh the reality that you're in pain and can't keep going as you are. You have to be brave and just let go of the rope. Let it fall and accept that if you were meant to hold onto that rope, then it wouldn't be as painful as it is. The pain is an indicator that it's not something you're meant to hold onto. Actually, it's an indicator that it's something you need to let go of. Flow with the energy of life, like a leaf in the wind, and let the rope go.

So I challenge you with this: review what is filling your body with negative vibes, what is maxing out your frustration capacity. And decide what you want removed versus what you want to keep and heal. Then be the badass you are and take that trash out! Whether it be people in your life, a job, school, debt, or whatever. Identify it and find a way to get rid of it. You may not be able to do it right away; you might need to make a plan instead…even a long-term plan. Do it though–do whatever you need to do. Even if it's something you can't eliminate right away, your awareness and belief in the plan can provide enough of an energy release to get you by until that plan can be fully executed. A plan can be your light to follow in the darkness. Just keep in mind that your life didn't get fucked in a day, and it won't get unfucked in a day either. But it will get unfucked, if you commit to removing what you no longer need in your life.

Once you've cleared as much toxic shit out of your life as you can, fill that open space with things that fill you with positive vibes. Be careful, of course, to learn from your mistakes and not backfill with more toxic shit. If you're not sure you can do that yet, then hold off until you're clear on what that looks like for you. You can keep open space if you need; that's totally fine. It may even be good for you. Eventually, though, you'll need to fill any voids with positive influences. Before you know it, you'll find your vibe is permanently shifting to the positive side of the spectrum.

A friend once taught me an awesome ritual to help with both taking the trash out as well as backfilling with the good stuff. Just to warn you, though, it may seem a little silly at first, but I swear it works! It isn't something that works immediately necessarily, but I've found it certainly does work.

Here's how it goes. This ritual is executed in two parts. The first part occurs on the full moon of each month. On that evening write down on a piece of paper all the things you desire to eliminate from your life. You then take that piece of paper outside and burn it in a fire-safe space/receptacle. The goal is to burn these things out of your life. Once it's done burning, you dump the ashes onto the dirt and pour water on them. The water ensures the fire is out, but it also helps return what you burned to the earth, where it can be broken down and reborn again into something new and positive.

The second part of the ritual occurs on the new moon of each month. On that evening, you write down all the things you want to attract into your life and keep that list someplace safe. The goal in keeping this list is it acts a representation of physically holding onto the things you want in your life. For this part of the ritual, you will traditionally use a piece of paper, but I personally opt to email myself the list as I'm not one to keep many things, including pieces of paper. I've heard that some people will write the list in a journal instead, which is totally fine. Ultimately it's up to you as long as the basis of the idea is maintained, which is writing down what you want to attract into your life and keeping that. Overall the idea is a cleansing and filling technique. First dump out, then refill. It flows with the moon, it brings the tide in, and then takes the tide out.

Huddle Up, Team Me

Another technique in bringing down your frustration levels is to have a support team you can talk to, people you trust and can be honest with. It could be a best friend, a family member, a therapist, etcetera. The key part is that you trust them–trust them in a way that you can tell them anything and know they won't judge you. They will listen without prejudice and be there for you when you need them.

I'm not a particularly social person, but I do have some really amazing friends–friends I can vent to and trust without hesitation. However, I still find it helpful to speak to a therapist on a regular basis to help reduce my frustration levels. Over the years I had tried several therapists, but most didn't hack it for me in the long run. I didn't trust them and didn't connect with them vibe-wise. Don't get me wrong; some offered great advice and techniques. But they just weren't great fits so were limited in how much they could help me. Eventually I learned to follow my feels to someone I felt in my soul that I could trust. It wasn't about a specific educational background, what type of therapy they offered, or how many years they had been in practice. It was all about vibe and trust.

Once I found my therapist–her name is Katie, by the way–I knew she would be able to help me. I knew it from the moment I saw her picture on a therapist search website. I felt a comfort with her. So I reached out, and after several years, I still talk to her weekly. I don't *need* to speak with her weekly, but I like to; I choose to. She's a cool chick who hears me. She understands what I'm saying, even if I don't choose the best words to describe it. She even picks up on what I'm not saying. What more could I ask for?! Answer: Nothing! She's awesome!

My weekly conversations with Katie help me release energy that builds up throughout the week. It's like being an RV and pulling up to a waste disposal station for a weekly clean out of the stanky shit that's been filling up my tank. We don't always talk about heavy stuff either. Sometimes we chew the fat with lighthearted banter about places we've traveled to or want to. The subject matter we discuss almost doesn't matter. There's an energy exchange between us, and words are simply the vessel that energy travels on. The words we choose to connect through are varied and ultimately irrelevant. She's a gifted soul who has the ability to suck bad vibes out of me and toss them aside once she gets them. She's an angel indeed. She's my soul sister who has my back when I need her.

On occasion I even speak to a psychic. The nice thing about a true psychic is they're inherently sensitive souls who have a talent for picking up on your vibes. And they usually don't hold back since they've long eliminated the fears that prevent a nonprofessional intuitive from sharing what they see. Plus, they have a knack for hearing whispers from either your or their spirit guides. For me the actual psychic part of the conversation isn't really about predicting the future. It's about them seeing something that I'm missing or not understanding clearly, something that's not necessarily physical. It's more energetic. I find psychics to be great allies in managing negative energy on so many levels.

I've been very fortunate to have worked with several amazing psychics over the years. I normally don't speak to them weekly, as I do with Katie. And I don't typically vent anything going on in my life either. I mostly listen to what they have to say and see what they pick up on. That's where they shine. If necessary I'll bring up a particular subject to see what they pick up on. I don't push, though, because my philosophy is to let the info flow. The info that's meant to flow to you will. I accept that and move on. Most of the time, though, I don't even have to ask anything. They bring up the important stuff without me having to ask. Psychics have proven to be great members of my support team, Team Me.

Whoever you decide to put on your support team, take care of them. If they're friends or family, then be one of their support team members as well—and be an honorable and trustworthy one at that. That way you pay them back for the good they've done for you. If they're a professional, like a therapist or a psychic, then leave them positive reviews or share your experience to others in working with them. That's one of the few ways you'll ever be able to pay them back for their assistance. Therapists don't take tips, but psychics typically do. Give them a healthy tip to say thank you. You inevitably expose them to a lot of your shit when you speak with them; show your appreciation to them in any way you can. By doing so, you'll be an angel to them and end up filling yourself with positive vibes in the process.

The Apology

As this long and complex lesson comes to an end, I'd like to bring your attention back to the subject that it began with: the movie *Bad Words*.[22] I had mentioned the part in the opening scene of the movie where Guy Trilby appeared to be speaking to you the viewer. When I mentioned that aspect of the scene, it may not have been clear why I was bringing his words to your attention. Well, I did it because it meant something in the big picture. Just as many things do, even though you may not understand it in the moment.

As the movie proceeds, Guy continues speaking over and throughout various scenes, which cumulatively turn out to not be a message directed to you at all. Piece by piece, you get to hear what turns out to be a letter. A letter he is writing to the person who hurt his feelings, the person who inspired the eruption of his anger. This letter is the part I referred to as you getting to see the beginnings of healing. And that's why I would like to share the remaining portion of his letter with you now:

> I had plenty of opportunities to stop what I was doing. To make a good decision. But that would have required the kind of lessons that I was never taught. Obviously if I could figure out a way to be less stubborn, the right way to fix things would be easier to see. The closer I got to the end, the more I thought about the goal. And the more I thought about the win. With the humiliation part taken care of and the favorite child all but killed, maybe I already had my win. I don't know if I should have done things differently. Like I said I'm not good at a lot of things. Maybe there should have been a screaming match. A fight. Maybe some tears. But I guess I just want to move on and let you do the same. What's done is done. I can't change what happened. All I can do, all I want to do, is leave you with this apology. This note, which started with me telling you that my feelings were hurt. And as much as I'd like to hurt your feelings and call you names, they're just words, and it wouldn't change a thing. That's not what this note was for. Hopefully it has explained why I did what I did and maybe even have you understand. If not, that's fine.[22]

I share Guy's words with you because it once again highlights how the universe speaks to us through creativity. How you can find guidance to life's many challenges through creativity if you open your awareness to it. This is the language of the universe and of your spirit guides. Listen to them whisper to you, hear them guide you through your challenges.

In this case, Guy found healing by releasing the sadness, fear, trauma, and powerlessness that created so much frustrated energy within him. What he finds is that just a simple letter to his offender helped him heal and release his frustrated energy more so than his anger-based actions ever did. There's wisdom in that. Maybe writing a letter will do the same for you. Or maybe talking with someone will. Or maybe going for a walk will do it or even beating the shit out of a punching bag. Or maybe a combination of all of them. Whatever it is that peacefully releases the frustrated energy for you...go for it. Follow your heart, follow your peace, and listen for the whispers of wisdom that guide you. It's down that path that you will find the key you need to move onto your next evolution, the key to permanently heal from those traumas that power your bad words.

LESSON 8:

OMG, I've Gotta Pee!

When You Gotta Go, You Gotta Go

Many of life's challenges exist solely in our physical minds, like impatience, for example. Oftentimes physically we don't have full control of our life experiences, which can cause our avatars to feel the sensation of impatience, since it's unable to dictate the timeline and/or operational road map for a particular life event to take place. That impatience, or perceived lack of control, can create a brain-based desire to want, or even to force, an event to occur in the timeline and way that fits our own physical self-focused needs.

In some cases our physical selves are in complete control of a life event, both in the sense of determining feasibility as well as in operational execution. Like if you need to pee and can't hold it any longer. The physical brain is sensing alarms telling it that your bladder is near capacity and that any further delay of bodily fluid evacuation will result in pain and potential physical damage. Fortunately your need to pee generally doesn't impact anyone but yourself, so you can take care of business whenever and in whatever way you so physically choose. Impatience typically isn't involved in that since our physical selves are in full control of said event.

Of course there are variables that can impact other people in such a scenario, such as if you're caring for a young child and your temporary departure to relieve yourself inevitably impacts them. But that's a fairly localized issue that can easily be resolved within the limited awareness of your physical self. For example, asking someone else to watch the child while you have a tinkle solves the problem with minimal impact on a broad scale. Of course that action will impact the person who you ask to watch the child, but again, it's another localized issue with minimal impact in the larger scale of your life, or anyone else's for that matter.

The flip side of that is when your physical self determines it has a need or desire, yet fulfilment of that need/desire will impact life in ways our brains can't even fathom or even care about. For example, you're low on money, and your mind determines that winning the lottery is an optimal way to resolve that issue. Minimal investment with a large return. OMG, how lovely would that be? Just collect your money and be free to enjoy this life as you physically see fit. Yes indeed, it's a great plan! Let's make it happen! Ooh, fantastic! The lottery is tonight! I'll pick up a ticket this afternoon and win this evening! Easy peasy, lemon squeezy!

However, such an event impacts so many aspects of life outside of ourselves that the determination of whether it can be facilitated or not can't be exclusively held within our physical selves. Our avatars simply don't have the awareness or the ability to become aware of the infinite number of impact points that event would cause throughout life. Not just to our own lives, but other lives as well. Not to mention that our avatars generally haven't evolved to the point where we truly give a fuck how such a thing would impact anyone else. We just want what we want, and that's where our physical focus naturally is. So the determination of fulfilling an event such as this must land outside of our self-focused physical minds. This is where our spiritual selves and the universe step in. And with that comes the physical perception of a lack of control and subsequent sensation of impatience.

In such a scenario, we physically have limited control to make the desired event occur. I mean, we can certainly decide to purchase the lottery ticket, and we can make that purchase whenever we physically choose. Again those choices are fairly localized with minimal impact in the grander scheme of things. But the actual decision to win the lottery falls completely outside our physical selves.

Some may say that the choice in who wins is determined completely by chance. Others may say that an evil overlord makes the decision since gambling is, in their perception, evil. And there's a whole other group who might say it's their God alone who blesses them with such a decision. Truth be told, the choice isn't random and isn't chosen by anyone other than your higher spiritual self. Certainly the universe (or God if you prefer that term) plays a role in the decision, but ultimately it's the spiritual you who will approve or reject such a desire. And that decision is based on how that event will impact our lives, the lives of others, and this massive multiplayer virtual reality game we're all playing.

Now you may be thinking to yourself, Wait, wait, wait...I obviously can't physically control who wins the lottery, but you're saying I can spiritually? To which my answer is, yes! But–and it's a big but–it's not a matter of somehow convincing your higher self to make it happen. You–your higher spiritual self–are a highly evolved energy-based entity, capable of multidimensional travel, with a vast awareness and capacity to understand how any event can impact the grander scheme of this experience we're all living. Yes, you're a fucking badass! Think of your higher self as infinitely wise as how most people perceive their God. And with that in mind, if the spiritual you felt that winning the lottery would be a benefit overall, then you would have already planned it into your life. Meaning, if it's meant to be, then it will be.

So does this mean that you physically have no control over theoretically winning the lottery? No, not at all. You certainly have some physical control. Again you physically decide if you're going to purchase tickets, and you decide when you execute that. But you physically can't control if you actually win or not. There's a balance in there, a harmonious and almost symbiotic partnership between the physical you and the spiritual you. You spiritually draw the map, and you physically walk it. And to add an additional layer to that, you physically decide when and how fast to walk it.

With that being the case, there certainly are things we can do to physically find and embrace the noted balance and harmony, and in the process, numb the inherent physical sensations of impatience that accompany the reality that we physically are not in full control.

Keep in mind that our physical bodies are not who we are. These physical bodies are the vessel of our own design that we use to experience this reality. As spirits we are inhabiting our avatars, and while we're in them, we have limited access to our infinite knowledge and capabilities. So it's not like the spiritual you that exists within your avatar is a completely separate entity from the spiritual you that exists out in the ether. On the contrary we spiritually exist both in the physical and spiritual realms at the same time. We are the very same spirit that makes all the important life decisions that are outside our physical control.

I'd like to highlight something from that last paragraph before we move forward, which is that I noted we have limited physical access to our infinite spiritual knowledge and capabilities. I didn't say we have no physical access; I said we have limited access. The key ingredients in finding the balance and harmony between the physical and the spiritual is by understanding the control we have through each, embracing the physical access we do have to our infinite spiritual knowledge, and growing that access through our physical evolution. Through that you will feel a tremendous physical relief in any sensations of impatience as well as any feelings that you, as a whole being, are not in full control of your life.

Déjà Vu

Before we begin our physical lives in these organic earth suits I often refer to as avatars, I believe we, our spiritual selves, map out a plan for the lives we're about to experience. A plan that primarily revolves around the lessons you need to learn and teach in order to achieve your higher-level spiritual goals. I think of it as sitting down with your personal operations team and making a strategic plan on what exactly you're going to learn, how you're going to learn it, defining what your team (a.k.a. spirit guides) can assist you with, who will be your teachers, who will be your students, what sequence events should occur in, and so many other things that I couldn't possibly list them all. The plan is obviously highly detailed yet also flexible to allow for variables involving physical decisions (free will) that will inherently be made during execution of the plan.

The way I envision this plan is as a map of a three-dimensional universe in the shape of a sphere, where destined key events are strategically placed and are dynamically moving about the interior of that sphere. The space between each event represents time, and each event is connected by physical decisions that provide an infinite number of interconnected pathways between each key event. Essentially the key events are destined to occur, no matter what physical decisions you make. The decisions themselves can take you down countless numbers of potential paths, but ultimately all paths lead to the same place: the key event.

Of course, there's always an optimal path between each key event, but whether you take the optimal path or not is dependent on the physical decisions you, other people, and our society make as well as an infinite number of other variables that are impossible to comprehend in our physical minds. It's basically a dynamic map that's built to endure and adapt to our earthbound decision trees. When it comes down to it, though, no matter what physical decisions are made or by whom, you will hit the key events whether you physically intend to or not. The only question is, when will you hit them. And that is defined by our earthbound decisions.

When you make this plan, you see a preview of what's going to happen around the key events, simply because you're the leader of the team designing the plan. You know every event and every person involved in that event and every conceivable element of what needs to happen. But you can't carry all that knowledge forward into your avatar form, simply because that would undermine the goal of the journey, the knowledge you need to gain through it, and the physical decisions that are necessary along the way. Plus, your avatar isn't capable of comprehending and storing that type and amount of knowledge without malfunctioning. It would be like trying to load a terabyte of data onto a megabyte thumb drive. Only a fraction would load, and little would make sense because of the fragmentation that would inevitably occur. So nearly all aspects of the plan, including the key events, are locked away within your spiritual self, where your avatar doesn't have direct access to it.

There are a few exceptions to this not remembering rule though—one being if the path leading to a key event requires some familiarity in order to successfully navigate it. Another is if the key event contains some elements that you spiritually look forward to experiencing for one reason or another; that excitement tends to stick with you on a higher level and breaches both the physical and spiritual realms as well as time itself (i.e., the space between each key event). Another exception is that one of our goals of this journey is to physically evolve to a point where we can tap into the knowledge that's contained within our spiritual selves. So the further you physically evolve, the more access you gain to your spiritual knowledge that's locked away inside of you.

Physically speaking when you're either approaching or in the midst of a key life event, you can experience familiarities, or memories, of that event or its many details. This is an intentional wormhole that allows a relatively small and physically manageable amount of knowledge to come through to our physical selves.

This situation can be very perplexing for your brain. Knowledge is coming to it from your higher spiritual self, information which it has no physical reference to, information it's not pulling from its own senses or knowledge banks. Keep in mind that your brain is an organic computer. It analyzes the shit out of countless terabytes of physical data every second. Analysis is one of its primary functions, but receiving and analyzing spirit-based data can be disorienting for it until it learns how to process that type of data.

Some people don't experience these familiarities, or memories as I prefer to call them, at all, and that's ok. It's just where they are on their journey. However, most, if not all, who are drawn to read this book have inevitably evolved to a point where they experience spirit memories on a somewhat regular basis. And for some it may be on a frequent basis.

Most of us who experience these spirit memories sadly don't refer to them as such. We instead typically refer to them by the easily dismissible term *déjà vu*, which is a French word that appropriately translates to *already seen*. Don't get me wrong; that's a lovely term that isn't a bad way to describe it by any means. But it also doesn't tell the full story that desperately needs to be understood by the souls who experience them, which is how we're able to easily dismiss them.

These spirit memories often are triggered in the moment by seeing something you swear you've seen before, yet you're positive you haven't...physically anyway. The familiarity can be a downright trippy experience because it likely isn't one specific thing you're recognizing. Oftentimes it's a series of completely random yet specific things happening in quick succession.

For example, a person you just met in a coffee shop you've never been to before says something specific to you right when a particular song is playing overhead, and then someone spills their coffee on the ground off to the left of you. In that moment you remember the entire scene in the coffee shop. The person you're talking to, the outfit they're wearing, the smell of the coffee brewing, the exact spot you and everyone else are standing in, and your perspective in all of it. Trippy indeed–and undoubtedly a spirit memory.

This is the kind of event that someone will typically refer to as a déjà vu. For me, these are a sign that you're in the midst of a key life event. The coffee shop, in this case, likely isn't the event itself. It just happens to be in proximity or part of the event. The key life event may be something that is much grander than just the shop experience, like maybe it occurred shortly before or after a spiritual awakening, a death in the family, or the person you met in the coffee shop will play an important role in future events. Whatever the key life event is, the memory is being triggered in you because it was important enough to carry into this physical life.

There are other more subtle spirit memories that you can also experience, but they occur well in advance of a key event. These types of spirit memories can be the most powerful, as they're intended to guide you through a path and to another key event. I have a great example of this type of memory that I'll share with you shortly.

Even though these spirit memories aren't widely understood as memories, deep down people basically get it. We recognize that we've experienced something familiar to us on some level. What I've learned, however, is that there's so much more to it than that. What a spirit memory represents to me is that we're either approaching or in the midst of a key event that is/was destined to occur. Most importantly this memory represents an important milestone in our journey. It represents that we've reached a key moment and are leveling up.

The Addis Event

I began experiencing déjà vu at a very young age, and the experiences have continued throughout my life. Each time one occurred, it would inevitably catch my attention, and I couldn't help but be curious what they were. I subsequently spent years trying to understand them, paying close attention to when they came up, what exactly triggered them, and what I was feeling, seeing, and aware of, both physically and spiritually, in those moments. As my awareness and understanding of them grew so did the frequency and intensity of these events. Some were small for sure, but some were very powerful. So powerful that an eruption of excitement would overwhelm me when they occurred.

The awakening event I noted in lesson 5, where I awoke to all the lovely feelings, excitement, and hearing the voice speak to me, proved to be a key life event for me. I didn't connect the dots at the time but, looking back, I now realize I had experienced several powerful spiritual memories shortly before that event. I'll spare you the details of those memories as they're not relevant in the scope of this lesson, but the important thing is that awakening was a key life event that was destined to occur. And it was a massive one at that. One that marked a change for me in so many ways.

One of those ways was that I began rocket blasting through key events, one after another. And not just small ones either–big ones too...supermassive ones. That event triggered an important awakening in me to where I'm now feeling, and spiritually remembering, my way to and through the most direct paths between each event. I've gotten so good at it that I will literally stop my life and flip it upside down in order to avoid missing a direct path. And those paths and key life events are leading me somewhere important. I feel it so strongly and deeply within myself, and it fuels me each day. I don't remember the exact details of what that is, but I remember a rough idea, and it's enough to get me out of bed each morning and where I need to go.

One such path came upon me recently, and it led me to one of the most powerful key life events I've experienced so far. It's right up there with the awakening event I mentioned in lesson 5. This path was a dark one without doubt, but it was lined with many future based spiritual memories that guided me along my way and provided the light I so desperately needed to successfully navigate it.

Please note that some time has passed since I began writing this book. I wrote everything up to lesson 7 in early to mid-2021, during the thick of the pandemic. It's now the middle of 2023, and many things have changed in my life, mostly due to the many changes I've learned to make in order to stay on the most direct path to each key event. During this time I also had to take a break from writing, and once again, it all had to do with me following the paths as they dynamically changed based on the infinite variables that inherently occur.

This backstory begins shortly after I stopped writing, when a couple of friends who own a graphic arts business reached out to me with a job offer that would involve me traveling to Honduras and working with a team of people there. Going back to corporate-type work really wasn't what I wanted to do, though, especially after having discovered my divine inspirations in writing. But there was something about this offer that triggered me. It was the Honduras part, and I physically didn't know exactly why. But there was something deeply familiar about it in the spiritual sense. And the idea of traveling there was stoking a fire of excitement within me. So much so that I mentioned it to Katie in our weekly session that week.

Now keep in mind that at this point I had never been to Honduras, and all that I physically knew of the place was that it wasn't a very safe area. So physically my brain was fearful of traveling there. Spiritually, though, it was a totally different story. It very quickly became clear to me that I was going to Honduras at some point, and there was something very important for me there. The only question for me was when I would go and exactly what, or who, was drawing me there.

As I felt my way through that job offer, something felt off to me. It wasn't the right time, and that was clear to me. Physically my brain was confused because it had long evolved to accept this spiritual knowledge, but that same knowledge was also saying no. Not *no* forever, just no for now. That same spiritual knowledge ended up leading me to take a different job offer in Portland, Oregon. I honestly wasn't interested in going to Portland physically, but spiritually I knew it was the path I needed to take. It was the most direct path to the next key event, and that excited me.

When I accepted this job in Portland, I signed an agreement with the company stating that I would work and live there for a minimum of one year. Included in that agreement was a clause specifying that I would have to pay them back up to $16,000 in moving expenses if I broke the agreement. In my mind I had to stay there because paying that back would be a major issue for me, especially considering the amount of time I had been out of work prior to that. With that in mind, I also signed a one-year lease for an apartment on the outskirts of the city.

I subsequently moved to Portland and embraced the experience for what it was, a pathway. After about eight months, though, something happened. One fall afternoon while I was on a meditative walk, I felt a clear and powerful awakening of knowledge within me. It was an awakening along with a solid nudge of guidance from my spirit guides. It hit me hard and fast, and there was no doubt what it was or what I needed to do about it. I needed to leave Portland, along with the job, and go back to San Diego. And I needed to do it immediately.

I remember speaking to Katie that week and telling her what had happened. I explained to her how my brain was struggling with understanding what to do with the information, as I was obligated to stay in Portland for at least four more months. Yet despite that brain-based confusion, I was spiritually clear what needed to be done and what was about to occur. Katie was supportive as usual, of course, and at this point, was used to me making abrupt changes in my life. But I think even she was thrown for a loop when I informed her the following week that I had already put the move in motion.

A few days before, I had notified my boss that I was moving to San Diego and that the company's only option was to allow me to work remotely; otherwise, I would resign. I also notified the property management company that I would be breaking the lease. Even Katie was shocked that I had moved on this so quickly and so boldly. I explained to her that I planned on making the actual move in just a few weeks and that I had already begun selling or donating much that I had accumulated while I was there. That's how powerful this was for me. I needed to move right away, and I wasn't going to let anything get in the way of that. Not the job, not the contracts I had signed, and certainly not any possessions that weren't important in the big picture.

My path in Portland was complete, and as I told Katie, there was something very important coming, and I needed to move right away for it to happen. The on-ramp to my next path was coming fast, and there was little time to catch it. If I didn't move right away, then not only would I miss the path, but the path wouldn't open at all. I couldn't explain the details around that, but I knew that time was of the essence. I also warned Katie to be prepared because even more changes were coming. I said that confidently because I knew it as fact. Not physically, but spiritually. Spiritually I was remembering it.

About the time I moved, my employer got back to me regarding whether they were going to formally allow me to work remotely. I honestly didn't care if they did or not though. My brain wanted to worry about my income and whether I was going to have to pay my employer a bunch of money to leave. But I knew what I was doing was right, and because of that, I knew everything would fall into place. So I didn't allow my brain to overanalyze the details of what that would all look like. I just flowed with what I knew and allowed the pieces to come together. I had learned to follow my memories, my feels, and the guidance of my ops team. So I simply trusted in that.

My employer ended up agreeing to allow me to work remotely. However, one of the two friends I mentioned earlier had heard that I was moving back to San Diego, and that prompted him to call me. Turns out a need for a San Diego-based operations manager, who would be responsible for training a team of people in Honduras on behalf of one of his clients, had just arisen. He ended up offering me the position. At the exact same time, his client also reached out to me and offered me a similar position that would be involved with the same team in Honduras, just not in the exact same way.

This was very interesting to me. I had just made what appeared from the outside to be some absurdly crazy life moves, all on what would appear as a foolish whim. Crazy moves that, from a logical perspective, should have been disastrous. But now here I was with three job opportunities, and two of them involved the same team of people in Honduras, the very situation I had felt so drawn to the year before. And had I not moved when I did, then the opportunity would have never come about. On top of that, all three of these companies were aware of each other's offers, and subsequently came in fast and hard to compete. What an interesting play of events.

Needless to say, I wasn't interested in staying with my Portland employer. That was a no-brainer. I was so drawn to Honduras that they just weren't in the running for me. And I wasn't going to worry about potentially paying them back for the moving expenses either. That was just another detail that would work out exactly as it needed to. But of these two other offers involving Honduras–which should I take? They both involved the same team, and clearly what I was being drawn to involved that team. At that point I could spiritually see within my memories the option of taking two paths. Two paths that led to the same place, an exceptionally powerful key event. But one of those paths would lead me straight to my destination without any doubts. The other one had the possibility of a deviation. So it was an easy decision for me. I went with working for my friends.

Once I made the decision, I notified my Portland employer that I would be resigning. In that process they opted to not charge me for breaking the contract. I never found out why exactly; they just never pursued it. And the property management company only charged me a fee of a few hundred dollars for breaking the lease. So all was working out seamlessly. And time had proven that there was never anything to worry about.

With my path forward now solidified, I had already begun working remotely with one of the team members from Honduras. When I first started working with this person, I was very curious as to whether they would spark a spirit memory for me. Much to my dismay, they didn't. Don't get me wrong; this person is amazing, and we subsequently have become truly great friends. I absolutely adore this person to this day, but I had no memories of them. I was honestly bummed but knew there must be more to the story. So I let that go and moved forward. I thought maybe going to Honduras would be the trigger, like maybe I was going to move there, or maybe something was going to happen while I was visiting. Time would have to tell, but at this point there were no discussions of me taking the trip just yet. So I had to patiently wait.

Fast-forward a couple of months, and I was asked to join a call with one of my friends/new bosses and a newer Honduras team member who I hadn't worked with yet. Interestingly this new person had been going through the interviewing and hiring process at the same time I abruptly decided to leave Portland. I wasn't aware of that until much later, and at this point wasn't expecting much from the meeting other than having an introduction to them. I had it set in my mind that I needed to go to Honduras to figure out what this draw was so just didn't have any expectations with this meeting in any way.

The call started with nothing out of the ordinary. My boss talked momentarily, and then I had to introduce myself to this new team member, which I honestly was little nervous about just because I can be socially anxious. And I wasn't positive I knew how to properly pronounce her name. So I started out by saying hello and asked if I was saying her name, Addis, correctly. In a voice that I immediately recognized and felt I had heard a million times before, she simply replied, saying, "Yes!"

That was it! In that moment with just that one little word, I was hit so hard with an intense wave of energy that it, spiritually speaking, knocked me to the ground. I had experienced a few exceptionally powerful connections with people in my life but nothing like this. Not even close.

In that moment I remembered Addis. I remembered her voice and every bit of who she is, was, and will be. I remembered her beauty, kindness, and sincerity. I remembered her strength, wisdom, and love. In that moment, I remembered this gentle yet powerful soul who has a goofy, quirky, and wicked sense of humor and the sweetest and most contagious laugh you could ever imagine hearing. I also remembered her beautiful shadows, the dark corners where she hides herself away so she can blend in with the crowd. My dear friend Addis, who I've looked forward to meeting in this life, who represented the coming of a supermassive key event for me, who was so kind to join up with me on this journey and help me as I make it through this event, and level up as I complete and publish this book. Addis is the person who triggered me to start writing again, and the person who's inspiring these words right now. She inspired this entire lesson.

It's now been a few months since that moment, and Addis and I very quickly became powerful friends, long before we eventually met in person. We share things with each other that we don't share with anyone else; we understand each other is a way that's unexplainable with words, and we trust each other without any fear. So much so that, within a week of our noted introduction, I sent her a copy of this book up to lesson 7, which was where I had previously paused. She was the first and only person I allowed to read what I had written up to that point. It was raw and unedited. That's how much I knew and trusted her. That deep spiritual connection between us is why I had such powerful memories of her and why I was so excited to cross paths with her in this life. She is a goddess without question, and one I feel so fortunate to call my soul friend.

Do You Trust Me?

I shared this event about Addis not only to be an example of a spirit memory that occurs in advance of a key event but also to highlight how spiritual memories can help guide you along your path if you're willing to listen and trust in them—and ultimately trust in yourself. These memories are *your* memories. Memories of key events that *you* designed and planned for. Seeing those spirit memories turn into physical realities means *you* are achieving *your* goals. *You* are successfully navigating to *your* endgame destination.

The balance and harmony between the control you have spiritually and physically, which I mentioned earlier, can be found in the knowing that you spiritually drew this map you are physically following. The control you so desperately desire is already within you.

You just need to trust yourself, the plan that you designed, and your ops team, who work tirelessly to help you with every step of this very long journey.

Once you understand and accept that nothing is random, that there's no luck, no mystical old man sitting in the clouds deciding your fate, no evil overlord taking pleasure in making your life difficult, no amount of physical forcing that will take you anywhere you don't spiritually want to go, and that the only way out of the darkness is by following the lights that line the paths you walk upon—then and only then will you numb the physical sensation of impatience and find the balance between the physical you and the spiritual you. This is when you will be flowing with life and rocket blasting through the lessons you chose to take, the lessons that will elevate you to the destination you seek. The lessons that will bring you home.

Shit Stinks

On paper this event I shared about Addis and I finding each other may sound as if it was relatively fast and easy for me. But I promise you it wasn't. I shared with you the highlights which, in the big picture, are what I've been focused on. The details I couldn't share though; those were hard. That entire path was dark, endlessly tiring, and lonely as fuck for me. But those spirit memories kept me going. They were a light off in the distance that I could stay focused on, as time passed ever so slowly. And the dark paths didn't end for me when Addis and I met either.

Honestly, this corporate job I'm working at in this moment...I don't want to do it. I never did. And I'm not going to stay in it much longer. I know that without a doubt. I remember it. I hate corporate jobs, even ones where I work for friends. The only reason I accepted the job was because it would bring me to Addis, my light, and push me onto my current trajectory, which has so many more wonderful things coming for the both of us, a much easier and brighter path without doubt. But the job I'm at and the path I'm on, ugh! It's hard, painfully long, and unpleasant as fuck in many ways. But it's the path. It's the path I created, the path I remember, and the path I trust. The path that is leading me where I chose to go, where I want to go, and where I'm drawn to go. That doesn't make it easy or quick, but it does get me through it. And the lights along that path, make it all worth it. The darkness can be forgotten, but the light stays with me...forever engrained in my memory.

I don't remember the exact details of what Addis and I will experience in the future. What I do know is that we'll experience some amazing and wonderful things. I remember that very clearly. I can honestly say that I love Addis in the purest of ways, and there isn't anything I wouldn't do for her, including walking the darkest, toughest, and loneliest paths in order to meet up with her.

Warning! Warning! Bladder Is Full!

Patience, acceptance, and self-trust...those are important lessons to learn, especially when you've been waiting so long and have worked so hard for what you desire. Yes, you're a brave soul indeed my friend. And you have endured so much time and so much pain to hold yourself together so many times when you felt you were on the verge of falling apart. You're doing it though; you're making it through. You've made it through so much already, and you can continue making it through. You can and will make it. Even when your bladder is filled to the rim, and you absolutely can't hold it any longer. When you're on the brink of springing a leak and think to yourself, OMG, I've gotta pee!

LESSON 9:

Guardians of Your Galaxy

Aww, Gawrsh

My avatar's mind is an interesting one indeed. It's very rational and calm, yet it questions everything to a point that, at times, it can be a bit chaotic to experience. It takes a tremendous effort for me to keep it in check and ensure it doesn't go off the deep end. I'm very thankful for it, though, because it's that mind that's been able to digest, analyze, and understand all the spiritual data that I and my ops team have provided it, especially for the subject matter that's been covered in this book. It undoubtedly has proven to be a powerful communications conduit between the spiritual and physical worlds.

One of the subjects that we–I and my spirit guides–have spent a large amount of time training my avatar's mind to understand is the subject of spirit guides themselves. Who are they? What are they? Why do they do what they do? What is it they do? How do they communicate? Why can't we communicate with them physically? Or can we? I could go on for days with all the questions that have been analyzed by this mind I'm physically communicating to you through, but I obviously can't do that. What I can do, though, is get into some core elements and share with you what my avatar's mind has figured out so far.

Before I proceed, though, I just want to take a moment to express how excited I am to write about spirit guides. I knew from the get-go that an entire lesson would be dedicated to them, and that it needed to be the second to the last lesson in the book. I've thought about this lesson throughout my writing and have anticipated this moment all along, this moment where I get to shine a spotlight on these beautiful souls who work tirelessly to assist us on our journeys and to help us achieve our life goals. This lesson is my way of thanking them for all they do for us.

Mi Familia

Throughout my life I've noticed something that I used to blow off as an insecurity but later found to be a fascinating aspect of what I've experienced. What I noticed was that I always seemed invisible to most other people. And I mean that both literally and figuratively.

I'm not exaggerating when I say this. I've frequently experienced people walking straight into me and then apologizing afterward, saying they never saw me, even though I was literally right in front of them. And when people don't run into me, I'm always dodging them, crowd or not, because I've become so hyperaware of the fact that they simply don't see me. I also frequently experience having lights turned off on me while I'm in a room in clear view, frequently help people without them being remotely aware of it, and scare the shit out of people because, as they say, I'm like a ghost and just show up out of nowhere. And I'm not even gonna get started on the number of times my birthday has been forgotten or gone unnoticed.

Please don't get me wrong, I'm not saying all this to evoke pity of some kind. No, no, no...not one bit. Trust me—I left my pity party long ago. But as with anything else in life, there's meaning behind everything, and I'm confident many people will be able to relate to at least some of these experiences. And if people can relate, then there's an opportunity for learning through sharing.

If these types of experiences happened on occasion, then I could easily dismiss them. But they've happened so often and so consistently that I simply can't ignore them, and it certainly couldn't be coincidence. Like I mentioned, I used to blow it off as maybe an insecurity; maybe it was something wrong with me, or maybe I'm just such an introvert that I brought it on myself. As I evolved, though, and I moved beyond the tragedy and trauma of those experiences, an awareness came to me. Maybe it wasn't that I was forgettable or meant so little to people that I could be so easily dismissed. Maybe it was a matrix kind of thing where my code was written to be a ghost in the typical world, and I could only be truly seen by those who walk in the shadows of that world. Maybe I was supposed to be invisible.

I remember one day, after having one too many of those previously mentioned experiences, asking my spirit guides for help in understanding what the point of it was. Like what did I need to learn from these experiences? I followed that guidance request up with a genuine and heartfelt thank you, as I typically do. My heart was so thankful in that moment for all that my spirit guides do that I also began thanking them for all they do that I'm not even aware of. You know—the stuff I don't ask for, yet they do anyway. Moments later, as often happens after I ask for guidance, an awareness hit me.

I began pondering all the things that my spirit guides do for me that I'm unaware of. The idea was enlightening for me actually. In that moment I realized that they have a tough fucking job because most of what they do goes unrecognized by those they do it for. And I'm someone who thanks them regularly, yet they probably do so much more that I'm not even aware of. I then started imagining all the people in this world who either don't believe in their spirit guides, simply aren't aware of them, or just don't pay any attention to what they do. Damn! Can you imagine? I wondered if what they do is hard on them. Here I've pissed and moaned about what I've experienced when they obviously experience so much worse.

This awareness eventually brought me to an understanding. Maybe the reason I was having the experiences of being invisible to people in the typical world was because it's a form of training. Training that provides all the ingredients to trigger a spiritual evolution that will allow me to one day become a spirit guide myself.

Wow! My mind was blown right there! Prior to that moment, I honestly hadn't considered that it must take some intense training to become a spirit guide. I can only imagine it must take lifetimes of being invisible to people, lifetimes of trauma associated with those experiences, and lifetimes of healing in order to evolve to a point where a person can selflessly help someone, day in and day out, regardless of whether they're acknowledged for their efforts or not. It must take a spirit who's so experienced, evolved, and healed that they've learned how to hold only pure love in their hearts. A pure love so undiluted that they can give it every day without getting any back, or even minding if they get it back or not. Wow again…I have so much respect for my spirit guides! So much so that I prefer to call them my spirit family.

Nou Ani Anquietas

Our spirit guides are the operations team that we assembled to assist us throughout our life journeys. They are ancient souls who have lived many lives themselves and have a deep understanding and appreciation for the work we're doing. Some may have lived as physical relatives to our avatars, but most have not. Regardless they no doubt are members of our spirit families and care deeply for us, almost in a parental or older sibling kind of way.

Physically speaking I can't yet fully remember what the experience is like in the spiritual realm, where our higher selves and our spirit guides reside. But I like to imagine there being some sort of command center, maybe something like the equivalent to a *Stargate Command* as was seen in the movie *Stargate*, and subsequent television series *Stargate SG1*, *Stargate Atlantis*, and *Stargate Universe*. Unlike *Stargate Command*, though, I don't really see it being in a dimly lit underground military facility. I see it being based in light and unfathomably futuristic, where it's a trillion years in our physical future with organic based technologies we can't even begin to imagine. And instead of it being called *Stargate Command*, it's called *Earthgate Command*, lol!

In all seriousness, spirit guides work closely together to monitor our experiences and guide us at any turn where they can be of assistance. Life's challenges can obviously be difficult, and you may question if they're truly there or not since you can't physically see, hear, or experience them. But I promise you, your spirit guides are beside you every step of the way. Not a moment goes by that they aren't listening for your calls and longing to answer them. The question shouldn't be if they're there or not; it really should be if you're hearing and seeing their guidance.

At any given moment in our lives, we have a minimum of one, and frequently multiple, spirit guides helping us. I haven't definitively nailed down if there are specialties among the ranks, but the evidence thus far indicates there are. I know in my case, I clearly have a core group that I work with daily, and there's one that I communicate with most often. There's one very powerful soul who's exceptionally good at communicating in a way that not only grabs my attention but my avatar's as well.

Over time I've learned to recognize my spirit guide's communications. We've whittled it down to an easily recognizable science, both spiritually and physically. And some of those communications are a blend that need to be recognized on both levels to be fully understood. My team and I have gotten so good at communicating with each other that we can call at any moment and trust that the other hears it.

When my spirit guides reach out to me, they do so in a variety of methods that greatly depend on what's physically available around me to connect through, the path I'm on, and the frequency I'm tuned into. Their communication choice is always unpredictable but highly consistent. It's that consistency that has given me the ability to quickly catch wind of their whispers. And whispers they are indeed. Perk your ears up, kids, and I shall share with you my spirit guides most chosen communication modalities.

Baby, Don't Forget My Number

I regularly see number patterns and synchronicities on time displays, timers, counters, spreadsheets, speedometers, receipts, invoices, etcetera, most often in repeating three-digit patterns (111, 222, 333, etcetera), though they can be in other pattern types as well. These number patterns are messages from my spirit guides telling me that what I'm experiencing, or will soon experience, is exactly as it needs to be. In other words, this is right.

What I'm experiencing when I see these number patterns can be perceptually good, bad, or anywhere in between. Regardless it's intended to be a positive and supportive confirmation that this is right and to keep going. I hesitate to put the physical translation to a single word, but if I were to, that translation is essentially a "Yes!" (Please note the exclamation mark.)

Deciphering how to apply the message in the context of the situation at hand can be tricky since the communication is intended to be simple, yet my physical mind likes to make it more complex than it really is. I've learned that this type of communication from my spirit guides is not intended to provide specifics, so I remind my physical mind not to analyze to a point that it creates details that aren't there. Instead I focus it on the simplicity of the message. "Yes, this is right."

For example, let's say I see "333" while I'm thinking and feeling about someone I have a massive crush on. Is that supportive confirmation that me and this person are destined to be together? No, not specifically. It's a supportive confirmation that what I'm thinking and feeling in that moment is right in the big picture, and that it's important enough to warrant my spirit guides calling it out to me. That's it. Reading more into it would be inaccurate. So maybe me and this person will eventually be together. Or maybe we won't, but my interest in that person will lead me down an important path I need to take. Whatever it is that will eventually play out is not being communicated. What is being communicated is a warm hug saying that what I'm thinking and feeling in that moment is right in the big picture of my life plan, and basically to not fear it.

Number signs from my spirit guides carry a lot of weight with me. I think about it this way: they've expended their energy into creating a physical communication with me across dimensions, and I can't imagine that's a small task. They wouldn't do that if there wasn't something important to say. The fact they're communicating is a message all on its own; it adds amplification to the context it was delivered upon. My part is to hear it for what it is. Simple, positive, and supportive confirmation... Yes, this is right.

The various number patterns my spirit guides use to communicate with don't each carry different meanings, contrary to what's often noted on the internet and social media. What I've found is that they most often use the numbers that are available around me in the moment in which they're communicating. Whether they're patterns of ones, twos, threes, etcetera, doesn't change the physical translation. Put simply, they're aware of what I'm experiencing, are aware there's a clock near me, and are aware it's about to turn 1:11, so they whisper for me to look over at just the right moment. I then see 1:11 and know it's them saying, yes, this is right. It's not like 111 means one thing and 222 means another. All the number patterns carry the same simple physical translation... Yes, this is right.

Though each number pattern carries the same translation, I believe that each person can have specific numbers that are more amplified with them as individuals and can even be associated with a specific subject as well. For me, the number three falls into this category.

Over time I've clearly seen my spirit guides utilize the number three when communicating their most powerful messages of support. In order for my spirit guides to communicate a specific number pattern such as that, they must expend more energy in order to not only influence me to see it, but they must also influence the physical world to create the number three pattern itself. That effort provides additional amplification, which I certainly acknowledge and appreciate.

However, the number three may mean nothing to you, so your spirit guides may not use it in any specific context. Or maybe it does mean something to you; it's just something different. Twos or fives could be your special numbers, or maybe it's the number seven? You'll need to observe for consistencies in the messages to see which, if any, numbers have more power and/or carry any specific context to you. And the way you'll know is, you'll feel it in the energy the message triggers within you.

Number synchronicities are subtle yet powerful messages from your spirit guides. Their physical translation is simple, yet they can carry deeper and more powerful spiritual and energetic meanings. Physically understanding that deeper meaning takes time and evolution, but you can figure it all out when you open yourself to the awareness and feel for that meaning.

Somewhere Over the Rainbow

I've noted several times now that my spirit guides whisper messages to me, and I say whisper because the communications are subtle and not meant to stick out. For most people the messages are intended to physically influence without conscious awareness by the recipient. Just subtle nudges to guide their movement in this life. For sensitive souls, though, these messages are not only designed to influence our physical movements but are also meant to be observed and understood on a conscious level as well. They're meant to be heard by those who are open to hearing them. As you physically evolve, your ability to be aware of these messages inherently amplifies.

Just as your spirit guides can whisper for you to look over at the clock that's about to turn 1:11 p.m., they can also whisper to call your attention to other physically based things that will convey their messages as well, physical things that most other people wouldn't pay a bit of attention to. Sensitive souls, however, are capable of understanding the deeper message conveyed beneath the surface of what others can't even see.

One of the more frequent communication means from my spirit guides are songs randomly popping into my mind. I can't tell you how many times a particular part of a song will pop into my mind out of the blue. And most often it's a song I haven't heard in forever or was never a big fan of in the first place. These are not random coincidences. They're communications from my spirit guides, and communications I always pay attention for.

I remember one such occasion on the day I moved from San Diego to Portland. It was the first day I was in the city after making the sixteen-hour drive and unloading all my belongings into my new place. It was a typically rainy day, and I needed some household goods so headed over to the local store. At this point I had just made a major move that was one thousand miles away from my son and the sunny locale I had spent my entire life in. I was excited for the path I was on and was confident I had made the right decision to move. But I was also alone, overwhelmed with a significant amount of change in a short period of time, and coming to terms with the physical realities around me.

As I was driving to the store, a well of emotions erupted from within me, and tears began flowing out of my eyes. I began to question everything. Maybe I misunderstood my path, maybe I made a mistake, what kind of father was I for leaving my son behind in California? Ugh! I was a mess of doubt in that moment. Just then, as

I was trying to wipe the tears away so I could see where I was driving, the song "Somewhere Over the Rainbow"[23] started playing in my mind, specifically the part that says "Somewhere over the rainbow, skies are blue. And the dreams that you dare to dream really do come true."[23]

It only took a moment for the song to catch my attention. I hadn't heard that song in a very long time, and I was never much of a fan of it in the first place. So it wasn't like I had just heard it recently and was playing in my mind because of that, or like it was a favorite song that plays in my mind regularly or anything. There was something special about this song popping into my mind.

As the reality was starting to hit me that this might be a communication from my spirit guides, I turned a corner and could see my destination off in the distance through the rain-splattered windshield. As I turned on the windshield wipers to clear my view of the store, a real-life rainbow appeared in the sky before me, right over the store I was headed to.

In that moment I had no doubt that I just received a very heartfelt and powerful message of support from my spirit guides. I took it as a confirmation that I was on the right path, and that they were confirming that the skies were blue ahead of me, somewhere over that rainbow.

To add a little more intrigue and power to the story I just shared, the version of that song that played in my mind that day was an interesting one. It wasn't the commonly known Judy Garland version[23] or even the also well-known Israel Kamakawiwo'ole version[24] either. Yet the version I was hearing in my mind was very familiar to me. So familiar I felt I had heard it countless times. But I didn't like that song and didn't even have it on a playlist. So how in the world was I hearing a version in my mind that was superfamiliar, yet I couldn't place it and couldn't think of anytime I would have heard it? This was something that I needed to investigate further.

I remember sharing this experience with Katie and telling her how I had subsequently listened to every version of that song, popular or not, I could find. Nothing even remotely similar matched what I heard in my mind that day. I told her it was haunting me because I know this voice but couldn't place it. I recognized the voice and the version of the song, which had a very specific sound and arrangement, but I couldn't find any evidence it existed, or that I had ever heard it…yet.

Fast-forward almost a year into the future to January 20, 2023, at 2:23 p.m. when I finally stumble upon the version of "Somewhere Over the Rainbow"[25] that I had heard in my mind that pivotal day almost a year earlier. It was a TikTok post from fellow sensitive soul Ariana Grande that she had recorded a cappella in her kitchen and had just posted that day, the very same day my first trip to Honduras was finally being booked. Coincidence? Nope…no way. And I recognized it in that moment. So much so that I took a screen grab of the post so I could always remember that important moment.

See–subtle whispers. This is how my spirit guides communicate with me. They whisper messages to support me and keep me going where I need to go. This is the kind of stuff that's easy to blow off and easy for others to dismiss. But if you open your mind and listen for those whispers, you'll hear the messages they're conveying. The messages that help you remember your path, the lights along that path, and your way to the place you desire in the deepest parts of who you are.

Gotta Do What You Gotta Do

As you can see, the subtle communications from my spirit guides can come in many forms. Another of those forms is that of energy being infused within my avatar that doesn't originate from within it. What I mean by that is my spirit guides can trigger an energy—let's say anxiety—within my physical body to catch my attention on a specific subject and even influence me to take an action based upon it. This might sound a little shady at first glance, but trust me, it's never anything too intense, and the result is always positive and beneficial. Again they communicate with subtleties, which are intended in most cases to influence without conscious awareness. What better way to do that than to make you itch when they need you to scratch.

I had a recent communication from my spirit guides that was of this nature. On the day in question, I was having quite a lovely day that was filled with much laughter and enjoyment. And I really wasn't worried or stressed about anything. Addis and I had had some really funny conversations with each other that day, and I was making great progress with writing this very book. I was simply feeling great in that moment.

About midday I began feeling an energy within me that was hard to explain at first. It started out subtly. It was just sitting in the background, slowly filling my energetic capacity. Within an hour or so I was starting to feel a bit restless and was having a hard time focusing on tasks at hand. This caught my immediate attention, so I had my brain begin analyzing what was triggering it while I continued going about my business. By late afternoon the analysis had come up with nothing, yet I was now in a full-on mild state of anxiety. This now required my full spiritual attention to get to the bottom of it.

Based on the lack of data from my brain's analysis, I began to suspect this may be a communication from my ops team. The only way to find out for sure would be to meditate on it. It was the end of my corporate workday, so I decided to take a meditative walk to achieve this. If this anxious energy was the result of something physical within me, then a physical activity would dissipate much of that energy. If it was a communication, then the walk wouldn't help as nearly much since my team would continue refilling my avatar to achieve their goal. If the situation was the latter, then the meditative aspect would hopefully shed light on the communication.

After a forty-minute walk, it had become clear to me that the anxious energy was a communication, as I was feeling no different than before the walk. What was the communication though? I had hoped the meditative side of the walk would clarify that for me, but it didn't unfortunately. I mean, it helped for sure...I just didn't get this amazing clarity from it where I physically knew exactly what the situation was. At least I knew it was likely a communication though; that certainly got me going in the right direction.

At this point I was a bit stumped on what my team was trying to tell me. I wasn't concerned about that though; if they intended for me to learn the message through the meditative walk then I would have likely achieved it. That told me something all on its own. I'd had many similar experiences like this before so was familiar with what this all meant. It meant there was something they needed me to do, but I needed to investigate it in order to fulfill it. In other words I needed to investigate, or analyze, possible actions I might need to take in order to hear the message they were sending. The investigation was part of the action they were trying to influence me to execute.

Over the following two days I, of course, investigated and analyzed the situation as best I could. Unfortunately this was proving to be a long process and wasn't resolving quickly. And I was still feeling the anxious energy during much of that time. Wait...that was a clue! I wasn't feeling the energy all the time. I was only feeling this energy during the day. I wasn't feeling it at all in the evening and nighttime. Whatever it was I needed to do needed to occur during the day when I was working. Great! I had a lead!

At that point I decided to meditate again on the situation—this time a more traditional meditation. And in that I asked my spirit guides for assistance in understanding what I needed to learn from this situation.

As I meditated an awareness came to me. Leading up to all of this, I had been having some spirit memories awaken within me. Memories of once again being in Honduras. I had just had my first trip to Honduras a few months prior, but it was clear from those memories that I would be going back again and soon. Not only that, but it was an important trip as well; otherwise, I likely wouldn't have the spirit memories of it. However, there were some things going on business-wise where it made sense that I'd soon be taking a trip there. So I didn't think that there was anything specific I needed to do regarding that. But maybe there was.

As soon as that possibility hit me, I reached out to one of my bosses and asked about going to Honduras again. Long story short—it turned out that my action proved to be perfectly timed and resulted in me getting approved for a one month stay that began just a few days after Addis's birthday. Had I waited any longer to bring up the trip, then I'm confident it wouldn't have come to fruition the way and in the timeline it did—and most likely never would have happened at all.

After my action of reaching out to my boss about going to Honduras again, the anxious energy completely and immediately dissipated from my physical body. Turned out that was what my spirit guides were trying to get me to action. They knew the timeline involved, the importance of the trip, and that I needed to act quickly to jump onto that path. But they couldn't tell me to my face. They needed to influence me to do it, so they did what they had available–they triggered anxiety that they knew I would immediately start investigating and trying to resolve. And through that process I was able to put two and two together and understand the bigger picture as it related to the spirit memories I had been seeing.

This is a perfect example of how my spirit guides will use energy to communicate a message to me and nudge me in a particular direction when they can see I need the nudge. They use this type of communication when they know it's the best method to achieve the goal, it's capable of communicating a much more complex and layered message that will result in action on my part. Basically, they do what they gotta do.

Dealing with energy being infused into my physical body isn't always the most appealing communication experience; it can be downright challenging at times. But I'd much rather deal with that than with the delays of missing an important junction in my path or missing a direct path all together. My team knows that so will utilize this method when needed. I trust them so never doubt the need. Instead I do everything I can to help them help me. And I do that by being open; listening for their whispers; and investigating, meditating, executing tough actions, or anything else I need to do to make this journey a success.

Silent Lucidity

The three most powerful, and in some cases rarest, methods in which my spirit guides will communicate with me is through what I define as spiritual experiences, visions, and dreams. In these communications the messages are much more logically interactive, visual, and relatable in this physical world where my avatar's mind exists. Yet they also require my mind to receive spiritual data it has never physically experienced before, which can result in inaccurate or vague data interpretation and visual representations in my physical mind. In addition, I can only be shown certain information so as not to negatively interfere with the grander plan. This is why I believe these forms of communication can be more on the rare side. Basically they're kind of a double-edged sword. Better in some senses and worse in others.

To better understand this subject, I think it'll be best if I jump right into the deep end by defining each of the three communication methods...

Spiritual Experiences: The best way I can describe this is that it's an experience that can be dreamlike, yet you don't necessarily have to be asleep to experience it. You also may or may not physically recall many specifics of the experience, yet you receive a clear communication through it.

A perfect example of such an experience is the awakening event I mentioned in lesson 5. It wasn't a dream, and I don't physically remember much of what I experienced. All I remembered was what happened as I began to awaken—the voice I heard within me giving me guidance and the wonderful feelings that came along with the knowledge I was infused with yet couldn't recall. I believe that voice was one of my spirit guides communicating a very important and powerful message to me. It was an out-of-body experience that was primarily taking place within the spiritual side of me.

I've had a few other spiritual experiences in my life, two of which were while I was sleeping, yet I did recall much of the experience, and they clearly were not dreams. I also had one once while I was fully conscious sitting at a stoplight waiting for my turn to go. That one was very quick, and just a short burst of information downloaded into my awareness. I heard a voice of knowledge within me telling me to warn a colleague about a risk to her pregnancy. Of course I followed that guidance, despite the natural fear my mind had that my colleague would think I was nuts. When I told her, she just about started crying and confessed that her doctor had been warning her that she needed to slow down, yet she hadn't followed their advice. She promised me she would, though, and subsequently did. Several months later she gave birth to a healthy baby boy.

Regardless of whether I'm fully awake, asleep, or in a meditative type of state, spiritual experiences are the rarest, most powerful, and the clearest communications I receive from my spirit guides. I don't know exactly why these experiences are so rare, though I can only imagine they must require a tremendous amount of skill and energy to perform. Regardless of the reasons, I very much appreciate and trust them when they do occur. Most importantly I listen to them. After all, actions speak louder than words.

Visions: This form of communication from my spirit guides always occurs while I'm physically awake and doesn't involve any perceptually verbal interactions. They are exclusively visual, though they often include physical sensations that can be very powerful. Most often these communications happen as a result of meditation, though I've experienced many that occur out of the apparent blue while performing normal daily activities; these seem triggered by something I physically experience. The communications are always flashes of imagery and knowledge that are intended to expand my awareness and/or brighten the path before me. The best way I can describe it is kind of like a fantasy that I'm not in control of. The flash occurs over a course of maybe a second, yet I feel like I get a solid ten seconds of data.

An example of a vision that pops out to me occurred many years ago while I was having a conversation with my former mother-in-law. She was visiting from out of town and expressed that she wished she could move into the same apartment building we were living in at the time. There were limited places that could be rented, and she expressed how impossible it seemed one would become available. I had a vision in that moment though.

A pathway illuminated in my mind, and I could see a clear and unobstructed path where she would indeed get to rent the place downstairs from us, though I saw her only staying for a short period of time. I in turn told her what I saw, which was that the guy who lived there would abruptly leave in about three months, and she would get to rent that place. I didn't bother to tell her it would only be temporary, as I could feel that information was intended for my awareness only. She was excited at the idea but also skeptical if it could really come true. Sure enough–three months later the guy gave notice to the owner of the property that he would be quickly vacating. She moved in a few weeks later and subsequently moved out about six months after that when the entire building was sold, and everyone was forced to move.

I'm sure that vision was given to me by my spirit guides for many reasons, and I doubt I know them all. I'm confident the main goal, though, was to prepare me for what was to come and basically show me that it was ok. Most people wouldn't want their mother-in-law moving into the same building as them, and I was no exception to that. Having that vision granted me peace about that event that surely would have been upsetting otherwise. I knew it was temporary so made the best of it with that knowledge.

I think it's important to highlight that, in that vision, I was shown that my mother-in-law's stay would be short. But I wasn't shown that my stay would also be impacted as well. There was a reason I wasn't shown that. I don't have specifics, but I'm sure it's because that knowledge would have negatively impacted the grander plan. Having such knowledge withheld can be challenging in my physical mind, but I spiritually understand why that had to be. And I respect the fact that my team couldn't reveal it. I trust them and the plan so obviously am on board with not fucking it up, regardless whether my physical mind likes it or not.

Visions from my spirit guides aren't always premonition-type communications. I remember once having a vision when a super-annoying coworker stopped by my desk one day. This guy was supernice but just one of those people that aren't very sharp, and you have to repeat the same information to them over and over again—and they still usually don't get it. One day the guy stopped by my desk and asked me things I had explained many times before. I was struggling not to chase him off with some rude behavior. Just then, a vision hit me.

A flash of knowledge of him being both physically and emotionally abused as a child was infused within my awareness, along with images of him as a child and the traumas that were inflicted on him, traumas I could still see on him at that moment. My tolerance for him increased exponentially in that moment and remained high until he eventually was fired from the company many months later.

Clearly my spirit guides communicated this information to help me have compassion for this guy who was a challenge to work with. The knowledge I was given enlightened me to understand the bigger picture of who he was and why his behaviors were what they were. It was a beautiful and kind gesture by my spirit guides without a doubt. I very much appreciated them for sharing it with me, as well as myself, both spiritually and physically, for hearing and understanding the message.

Visions come in many shapes and sizes, and the examples I provided here are just a small sampling of my experiences. Regardless of what they look like, the subject matter they're about, or the perceptual importance they may carry, all visions are gifts intended to assist you on your path. They're a gift from your spirit guides, ops team, friends, and family. Honor that gift by being aware of them and following their guidance as best you can.

Dreams: When we're drifting off to and awakening from sleep, our physical minds briefly enter a semiconscious state that is optimal for us, as spirits, to receive communications from our spirit guides and the universe. During this brief time, our spirits are fully present in our avatars but not hindered as much by the constraints that normally occur while we're contained within it. The way I think of it is that state is basically the meditative state we work so hard to reach while awake, yet when we're drifting off or waking up, we—at least for a short period of time—automatically go into it without much effort. It's kind of a cheat in a sense, lol! However, there's a drawback that comes along with this easy access meditative state, which I'll explain momentarily after I lay some groundwork for that explanation.

Once our physical minds have fully transitioned into sleep mode and our bodies are busy recovering from our conscious experience from that day, the brain begins running a data analysis and indexing program that partially operates by converting some of the accumulated data into simulations within said mind (a.k.a. dreams). The subject matter, or data, involved in these simulations can be very similar to conscious life experiences, which in turn can also be pleasant, boring, weird as shit, or even kinda fucked up, just like conscious physical life.

When your physical mind is running these simulations, it's basically further digesting, or reprocessing, data it has already run through previously. The process where your mind chooses which data will be turned into a simulation appears to be similar to any other thought process in our minds, in the sense that it's not always well organized and methodical. Sometimes it can be a bit chaotic and messy as it sorts through the data, which is why it's running through it in the first place, to understand, define, organize, and index said data.

This is where the drawback comes in that I noted a few moments ago, otherwise known as the inaccurate or vague data interpretation and visual representations I noted at the beginning of this section of the lesson.

You see, as we drift off to sleep, our mind begins loosening its grip on our spiritual selves. That loosening allows us, as spirits, to more easily receive a communication from our spirit guides. However, our brains are not fully asleep yet so continue processing data, including the communications, which is necessary so we can consciously be aware and remember them. But–and it's another big *but*–moments later our minds can slip into the full sleep experience where it begins running the previously noted data analysis and indexing program and generating the associated data simulations. This can result in a mixed awareness of communication and simulation within our physical minds, which can make it difficult to understand or accurately remember what the communication was. This is obviously no bueno!

The same situation can occur when you're going through the awakening process as well, except, this time, you'll have come out of the simulation and potentially into a received message. This situation is better than the drifting-off scenario since your mind isn't heading into a simulation, so there's less chance of data mix-ups. However, you're now coming out of that loosened grip state and into a very tight grip that can hit very fast and very hard. The result is you can be in the middle of a communication when you suddenly lose it. Kind of like a dropped call on your cell phone. So it's not as much a mixed-up data issue but rather a data loss one. Either way, there can be challenges associated with receiving dream-based spirit guide communications.

Despite the potential challenges of this communication method, it's still relatively easy and common to receive messages in this form, so my spirit guides will still utilize it when they feel its appropriate. Typically I don't have much of an issue with these communications when I receive them, but I have to be very aware that confusion or gaps in the messages can occur. To prevent that, I must act quickly and intentionally to remember and sort out the communications as quickly as I can after I'm fully conscious; otherwise, the loss and confusion can set in very quickly. My team assists me with this by typically sending messages upon awakening rather than drifting off. If they do communicate while I'm drifting off, then they'll always trigger me to wake up immediately after it so I can consciously process the information before I go back to sleep.

As far as how these communications function, they're actually very similar to what I experience with visions. The difference is that they only occur while I drift in or out of sleep, and instead of them being flashes of imagery, they appear more like flashes of a dream even though they clearly aren't dreams. Just like visions, though, they're infused with the same knowledge that's intended to expand my awareness and/or brighten the path before me. These types of messages are a blessing like any other, and despite the challenges that can occur with them, I very much appreciate and look forward to receiving them when they arrive.

Aww...It's So Cute ☺

Before I begin wrapping up this lesson, there's one more form of subtle communication I receive regularly from my team that stands alone in its uniqueness in how the message is communicated. That communication comes in the form of being visited by a spirit animal.

Unlike other communication methods, when I'm visited by a spirit animal, I don't see images, hear sound, or get infused with knowledge. All I experience really is that the animal comes upon me and catches my attention. I get a strong vibe that they're saying hello to me. They may only stay for a moment, or they may stay for a long period of time, but either way, they simply show themselves to let me know they're with me, and I'm being supported.

This type of message is a simple communication that's very similar to the number patterns I mentioned earlier. What I mean by that is that they're not intended to communicate a lot of information; they appear simply as a form of support and a reminder that your team is with you. Your spirit guides have asked the animal to risk their lives in showing themselves to you. It could be a bird, a mammal, an insect, or even a fish. Whatever type of animal it is, it was sent intentionally, and that carries a lot of meaning all on its own.

I'm not an expert at knowing what meaning each animal can potentially represent, though I do believe they can carry specific messages or representations. I typically just google the animal and see what I can find from other sensitives who have more awareness of the subject than I do. I can't say those people are correct or not, but it at least helps me get an idea of what the intended message is.

Of course I always follow my own feels as to whether what I read is correct or not. Between all of that, I can get a pretty good idea of why I was visited. No matter what, though, I know it's always positive support and that helps me even if I can't identify the specific message.

I mentioned yellow butterflies in lesson 4, and that is a great example of being visited by a spirit animal. Like I said when I see one, I know they're there to help carry my worries away. Another great example is about seven months ago, while I was still living in Portland, I spoke with a psychic who told me that a dragonfly spirit animal had arrived in my life to help usher in some powerful changes that would play a major role in my future path. I hadn't seen a dragonfly in forever but believed what she told me. After the session I decided to go on a meditative walk to process everything she said. Just two minutes into the walk, a dragonfly flew up to me and hovered inches from my face for a moment. Even I was in shock with the timing of that. The dragonfly then flew around me three or four times, hovered again, and then took off. And I haven't seen one since. It wasn't long thereafter that I began having spirit memories and other nudges from my spirit guides inspiring me to move to back to San Diego, which obviously led to me and Addis eventually meeting, and of course, me writing these words right now. Coincidence? Never!

I have to remind myself that spirit animals aren't always the rare, beautiful, or mystical types. I recently was walking into the front entrance of where I'm currently living and found an obscenely large lizard parked in the shade and blocking my path. It immediately caught my attention because of its unusual size and the fact that it was sitting in the middle of the shaded pathway, completely unstartled by my presence. Lizards are common in this area, and they regularly sunbathe. But this was just different. I assumed it would scurry off as soon as I approached it, but it didn't. It just sat there starring straight at me. I then began to step over it and was cautious, as I thought for sure it would run off at the sight of my foot stepping over it. But no–it remained exactly in place. I then was concerned it was injured so leaned down to get a better look. It stared so intently at me that I couldn't help but then realize that it was a message from my spirit guides.

Even last night while I was writing this very lesson, a gnat kept flying around me. It had been doing that every day this week while I wrote. Initially I thought it was just an annoying gnat that I should swat away. But then something hit me…a nudge. I didn't have any fruit in the house at all, and no food sitting out. And why was it only showing up while I was writing? I started to wonder if a gnat could be a spirit animal. So I googled it, and sure enough, I found information stating that gnats can indeed be spirit guides. The specific meaning behind it really didn't matter in that moment. I knew the gnat was there to show support, I knew it was there intentionally, and I knew it was a message from my spirit guides.

One last example is that of doves. I can't tell you how many times I've sat alone, longing and aching to find my soulmate. And how many times I'll hear the coos of doves coming from nearby trees and rooftops in those moments. It happens so often and so consistently that I know it's a powerful message from my spirit guides. They're letting me know they hear and feel me and are telling me to hang on and not give up. She's down this path, and we're destined to be together again. By the way as I wrote that last sentence, I looked up to see what time it was for the first time in a few hours. It was 3:33 p.m.

10-4, Good Buddy

I've obviously spent most of this lesson discussing the many ways in which my spirit guides communicate with me. But how about how I'm able to communicate with them? Well, it's pretty simple actually. I simply do what they do.

Anytime I use a microwave to warm something up, I'll set the timer to a repeating number pattern. Instead of setting it for 1:00, I'll set it for 1:11. Instead of 2:00, I'll do 2:22, etcetera. Or if I'm pumping gas into my car, I might purposely stop the pump at a specific price, say $44.44 or something like that. It's not fancy, but it gets the job done. I'm not sure how effective it is, but I try, and I know they see and appreciate it.

Another thing I do is I acknowledge them anytime I see one of their messages. I might simply feel a powerful thank you in the depths of who I am that I know they will feel. Or if I see a number, for example, I might give a little wink to send a physical acknowledgement to them. It's not much, but it's something and the best I can do, given the physical limitations that exist in communicating across dimensions.

The last and arguably the most important way I communicate back to my spirit guides is simply by talking with them. I literally speak with them out loud. I obviously can't hear them speak back in the same fashion, but I truly believe they can hear me. Some might call this prayer, but I just call it conversation. When I pick up a message, I'll say, "Thank you" out loud or in a whisper to let them know I received it. Or I'll acknowledge it but also add in a question asking for clarification if I'm not clear what I'm picking up on. And if there's something I'm desiring assistance with or guidance on, I simply ask. The very act of asking is acknowledgement all on its own. And I'm confident they appreciate it.

Psst...Avast There

If you can't tell by now, I'm a true believer in my family of spirit guides. All I've noted in this lesson was written with passion and great admiration for them. And the interesting thing is, nobody taught me any of this. Not any religion or any guru, not a book or a physical family member. All I've learned about my spirit guides has come from direct experience and from the desire to understand how everything works. I feel my spirit family every single day, and I feel their support and love. I have no doubt about their existence or their love and support for me.

You might notice that throughout this lesson I've referred specifically to *my* spirit guides and how *they* work, how *they* communicate, and what *they* do. I chose my words with intention because I don't know your spirit guides so can't say that they communicate in the exact same ways. I very much suspect they do, but I wanted to leave the door open for you to figure that out on your own. I actually encourage you to figure that out for yourself. As with anything else, it simply takes desire, openness, effort, and time to do so. Once you do, though, you'll find yourself living in an enlightened world full of support, love, hope, kindness, and wisdom. You'll find that your spirit guides are your spirit family, your mentors, your operations team, and your friends. You'll find that they truly are the guardians of your galaxy.

LESSON 10:

50 Percent Namaste, 50 Percent Fuck You

To All Who Come to This Happy Place, Welcome

Well, here we are, kids...the tenth and final lesson. Based on the title of the lesson, and of course, the book as well, do you have any ideas as to what the primary focus of this lesson will be? Let me give you a few hints...it's been sprinkled throughout every lesson in the book, sometimes quite aggressively. And even when it's not mentioned specifically, it's there, sitting in the shadows, waiting patiently to be illuminated and understood. It resides in both the happiness and sadness you must feel, the pleasure and pain you must experience, and the satisfaction and hunger you must endure. It's the only vehicle capable of navigating both the light and the dark of this existence. It...is *balance*.

Throughout this book you've heard me repeatedly discuss balance, and that wasn't by coincidence. Life wasn't designed to be easy; it was designed to be learned from. And learning can be fucking hard at times. I'm not going to sugarcoat that. But not everything in life is hard, not all learning is hard. There are many aspects of life and learning that are easy, enjoyable, funny, and even beautiful. You'll never be able to avoid all difficulties in life and learning, but you can intentionally experience the ease, joy, and beauty within them. And when you do that, you'll counteract the difficulty with enjoyment and find yourself living a balanced life upon the sun-drenched lands of happiness.

True happiness isn't found when everything is easy; it's found against the backdrop of difficulty. No different than how light is seen against the backdrop of darkness. Without darkness there's no way to physically perceive light other than it being undefined and blinding. The same happens in reverse. Without light, darkness is undefined and appears empty. Light and dark need each other to provide definition for one another. Contrast is necessary for visibility, definition, and clarity.

Imagine for a moment if you were watching a movie but the projection was all light, and no dark was contained within it. You wouldn't be able to see anything on screen; it would appear as a bright cloud of nothing. In reverse if the projection had no light, all you'd see is an empty cloud of darkness. When you put the two together, though, they work in harmony to weave through one other and define and contrast each other, providing the definition and clarity to perceive the details within each. Life is no different.

Throughout my life I struggled with experiencing happiness. Of course I had experienced difficulties, but that wasn't the issue–it wasn't even that I experienced too many of them. The issue was that I had insufficient positive aspects in my life to counterbalance the difficulties. At the end of each day, I went to sleep feeling like that day had been the worst day since the day before. My life was a cloud of darkness, with limited visibility, definition, and clarity.

The turning point for me was when I finally learned I had the ability to illuminate the darkness that engulfed my world. I could fill it with things that brought smiles, warmth, and beauty to it. The more I added, the more illuminated my world became, allowing me to see what had been there all along–things that had been hidden from my view because there wasn't enough light around me to reflect upon them.

This turning point didn't remove darkness from my world; it added light to it, providing the balance it desperately needed. The darkness is the difficult lessons I chose to learn; the light is the love, laughter, and peace that illuminates my path through that darkness. Within that there is balance, and balance is how I found my way to true happiness.

I mentioned earlier that light and dark are necessary for visibility, definition, and clarity. Well there's one more element in that mix. The contrast of the light and dark will provide you with a grayscale view. Happiness provides the color. And with that you will have a balanced and beautiful image to gaze upon.

Goob

Recently, my spirit guides reached out to me and whispered some guidance regarding this lesson, guidance they knew I'd hear and pay close attention to since they utilized Addis to communicate it. It's a message they wanted me to pass onto you, which I will do without hesitation.

When it comes to the corporate work that Addis and I work together on, everyone within the company uses Skype to message back and forth. One of the functions of that app allows the user to upload a profile picture. Addis and I both hate using real pictures of ourselves and find it entertaining to use other images as substitutes. One day Addis and one of her best friends, Katherine, changed their profile pics to cartoon characters that I recognized but couldn't immediately place. Moments later Addis sent me a pic of a character she wanted me to update mine to so our profile images would all be in sync. This is what caught my attention.

With the characters looking familiar yet I couldn't place in my mind, I heard the whispers of my spirit guides calling to me to figure out where the images originated from. It didn't take long to find the source, and as I did, I immediately recognized it. The characters were from a 2007 Disney® movie titled *Meet the Robinsons®*.[26] I had seen that movie shortly after it was released and really enjoyed it. But I hadn't seen it since then, and that's why the characters were familiar. As soon as I identified the movie, I felt a strong vibe that I should watch it, which I did later that evening.

I had been writing lesson 9 at the time and had a vague plan to use a storyline from the movie Moana®[27] in lesson 10. After I watched *Meet the Robinsons®*,[26] though, it was clear to me that my spirit guides had a different idea. I hadn't begun writing this lesson, though, so I honestly didn't know how or even if it would fit in. But it stuck with me, and I made some notes about it that I could use when and if the time came. Fast-forward to now. As I approached this moment, I began contemplating what creative storyline I should use to integrate into this lesson. Now that I've written what I have thus far, I understand why my spirit guides whispered to me that day, why they brought my attention to that movie. It makes so much sense that it astonishes even me.

Before I proceed I'd like to give a quick thank you to my spirit guides and Addis for inspiring this. I also feel it necessary to note that I will need to give a spoiler to the movie. I won't spoil the movie overall by any means and will approach what I say very carefully to keep it limited to the message of this lesson. If you haven't seen the movie yet, I highly recommend you do, and I promise that what I'm about to say won't spoil the experience.

Meet the Robinsons®[26] is about Lewis Robinson, a twelve-year-old boy and aspiring inventor, who has grown up in an orphanage because his mother abandoned him there when he was just a baby. You quickly learn how Lewis longs to be part of a family yet is always rejected by potential adoptive parents because he doesn't fit the mold of what they're looking for. He's a nerd who's always fantasizing about new inventions to make the world a better place, like moving sidewalks and flying cars, rather than being focused on sports or more typical activities of a twelve-year-old boy.

One day after being rejected by the Harringtons, the 124th potential adoptive parents to reject him, he decides that the only person who's capable of loving him is his biological mother. He concludes that she likely only abandoned him because she had to, not because she wanted to or didn't love him. With that in mind, he decides he needs to find her, but nobody knows who she is since she literally left him on the porch of the orphanage twelve years earlier. Well there was one person who saw her actually...he did–he just couldn't remember her since he was just a baby when he last saw her. So he decides to put all his divinely inspired energy toward an invention that would allow him to display his memories on a TV screen, where he could use that image to find his mother.

The movie carries on with an action-packed and hilarious storyline, where Lewis gets to travel through time into the future to help catch a bad guy who stole a time machine. During that adventure he meets a cast of characters who are wild, funny, and crazy all at the same time. I won't go into much else about the movie from here other than one spoiler that I'm about to share.

By the end of the movie, Lewis finds the family he's desperately been looking for, but it isn't his biological mother. All his life he's felt alone and–in my words–in a cloud of darkness. But he isn't alone; he has had his friend Goob, who was his roommate at the orphanage. Through his time travels, he gets to see all the wonderful people who will become a part of his life as a direct result of him being an orphan, the people who he will choose to become his family and the people that choose him as their family.

Turns out, twelve-year-old Lewis's problem isn't his mother abandoning him or being rejected by the 124 potential adoptive parents– or even that he didn't fit in with others. His problem is that his life is full of darkness, and he just needs a little light to illuminate his path and guide him to his enormously bright future. His life is out of balance. Once he is able to see the light that was already around him and opens his awareness to the light that he is walking toward, he finds himself feeling something he hasn't truly felt before...happiness. He has found the balance between the light and the dark and is able to experience true happiness because of it.

Throughout the movie you hear a phrase that's very important to the future Lewis Robinson. The phrase is "Keep moving forward."[26] That phrase becomes his motto as he becomes a world-renowned inventor and improver of lives. At the end of the movie, you learn that phrase was taken from a quote by a real-life person. That quote goes like this:

"Around here, however, we don't look backwards for very long. We keep moving forward, opening up new doors and doing new things...and curiosity keeps leading us down new paths."[26] – Walt Disney®

I bring this story and quote to your awareness with intention and with divine inspiration. For we can never give up, we must keep moving forward one step at a time. Only look back momentarily to see where you've been and appreciate the journey you've taken. Beyond that focus on where you are and your next step in where you're going. Look for the light around you and use it to keep your balance and to see your way into the future. A future that is balanced, beautiful, and happy, should you bravely choose to focus on it.

The Path

I have to be honest with you about something. The lessons in this book weren't written by me; they were written by the divine universe through me. I merely have been the conduit that has translated the wisdom of the universe into physical words. Words that you have now read and will need to judge to determine how they fit into your life, how accurate they are to you, or whether I'm just some crackpot who's spewing a bunch of bullshit. On that journey please remember the following...

Actions and vibes speak louder than words: A person can manipulate and lie to you using words, or they can tell you the complete or partial truth. The only way to know the truth behind those words is to observe the actions associated with them and feel for the vibes being emitted by those who are wielding them. Find the balance between what they say is the truth, what you feel is the truth, and what actions show you is the truth. Actions and vibes will illuminate the truth along your path.

You are not your thoughts: Your brain is a very powerful CPU for the organic machine you use to travel this physical world in. Though it's powerful, it's not perfect. That power can turn chaotic when out of balance. It makes mistakes, it can be fooled, it can misunderstand, it sees much in this physical world, but it also is blind to that of the spiritual world. As spirits we must compassionately help our avatars learn to see beyond that which is physical. In that process we must keep a strong grasp on the true reality that we are not the thoughts of our avatars; those thoughts are simply part of the functionality of these organic machines. Those thoughts are data, information we need to be aware of, appreciate, and take into consideration. But that data is not us; it is not who we are.

Flow with life like a leaf in the wind: There is a flow to life, an energy that takes us from one destination to the next. You can resist the flow if you'd like; you have the free will to do so. However, the energy is there to move us through this experience. It's in place to guide us down the paths we've chosen. The energy of life is made of you, of your spirit guides, and of the universe. It's not something you need to fear or resist. It's something you can trust and rely upon. If you resist the flow, then you'll simply be making the flow more turbulent and find yourself crashing and stumbling your way through life. When you find balance in the control you have physically vs. spiritually, as well as the things you don't have control of, then you flow with life with ease and grace. You will find peace with what was, what is, and what will be.

Beauty is in the eyes of the beholder: The foundation for how you perceive your life and the world around you is your physical knowledge and spiritual awareness. The more open your physical mind is and the more aware you are spiritually, the stronger that foundation becomes. What you choose to do with that knowledge and awareness is completely up to you. Others may try to manipulate your perception; they may even try to control it, but they cannot do that unless you allow them to. There is no way for anyone to force you to believe something if you really don't believe it. This is your power.

Society tells us that green means go, and red means stop. Is it true? No, not really. Green and red only mean what you perceive them to mean. In the physical world, there's a meaningful function to the perception of those colors, and that's ok as long as you're aware of it. But you must keep in mind that there's no true meaning behind green and red. The same applies to light and dark. Society tells us that light is good, and dark is bad. That is just a perception in your mind though. The truth is, light and dark are equals. They're the same thing, just on different ends of the spectrum. Neither is good, and neither is bad. They just are. It's up to you to question these things; you must question everything so you have the full picture. Once you have that, then you get to choose what to believe and what to focus on. This is your freedom.

Being aware of the whole truth yet choosing to focus on what makes you feel good and what brings love and kindness to the forefront of your life and to others' lives is the pathway to being in balance; it's the gateway to happiness. This is your wisdom.

Everyone is weird: You are different, and that's ok. I am different, and that's ok too. We are all different from each other, and that makes us all weirdos to one another. Our avatars are naturally full of all kinds of insecurities, and that's also ok. There's nothing wrong with having insecurities, and there's nothing wrong with being weird. We designed our avatars to analyze our physical selves and run a comparison program that serves to help us survive this competitive world. That analysis is powerful and serves a beneficial purpose, but it can also spin out of control and turn into negative self-analysis that isn't beneficial. It's up to us as spirits to monitor that analysis and ensure it remains in beneficial territory. When it does stray, we must be compassionate with our avatars and ourselves; we must love ourselves fully and completely to maintain balance. By doing so we'll inevitably gain compassion for others and help the entire world achieve the balance it desperately needs.

Let it go: Stress and fear are standard functionality of your avatar, so experiencing them is something that is bound to happen throughout your life. However, if you don't manage that stress, it will build up and begin wreaking havoc on your mind and body and impact how they're able to function and support you in this world. Adding stimulants, missing sleep, and taking on more than you can handle will serve to only compound that stress and fear, will inevitably lead to anxiety and panic attacks, and can even elevate to the point of a near critical system failure. This can trigger an automatic reboot into safe mode, all of which are terribly unpleasant and traumatizing experiences. Prevention is the best medicine when it comes to stress and fear, which involves a heavy dose of the magical ingredients of balance and compassion. By letting go of excess stressors and fears and utilizing self-compassion, you'll be able to prevent anxiety and panic attacks, and add significant leverage to your scales of balance.

Bad words: Anger comes in many forms, but all are born from one puppet master…frustration. Frustration is when energy is building up in your body with no outlet; anger is the release of that frustrated energy. Your avatar is designed to allow energy to build up and be released when it hits its maximum storage capacity. The result is an angry outburst, which by design is there to keep you and all you care about safe. Anger is a defensive mechanism that protects your avatar from a threat, whether it be legitimate or only perceived. It even protects from an energetic overload that could permanently damage your avatar. Regardless of what causes energy to frustrate within you, you must find a healthy way to release it to prevent anger when it's not appropriate. For without frustration there is no anger. When you find the ways to allow energy to not only flow into you but also flow out of you, you will find the balance in your inner world. And the balance of your inner world will create balance in your outer world. You will let go of societies mind fuck and find yourself living in the proverbial heaven.

OMG, I've got to pee: The lives we live are often long and full of challenges. Getting through our lives can trigger a sense of impatience, which is basically a desire for more physical control. We physically want things to happen and to happen when they make sense within our own physical awareness. But there's so much beyond that physical awareness that we can't even begin to logically comprehend. The dissolution of impatience comes when we become aware and accept that we, our spiritual selves, designed the lives we live, and that we already have the control we physically desire. The control we don't have physically is within us spiritually. We spiritually defined the paths we walk upon and drew the maps necessary to navigate them. We have an operations team by our side, helping guide us down those dark paths. And we have memories of key life events that are destined to occur, memories we physically can use to navigate and illuminate the paths between the key events. There is balance in the control we have physically versus spiritually. Balance that is achieved when we learn to trust our whole selves, the paths we designed, our support team, and the memories we embedded within to guide us home.

Guardians of your galaxy: We are not alone in this life and journey we are partaking in. Even if we don't have physical people around us, we do have our spirit family with us...always. Our spirit guides are our family in the truest sense. They love and care for us without selfish interest or agenda and without need for payment or reciprocation. They have only one goal in mind...to help and support us. In an effort to support us, they will send subtle communications that you can pick up on if you open your mind and awareness to them. These communications take effort on their part, which shouldn't be taken lightly. If they're taking the time to communicate, it means there's something important being said. Listen for them, feel for them, and trust in them. And know that you're never truly alone; they're always with you, and they will always love you, no matter what.

50 percent namaste, 50 percent fuck you: The lives we live are about learning and teaching. Sometimes we're the students, and sometimes we're the teachers. Either way, it's about learning, and learning can be difficult and challenging whether you're the student or the teacher. But not all learning is difficult; there's so much out there that's enjoyable, peaceful, and beautiful. The trick to making your way through this journey is by finding balance throughout the lessons you face, to be aware of and appreciate the darkness and the light, to fill your life with both to keep the scales balanced and in harmony. You need to be aware that what you're experiencing is simply a class that you chose to take, a class that you must pass before you can move on. You can drag your feet in the class if you'd like or even quit if you so choose. But that won't make the experience any better; it will actually make it harder since the timeline to completion will inevitably be extended. The best and fastest way around life is through it. And the pathway through it is happiness. Balance is the vehicle that will carry you through both light and dark; it's the gateway to happiness.

The Threshold

I mentioned in the introduction the metaphor of the cold and dark forest and how I found the path out of it. I also mentioned going back to leave path markers behind for the other wandering souls to find, so they could make their way out too. The reality behind those words is that I quite literally had to go back into the darkness in order to lay the path markers (i.e., write the lessons in this book) for you to use and find your way to the sun-drenched land of happiness. Every lesson required me to relive many of the life challenges I had already experienced and moved beyond. It was difficult but necessary, and I absolutely don't regret it one bit. But with the ending of this lesson and book upon us, I very much look forward to permanently exiting that cold and dark forest. This time I'm never going back.

The path markers have been laid, and now it's up to you to utilize those markers to find your way out. It's up to you to illuminate your darkness with whatever it is that makes you smile, laugh, feel warm and fuzzy inside, feel enjoyment, love, kindness, peace, or anything else that brightens your path. It's up to you to frequently examine your life and decide what can stay and what needs to go. It's up to you to clean out your life and climb out of any pit of despair you may find yourself in. It's up to you to walk your path, one...step...at a time.

I wish you so much love and peace on your journey home, and I will be with you in spirit and in this book the entire way. Your spirit guides and the universe will be with you the entire way as well. You are loved and supported whether you physically see it or not. Just look to your feels and to the lights that illuminate your path to feel the love all around you.

As I write these words now, I'm in San Pedro Sula, Honduras, staring at the beautiful mountains of Reserva de El Merendón. I'm standing on the edge of the proverbial cold and dark forest, ready to cross the threshold to the sun-drenched land of happiness. With the path markers laid, it's now time for me to say farewell my friend. I look forward to seeing you in the land of happiness; I look forward to welcoming you home and asking you how you're doing. To which you can proudly reply: "I'm 50 percent namaste, 50 percent fuck you."

The End

Acknowledgements

I would like to take this opportunity to thank some important people who played pivotal roles in the writing and publishing of this book...

Kindra Gans (Sister Kindra): You gave me a reading back in late 2020 that directly led to me writing this book. You said you saw me standing upon a stage and teaching many people around the world. I had never considered myself a teacher up to that point. Thank you for that knowledge and your continued support; I'm forever grateful to you, my friend.

Chloè Poulain (a.k.a. the Psychic Fairy): You are kind, loving, and an amazingly gifted psychic. I hit a patch of fog not too long ago (2023) and my spirit guides led me to you. You cleared that fog so I could once again clearly see my path to publishing this book. Thank you for that; I'm eternally grateful.

Katie Cordes, LCSW: I followed my feels to you and knew in my heart you could support me on the wild journey I could feel I was about to take. You've been a rock for me throughout the countless changes I've gone through. You've listened to me with compassion and without any judgment. You're an angel without doubt and one

I'm so thankful to have in my life. Thank you for supporting me on my journey to write this book.

My spirit guides: OMG, where would I be without you? You've always been there for me and there are no words to effectively thank you for all you've done. You've guided me through all the challenges and led me right to this point. I'm sure I'm a handful, but you love me anyway. All I can say is thank you and I love you.

Liam Hutchinson: You've had plenty of challenges in your life, yet you tackle them with an enthusiastic and contagious smile on your face and in your heart. I admire that so much! Everyone loves you, Bub, including me. I say I love you often, but my actions say it so much better. You've inspired me and many aspects of what I wrote in this book. Thank you for that inspiration and allowing me to share some of your life stories to teach others.

Addis Castellanos: I love you, kid! Without you I wouldn't have made my way to this point. You've been such an enormously bright light on my path. I saw you off in the distance for years; it takes an enormously powerful goddess to illuminate that brightly. Thank you for not only being here with me but also for trusting me and being my friend. I'll always have your back, I'll always be here for you, and I'll always love you. I truly look forward to what's coming next.

My girl: As of this moment, I don't definitively know your physical name or where in this world you are. But I feel you, baby; I always have. I feel your love like no other; it's a beacon that has guided me my entire life, to writing this book, and is leading me right to you. Our love for each other bridges time and space itself; we are quantumly entangled. Thank you for always being here with me spiritually, for believing in me, and for not giving up. I love you with all my heart, and I'll never give up on you.

My readers: Last but not least, thank you to everyone who has read this book. Thank you for listening to me, for being brave, and for not giving up. Thank you for investing your time into reading and feeling the energy behind the words I've been inspired to write. Thank you for spreading those words and the messages that you have taken away from this book. You are powerful souls my friends, and we together can combine our energies to expand the beauty of this human world and transform its entirety into the sun-drenched land of happiness it's destined to evolve into. We will create a world of peace, love, and happiness...together, as a team.

References

1. Carly Rae Jepsen, "Beautiful," track 9 on *Kiss (Deluxe Version)*, School Boy/Interscope Records®, 2012, songwriter(s): Justin Bieber, Toby Gad, and Alex Lambert, Apple Music®, https://music.apple.com/us/album/beautiful/1440873664?i=1440874163.

2. *Live Free or Die Hard*, directed by Len Wiseman (2007; 20th Century Fox®), Apple TV®, https://tv.apple.com/us/movie/live-free-or-die-hard/umc.cmc.532g428ovpfzjwubi7ydjlzok.

3. Enigma, "Back to the Rivers of Belief: Way to Eternity / Hallelujah / The Rivers of Belief," track 7 on *MCMXC A.D.*, Michael Cretu, 1990, songwriter(s): Michael Cretu, Fabrice Jean and Roger Cuitad, Apple Music®, https://music.apple.com/us/album/back-to-the-rivers-of-belief-way-to-eternity/712727641?i=712727721.

4. Enigma, "Return to Innocence," track 1 on *Return to Innocence EP*, Michael Cretu, 1993, songwriter(s): Michael Cretu, Kuo Ying-nan, and Kuo Hsiu-chu, Apple Music®, https://music.apple.com/us/album/return-to-innocence-radio-edit/1445293261?i=1445293265.

5. Christopher Cross, "Sailing," track 8 on *Christopher Cross*, Seeker Music®, 1979, songwriter(s): Christopher Cross, Apple

Music®, https://music.apple.com/us/album/sailing/1656697223?i=1656697235.

6. *NSYNC, "Sailing," track 12 on *'N Sync (International Version)*, Trans Continental Records®, 1997, songwriter(s): Christopher Cross, Apple Music®, https://music.apple.com/us/album/sailing/286006489?i=286006654.

7. Pet Shop Boys, "Go West (2003 Remaster)," track 1 (disk 1) on *PopArt: The Hits*, Parlophone Records, 2006, songwriter(s): Chris Lowe, Neil Tennant, Victor Willis, Henri Belolo, and Jacques Morali, Apple Music®, https://music.apple.com/us/album/go-west-2003-remaster/696887254?i=696888835.

8. Karol G, "Tusa," track 15 on *KG0516*, UMG Recordings, 2021, songwriter(s): Keityn, Karol G, Nicki Minaj, and Ovy on the Drums, Apple Music®, https://music.apple.com/us/album/tusa/1560071303?i=1560072127.

9. *What About Bob?*, directed by Frank Oz (1991; Touchstone Pictures), Apple TV®, https://tv.apple.com/us/movie/what-about-bob/umc.cmc.5glf7mtv57arohtkvgeoofrc3.

10. *Avatar: The Last Airbender®, The Complete Series,* directed by (varies by episode) (2017; Viacom®), Apple iTunes®, https://itunes.apple.com/us/tv-season/avatar-the-last-airbender-the-complete-series/id1310930993.

11. *The Legend of Korra®, The Complete Series,* directed by (varies by episode) (2012; Viacom®), Apple iTunes, https://itunes.apple.

com/us/tv-season/the-legend-of-korra-the-complete-series/id1099992483.

12. *The Legend of Korra®, Season 1, Episode 2, "A Leaf in the Wind,"* directed by Joaquim Dos Santos and Ki Hyun Ryu, written by Bryan Konietzko and Michael Dante DiMartino, aired April 14, 2012, on Nickelodeon®, Apple TV®, https://tv.apple.com/us/episode/a-leaf-in-the-wind/umc.cmc.6efgcyz66rfrdlt84eq9fh4bf?showId=umc.cmc.2lp0x595jjn9q1z06h8aadc25.

13. *Kung Fu Panda®*, directed by Mark Osborne and John Stevenson (2008; DreamWorks Animation®), Apple TV®, https://tv.apple.com/us/movie/kung-fu-panda/umc.cmc.34elthhr2qybuu3emdzn4d2fr.

14. The Party, "Yellow Butterfly" track 3 on *The Party's Over... Thanks for Coming*, Hollywood Records®, 1993, songwriter(s): Willie McNeil, Jay Colin, and Deedee Magno Hall, Apple Music®, https://music.apple.com/us/album/yellow-butterfly/1533823509?i=1533823514.

15. P!nk, "F**kin' Perfect," track 18 on *Greatest Hits...So Far!!!*, LaFace Records, 2010, songwriter(s): Shellback, Max Martin, and P!nk, Apple Music®, https://music.apple.com/us/album/f-kin-perfect/399891666?i=399891830.

16. Beck, "Loser," track 1 on *Mellow Gold*, Geffen Records, 1994, songwriter(s): Beck and Karl Stephenson, Apple Music®, https://music.apple.com/us/album/loser/1440636547?i=1440636710.

17. Flogging Molly, "The Worst Day Since Yesterday," track 3 on *Swagger*, SideOneDummy Records®, 2000, songwriter(s): Bridget Regan, Gary Schwindt, John Donovan, George Schwindt, Bob Schmidt, Nathen Maxwell, Matt Hensley, and Dave King, Apple Music®, https://music.apple.com/us/album/the-worst-day-since-yesterday/1630996871?i=1630996881.

18. Sarah McLachlan, "Don't Let Go," track 6 on *Rarities, B-Sides and Other Stuff, Vol. 2*, Arista Records, 2008, songwriter(s): Gavin Greenaway, Gretchen Peters, Robert John Lange, and Bryan Adams, Apple Music®, https://music.apple.com/us/album/dont-let-go/278796513?i=278796615.

19. Frozen, "Let It Go," track 5 on *Frozen (Original Motion Picture Soundtrack)*, Walt Disney Records®, 2013, songwriter(s): Kristen Anderson-Lopez and Robert Lopez, Apple Music®, https://music.apple.com/us/album/let-it-go/1440618177?i=728880409.

20. *Frozen*, directed by Chris Buck and Jennifer Lee (2013; Walt Disney Animation Studios®), Apple TV®, https://tv.apple.com/us/movie/frozen/umc.cmc.4b17gber8k76h90rzlulvrbcl.

21. Frozen, "Let It Go (Single Version)," track 10 on *Frozen (Original Motion Picture Soundtrack)*, Walt Disney Records®, 2013, songwriter(s): Kristen Anderson-Lopez and Robert Lopez, Apple Music®, https://music.apple.com/us/album/let-it-go-single-version/1440618177?i=728880418.

22. *Bad Words*, directed by Jason Bateman (2014; Focus Features®), Apple TV®, https://tv.apple.com/us/movie/bad-words/umc.cmc.2oh1c86fmw5vpe2tw6kx64ihh.

23. Judy Garland, "Over the Rainbow," track 2 on *The Wizard of Oz (Original Motion Picture Soundtrack)*, WaterTower Music, 1939, songwriter(s): Harold Arlen and E.Y. Harburg, Apple Music®, https://music.apple.com/us/album/over-the-rainbow/1454449430?i=1454449433.

24. Israel Kamakawiwo'ole, "Somewhere Over the Rainbow," track 10 on *Alone in IZ World*, Mountain Apple Company / BB, 2001, songwriter(s): Harold Arlen and E.Y. Harburg, Apple Music®, https://music.apple.com/us/album/somewhere-over-the-rainbow/6920402?i=6920394.

25. Ariana Grande, "Somewhere Over the Rainbow," songwriter(s): Harold Arlen and E.Y. Harburg, TikTok, https://www.tiktok.com/@arianagrande/video/7190646878030073134?is_from_webapp=1&sender_device=pc&web_id=7259131625895249450.

26. *Meet the Robinsons*®, directed by Stephen Anderson (2007; Walt Disney Pictures®), Disney+®, https://www.disneyplus.com/movies/meet-the-robinsons/3enZwQ8X7upX.

27. *Moana*®, directed by Ron Clements and John Musker (2016; Walt Disney Animation Studios®), Apple TV®, https://tv.apple.com/us/movie/moana/umc.cmc.13yhzauh3b57obklyle10aepi.

www.ingramcontent.com/pod-product-compliance
Lightning Source LLC
LaVergne TN
LVHW010640110826
845149LV00014B/2904

* 9 7 9 8 9 8 8 7 3 8 1 0 7 *